A.M.

8

D0876089

WITHDRAWN

The Roots of American Bureaucracy, 1830–1900

The Roots of American Bureaucracy, 1830–1900

William E. Nelson

Harvard University Press

Cambridge, Massachusetts, and London, England

1982

Library of Congress Cataloging in Publication Data

Nelson, William Edward, 1940–
    The roots of American bureaucracy, 1830–1900.

    Includes bibliographical references and index.
    1. United States — Constitutional history. 2. United
States — Politics and government — 19th century.
3. Bureaucracy — United States — History — 19th century.
I. Title.
JK216.N44   320.973   82-6214
ISBN 0-674-77945-2   AACR2

To my Mother and Father

Preface

THIS BOOK had its genesis in research into the ideology of the radical Republicans who so strenuously supported equality for blacks during the decade of Reconstruction. Early in the research, a conventional view of the radicals as self-interested Yankee capitalists bent on exploiting the South did not appear to capture their essential character. Instead, the preliminary research showed the radical Republicans to be heroic figures motivated by moral ideals to infuse American law and government with righteous principles. I set out in the spirit of a scientific historian to search for evidence to test which interpretation of the radicals was accurate.

The evidence raised two problems. One was the failure of the data to show conclusively what the true character of the radicals was. The data, although tending to confirm the perception of the radicals as moralists, did not fully refute the other view of them. The second problem was the radicals' failure generally to enact their moral principles into law. On the contrary, their legacy to the twentieth century was a series of institutions — the precursors of modern bureaucracy — that have an amoral character.

Although historical documentation was missing to prove that the radical Republicans were moral leaders rather than instruments of Yankee capitalism, the lessons provided by the political behavior of two of my personal moral tutors sustained my faith in the plausibility of the view. From childhood, I had observed my father, whether he was casting a vote for President or completing a tax return, continually ignore his own economic interests and act as a citizen in accordance with an Old Testament moral code inherited from his

Calvinist forebears. At the outset of my career, I had observed my professional mentor, Judge Edward Weinfeld, similarly ignore the dictates of expediency and interest so that he could help govern the nation in accordance with that same moral code. Both the judge and my father had shown that at least some people act as citizens and leaders of government on the basis of moral values.

Their examples made plausible my perception that the radicals of the Reconstruction era had acted on the basis of similar values. Their example also suggested that I ought not spend time proving the readily observable fact that self-interest is not the sole basis of human conduct. I could focus, instead, on the other problem that occurred as soon as the radicals were viewed as heroic moralists: the problem of how human suffering often results from decisions taken in the name of morality. I could, in particular, inquire why radical Reconstruction — a noble attempt to better the condition of mankind — was followed in American history by the Gilded Age — a time in which many people, including, paradoxically, the immigrant parents of my father and of Judge Weinfeld, endured deprivation and suffering. The inquiry resulted in this book.

No one can work on a scholarly project without incurring debts. The Society of Fellows of Harvard University provided me with a year of research time free from other responsibilities during which I began to expand an early article into a book. The Law Center Foundation of New York University provided research support that enabled me to complete the manuscript. I am grateful to both.

I am also grateful to the *Harvard Law Review,* the *Law and Society Review,* the *University of Pennsylvania Law Review,* and Fred B. Rothman & Company for permission to reprint articles or portions thereof. My deepest gratitude is reserved for the large number of colleagues and students who read or worked on various drafts of this book, among them Bruce Ackerman, Thomas Bender, Miriam Clark, William Duker, Jay Feinman, Harold Hyman, Robert Kaczorowski, Laura Kalman, Lewis Kornhauser, and John Reid. I am indebted to these fellow scholars for the labor, ideas, and support without which the book would never have been completed.

The writing of a book inevitably imposes inconvenience and sacrifice on the family of the author. This book has imposed far more than its share. I thank Elaine, Leila, and Gregory for bearing with me.

Contents

The Roots of American Bureaucracy, 1830–1900

Introduction:
Origins of Authority

Two ideals have commanded the attention of American political thinkers during much of the nation's history. One is the ideal of rule by popular majority. At the time the Constitution was being submitted to the states for ratification, James Madison observed in *The Federalist* that "the genius of the people of America" was "to rest all our political experiments on the capacity of mankind for self-government" and to create governmental institutions that derived their power "from the great body of the society, not from an inconsiderable proportion, or a favored class of it." As recently as 1980 a constitutional theorist concurred that "rule in accord with the consent of a majority of those governed is the core of the American governmental system."[1]

The second ideal, and one that has continually intruded upon the ideal of majoritarian self-rule, is that a just government must provide means for "defending the minority . . . from the tyranny of the majority." According to *The Federalist*, a just system of government must prevent "serious oppressions of the minor party in the community" and must protect "the rights of individuals from the effects of those ill humors, which the arts of designing men, or the influence of particular conjectures, sometimes disseminate among the people themselves." Students of American government today still agree that "the political theory ordained by the Constitution forbids popular majorities to abridge certain rights of individuals."[2]

This book examines how institutions of the federal government evolved during the nineteenth century in response to the two ideals of majoritarian self-rule and protection of individual and minority rights. Its thesis is that before the Civil War the institutions of the federal government evolved principally in response to the majoritarian ideal, whereas after the war the predominant force underlying institutional change at the federal level was a concern with preserving a pluralistic society in which individuals and minorities could thrive. The majoritarian ideal edged the United States toward a system of party government until the Civil War; thereafter a set of pluralistic concerns for the welfare of individuals and minorities led to the creation of bureaucratic institutions that persist today.

In the highly professionalized, bureaucratic state in America today, the power of government is generally brought to bear upon individuals by bureaucrats whose edicts are backed by police and ultimately military units capable of using physical force. These bureaucrats, full-time, salaried employees who usually make a career of government service, maintain a sharp separation between their official and private lives and occupy offices with clearly specified functions. The normative standards they enforce are frequently established and maintained by professional groups distinct from the general public. Access to and promotion within the bureaucracy and the professions, or even sustained conversation with either group, tends to be restricted to those who have internalized the desired normative standards either through long service or through the completion of formal courses of education.[3]

Government did not always work this way. In premodern America, power was exercised by those who conjoined private and public authority to perform undifferentiated leadership roles. Leaders were selected not because of their specialized expertise but because of their social position in the communities they were to govern. Once in power, they maintained close ties with the people they governed and with their people's normative values. Coercive instruments such as police forces were nonexistent or inchoate. In the mid-nineteenth century, the power of political leaders and hence the power of the people to whom leaders had close ties were mobilized through political parties and through governmental institutions designed to give rein to party power. Party organizations and their chieftains tended to dominate congressional proceedings and to exert a substantial influence on the selection and policies of executive and judicial officers. In antebellum America the democratic ideal of popular self-rule was translated into a reality of party governnment through the medium of yet a third concept — that of the rule of the majority.*

American government assumed most of its modern bureaucratic characteristics only in the last third of the nineteenth century. Although movement toward bureaucratization had begun earlier and would continue thereafter, these decades witnessed dramatic changes in all three branches of government. In the legislative branch, the period 1865–1900 saw the development of government by congressional committees led by senior congressmen who had made a profession of their political careers, as well as the appearance of communication networks and loyalties across party lines in lieu of strict accountability to the electorate through the party caucus. Specialization of function and respect for expertise, two classic bench-marks of bureaucracy, began to characterize the late nineteenth-century Congress. The executive branch in the same years saw the birth of the independent regulatory commission with close ties to those it regulates and increasing numbers of other middle-level bureaucrats immediately accountable to neither the public nor even the president. Even the late nineteenth-century judiciary became somewhat bureaucratized. Professional expertise became a practical prerequisite for ascendance to the bench, and another characteristic of bureaucracy — adherence to formal, objective, and neutral standards of reasoning — became the model for judicial decisionmaking. Important changes also occurred outside government. For example, legal education and the practice of law in general underwent extensive professionalization beginning in the 1870s, as did medical education and the practice of medicine slightly later. Numerous other professions also emerged in the final decades of the century, especially in the academic world. Indeed, the entire American educational system underwent a revolution in that period.[4]

*The three concepts of democracy, majority rule, and party government must be kept distinct. Democracy in this context is best defined as any polity in which the people freely select their rulers. Majority rule can be defined as a system of government in which at least the members of the legislative branch are elected to office by one more than half the people who are eligible to vote and who do in fact vote; a majoritarian system will not necessarily be a democratic one if the franchise is narrowly restricted. Party government can be defined as a system of government in which officials are selected and maintained in office by a political organization, usually from among its members. A system of party government can be democratic and majoritarian, as in modern Great Britain; majoritarian but not democratic, as in mid-nineteenth-century Great Britain; or neither, as in the Soviet Union.

The overall pattern of change in the structure and processes of government was immensely complex — too complex to be described completely in a single volume. I will not attempt a full description, for others have already described in detail the changes that occurred in many of the institutions of nineteenth-century government.[5] My aim instead is to ask why the bureaucratic state was born in America when it was — in the late nineteenth century. A subsidiary aim is to suggest how the various changes in government, which others have examined discretely, in fact occurred simultaneously and may have been related to one another as part of a larger pattern of change.

What factors transformed the mid-century party system of government into the bureaucratic system of the late nineteenth century? Max Weber's classic answer to this question has emphasized two factors. The first was the growing complexity and specialization of modern culture, particularly the emergence of a money economy. Modern societies demand a greater quantity and higher quality of administration carried on by personally detached and strictly objective experts. The second factor, in Weber's analysis, is the leveling of economic and social differences accompanying the rise of modern mass democracy. Democratic theory demands that the law treat all citizens as formally equal, which means that legally sanctioned privileges must be eliminated and legal guarantees provided against official arbitrariness. American democratic theory, of course, also imposes other demands on the political system, among them the requirement that majorities be capable of fixing public policies in accordance with their own value priorities. Weber, however, focuses on formal legal equality, not the power of majorities, as the democratic trait linked most closely with the rise of bureaucracy, because, he claims, formal equality can be attained only by bureaucratic administration of government, not by discretionary administration in the service of some substantive ethical ideal, whereas majoritarian self-rule can occur in the absence of bureaucratization.[6]

If the factors that Weber cites are understood to be necessary but not sufficient conditions for the emergence of bureaucracy, then his analysis is consistent with the facts of American history. Before the last third of the nineteenth century, the United States had become a complex and highly specialized society with a money economy. Moreover, American democracy was well developed, and there were widespread, powerfully voiced demands for the elimination of legally sanctioned privilege and for legal guarantees against official arbitrariness. American society had assumed these characteristics, however, as early as the 1820s or 1830s — about a half century before any significant federal bureaucracy or any state-level bureaucracy whatever existed.[7] Accordingly, some additional factor missing from Weber's analysis is needed to explain the birth of bureaucracy in the United States.

The additional factor was an outgrowth of the tension between the idea of majority self-rule and the concern for protecting individual and minority rights. The early steps toward bureaucracy in America were taken by a small though loosely knit group of elite, reform-minded political and intellectual leaders — the mugwumps or genteel reformers of the last half of the nineteenth century. No complete list of the members of this somewhat amorphous reform movement exists, but the following dozen were typical: Henry Adams, Charles Francis Adams, Jr., John W. Burgess, Grover Cleveland, Thomas M. Cooley, Charles W. Eliot, Richard T. Ely, Rutherford B. Hayes, Christopher Columbus Langdell, Theodore Roosevelt, Carl Schurz, and Samuel J. Tilden. They and others played an important role in bringing about the changes in government associated with the birth of modern American bureaucracy.[8]

The proclaimed purpose of the reformers was to provide individuals and minorities with protection against what they perceived to be an increased threat of majoritarian tyranny. They would have rejected Weber's view that bureaucratization of administration through civil service reform constituted a "replacement of competing sources of authority by a single source, that is a concentration of power." They would also have rejected Weber's contention that "concentration [of power] was a typical feature of bureaucracy"; they viewed bureaucracy, instead, as a device for preventing just such a concentration.[9] The late nineteenth-century reformers were not simply searching for order and rationality in an increasingly complex, industrialized world,[10] nor did modern American bureaucracy emerge only as a centralizing response to that chaotic world. Instead, the builders of the bureaucratic state strove to prevent centralization and concentration of power and to institutionalize pluralism. Their model was provided not by the sociologists of the twentieth century, with their concern for structure and efficiency, but by the founding fathers of the eighteenth, whose concern was that popular power be limited by popular rights.

Chapter 1 will begin the analysis of how nineteenth-century government evolved in response to the continuing dialogue between majority power and minority rights. It examines in detail the workings of pre–Civil War government, which was, in essence, a system of party democracy with partisan divisions along well-marked ideological and group lines and with the outcome of those divisions determined by majority vote. After I examine how the antebellum system worked toward concentrating power, I will turn in Chapter 2 to the important rhetorical objections raised against this tendency, primarily by antislavery political leaders both before and after the war. There, I focus on the objection that popular majorities tended to ignore moral precepts that properly constituted a source of law.

Chapter 3 presents the attempts of reformers, many of whom had antislavery backgrounds, to restore morality to government in the postwar era. It also shows how the failure of this attempt, together with transformations wrought in the federal system by the Civil War and Reconstruction, produced a crisis wherein a congressional majority, freed from constraints imposed by moral values and state power, threatened to abrogate minority and individual rights. Chapter 4 describes how the reformers, in response to this crisis, sought a new scientific morality whereby to limit governmental power. Finally, Chapter 5 shows how adherents to the old moral precepts and to the new scientific morality proposed to reorganize the institutions of government when, in the wake of the Civil War, a cohesive group of political partisans threatened to gain complete control of the federal government. Old-guard advocates of majoritarian democracy fought successfully to defeat many of these proposals. Nevertheless, out of this three-sided contest over how best to structure American government, the modern bureaucratic state—which was the precise ideal of none of the three groups—emerged.

The analysis in the following chapters does not subscribe to the commonly held historical interpretation that the reformers who created the bureaucratic state were seeking to preserve or perhaps even improve the socioeconomic position of the upper class at the expense of the lower classes. This interpretation is by no means inplausible. It is based on the facts that many reformers came from elite backgrounds and maintained elite associations and that nearly all reformers opposed any efforts by government to redistribute the nation's wealth from the rich to the poor. It is also based on historical hindsight as to the impact of reform proposals on the functioning of government in the twentieth century. These observations rest, in turn, on the implicit assumption that the results of the reform movement are evidence of the intentions of the reformers.[11]

Despite the supporting evidence, however, the hypothesis that the reformers were motivated by self-interest is subject to several difficulties. For one thing, it fails to take into account important questions concerning the size and composition of the late nineteenth-century reform elite. The received interpretation presupposes that a small elite, bound together by wealth and by fear of proletarian attacks on that wealth, seized control of the mechanisms of power and used those mechanisms to solidify its socioeconomic position.[12] The evidence for this supposition is not, however, unambiguous. A contrary possibility is that the late nineteenth-century elite was large and loosely tied together by common background and ideology rather than by economic interest. A third possibility is that the elite changed in size and character between the 1870s and the 1890s. Even assuming that the late nineteenth-century reform elite always remained small, cohesive, and bound together by economic fears and interest, the self-interest hypothesis fails to explain how that elite seized power and persuaded the American people to transform their political system from a democratic, majoritarian one into something resembling a bureaucratic oligarchy.

The self-interest hypothesis at best provides only a partial explanation for the birth of the bureaucratic state. But its ultimate failing is that it cannot be proved or disproved; we can never enter the minds or know the motives of people who have long since died. We can, however, analyze the rhetorical positions the reformers advanced to support their new system of government. This rhetoric may have reflected real motives, or it may have been simply a disguise for gross self-interest.

Nonetheless, analysis of the reformers' rhetoric is neither unimportant nor superficial. That rhetoric was addressed to what was and remains the central issue in American political thought — how to institutionalize a pluralistic form of government under which, in the words of Justice Holmes, "minorities" can "get an untroubled night's sleep."[13] Whether the motives of the reformers were benevolent or selfish, the fact remains that late in the century they persuaded at least some Americans that bureaucratization would institutionalize pluralism and thereby protect individuals and minorities from the power of the majority. Perhaps the thought and arguments of the reformers can also give us insight into how the modern, highly professionalized, bureaucratic state came into existence in America and hence about the essential nature of that state.

1

The Emergence of the Majoritarian Authority Structure

THE POLITICAL SYSTEM of mid-nineteenth-century America was a product of many forces, among them industrial and transportation technology. Technology made material progress possible, and the possibility of progress in turn generated numerous issues concerning the direction and the form it should take. Should a tariff be used to protect domestic industry? Should flowing streams be put to agricultural or to industrial use? Should roads, canals, or railroads be built to link communities? What precise route should a particular transportation improvement take? These and similar issues over which people were sharply divided often intruded into politics, requiring governmental decisionmaking of unprecedented complexity.[1]

Improvements in transportation and communication also led to an unprecedented spread of divergent ideas. In the eighteenth century, most people had taken their cosmology from the dominant church in their community: religious and intellectual dissent was the exception rather than the rule.[2] By the mid-nineteenth century, on the other hand, several churches existed on an equal legal and often social footing in most American communities, and itinerant revivalists recurrently introduced novel ideas into communities that had attained even a temporary religious equilibrium. Religion, moreover, retained considerable force in people's lives before the Civil War, and ideas of social reform remained intimately related to religious ones. A few people, such as the Mormon leader Joseph Smith, even died as a consequence of their religious beliefs and the social beliefs derived from them.[3] One might in summary say that competing ideologies existed in mid-nineteenth-century America and that these ideologies generated questions for the political process in a way similar to that in which the prospect of material progress raised issues.

Related to these two changes was a third, a transformation in the character of elite authority. A rapidly growing population, expanded economic opportunities productive of new wealth, and an implicit redefinition of the concept of upper class that accorded high status to anyone who earned enough money, whatever his social background,[4] increased the size of the upper class and, more important, gave new individuals entry to it. This change in the size and composition of the upper class tended to dilute the power and influence of individual aristocrats and made it more difficult for the upper class to preserve unity in the face of new issues and ideologies.

Such unity, however, was essential if deference to the elite was to provide the basis for government, as it may have throughout much of America during the eighteenth century.[5] But, whatever historians ultimately conclude about the power of aristocrats to enforce their values during the eighteenth century, it seems plain that factions within a large, divided upper class did not enjoy similar power in the nineteenth. The emergence early in the century of permanent divisions within the upper class, together with the appearance of new economic issues and the spread of novel religious and social ideas, inevitably transformed American politics and ultimately led to new structures of governance during the Jacksonian era.

The Majoritarian Ideal

Since the War for Independence the American polity had been premised, in theory if not in practice, on the idea that popular consent is the sole legitimate basis of government.[6] The mid-nineteenth century polity was a response to government's need to secure that consent at a time when new social questions were arising and old social structures collapsing: when those who were seeking to govern society needed to obtain as much support as possible for competing, often contradictory policies from an expanding electorate that was also subject to increasing ideological and socioeconomic division.

The consent of the people was the foundation on which the mid-nineteenth-century democratic polity was built. However, the concept of consent underwent redefinition. Popular consent could no longer mean, as it may have in eighteenth-century America, the free acceptance by the community as a whole of a social policy put forward by a single aristocratic elite.[7] With various interest groups advancing various social programs, it became possible for one segment of the community to attempt to impose its will upon another without the latter's consent. It was largely in the development of new devices for dealing with this possibility that the concept of consent received new meaning.

As it became more difficult to obtain the consent of the entire community, government responded to some matters by delegating to individuals the power to choose among alternatives. Consent was thereby redefined, at least in part, as an individual's affirmation and ratification of personal choice rather than the community's acceptance of a mandatory standard. In religion, for example, the legal system increasingly left the choice among beliefs to individuals rather than to entire communities when, through disestablishment, it ceased to use financial incentives to induce individuals to select one religion rather than another. A parallel movement occurred in other areas of moral control. Thus, there appears to have been a decline in the late eighteenth and early nineteenth centuries in the use of the criminal process to enforce community sexual proscriptions; although it cannot be said that all sanctions against fornication, adultery, and the like disappeared, formal criminal sanctions were used less often, and to that extent individuals in the nineteenth century had a greater choice in regard to sexual standards than they had in the eighteenth.[8]

Other sorts of matters over which government attempted regulation and ultimately coercion also became more limited. In the colonial period, local magistrates had regulated the details of individuals' economic lives.[9] In contrast, before the Civil War the federal government never assumed an extensive regulatory role; its most difficult enforcement tasks were the collection of its rather small revenue and the execution of the judgments of federal courts.[10] Whatever the precise burden of those tasks may have been, it was far less substantial than the burden assumed by colonial magistrates, who had attempted to enforce a coherent code affecting the minutiae of individuals' lives. Similarly, federal bureaucrats administering the regulatory state in the twentieth century would have a far heavier enforcement burden than their nineteenth-century counterparts. Only rarely did legislation like the embargo of 1807 extend the enforcement capacity of nineteenth-century federal officials, and even that legislation never fully tested the ultimate scope of federal power, for the embargo was repealed just as the Jefferson administration was beginning to take its most draconian steps to enforce it.[11]

Meanwhile, changes at the state level were transforming the states' role into one not vastly different from that of the federal government: the collection of revenue and the enforcement of judicial judgments.[12] By the early nineteenth century the old regulatory role of the states was withering away. Although some continued to attempt regulation of the economy, they found themselves confronting new economic phenomena that were much more difficult to control. As a result, many of their attempts at economic regulation failed. Massachusetts, for one, was only partially successful in its attempts to regulate banks, insurance companies, and railroads. Until the second half of the century, that state attempted enforcement through largely ineffective *ad hoc* legislative investigations occurring after the fact. Only in the 1850s were permanent boards established to oversee banks and insurance companies, followed in 1869 by a railroad commission that, in the view of modern commentators, had little effective power other than to investigate and publicize wrongdoing.[13] Other states had even less success. When Wisconsin, for example, sought in 1874 to establish a railroad commission with wide enforcement powers, the railroads openly directed their agents to disregard its orders and secured repeal of the enabling legislation in 1875.[14] Similarly, in Pennsylvania, various nineteenth-century commentators observed that the banking laws were "practically disregarded," "shamefully evaded," "contemptuously trampled on," and "daily violated with impunity";[15] like Massachusetts, Pennsylvania often sought to enforce banking and other regulatory laws solely through *post hoc* legislative investigations, with the result that regulatory programs were usually confined to the theoretical sphere. Even in New York in the post–Civil War era, a reform legislature met with only mixed success in the enforcement of its programs. The nation's first tenement house law was a dead letter within three years of its enactment, and an attempt to create a professional fire department succeeded only after initial rioting by old volunteer fire groups had been suppressed. On the other hand, a newly established Metropolitan Board of Health, armed with extensive power to inspect and disinfect houses and to quarantine individuals, achieved striking success in improving New York City's sanitation and in saving lives during a cholera epidemic there in 1866. During an eight-month period in that year, the board issued over thirty-one thousand orders, most of them requiring the cleaning and disinfecting of privies, cellars, yards, and the like — a remarkable feat of enforcement for the nineteenth century. Perhaps the board was so successful because its orders were backed by an implicit sanction of death, although even that sanction would not prompt Congress in mid-century to give federal authorities jurisdiction to deal with cholera.[16]

The narrowing of government's regulatory effort in the mid-nineteenth century was part of a broader change in the nature of government's total social role. The other element in that broad change was a vast increase in governmental grants and other forms of aid to promote economic growth. The federal government, for example, sold and gave away huge segments of the public domain. Much of the land went to individuals who settled it for farming, but large tracts were also awarded to entrepreneurs seeking to exploit timber and mineral wealth and to railroads as an inducement to construct transcontinental lines.[17] States were even more active than the federal government in promoting growth. The most noteworthy state investment was New York's Erie Canal, which several other states, notably Ohio and Pennsylvania, sought to emulate. In the first three decades of the century, virtually every state and locality in the nation sought to aid the economy by building roads and encouraging the construction of privately owned turnpikes, while in the decades that followed, similar state and municipal efforts took the form of buying stock and making loans to railroads.[18] Nor were state efforts limited to the construction of transportation facilities; Pennsylvania, for example, sought to aid the economy by investing in banks, and Massachusetts sought to promote industry by granting monopolistic privileges to mills.[19] Although grants were sometimes accompanied by regulations to ensure that the objects of the grants were attained, grants differed from more general forms of regulation in at least one significant way — namely, regulation could be applied uniformly to all citizens whereas grants, especially those that conferred monopolistic benefits in order to accomplish their developmental objectives, could be awarded to only one of several applicants. The increase in grants, occurring in conjunction with the narrowing scope of regulation, transformed government's primary role from one of ensuring the maintenance of uniform standards of moral and economic behavior throughout the community into one of allocating valuable resources among contending economic interests. This change in the role of government necessarily produced a corresponding change in the role of its officials: those who had once been charged with the maintenance of essentially moral values became distributors of government lucre among the various interests contending for it.

One response of officials who were authorized to dispose of valuable government-owned resources was to donate those resources to whatever individuals sought them; the recipients were thereby left with power to choose how the resources would be used. The federal government, as we have just seen, did this with much of the public domain. No society, however, can leave to individual determination every issue of social policy, no matter how hard it tries. Important questions always remain concerning the allocation of scarce resources—questions that cannot be resolved by letting individuals do whatever they will. There are also times when government must undertake minimal regulation of economic and moral conduct.

On those matters on which every individual could not be left entirely free, many political thinkers of the 1830s and 1840s believed that government must nonetheless treat every individual equally. Two principles followed from this concern for equal treatment. The first was the principle that government ought not to take economic action through either the enactment or the enforcement of laws that would favor one individual more than another and that therefore all government aid to the economy should be scrutinized closely to ensure that government treated all citizens equally by conferring on all the benefits that it conferred on some. On the national level, for example, President Jackson vetoed the 1832 bill rechartering the national bank partly because the grant of a banking monopoly extended a governmental favor or privilege to only some citizens.[20] In many states during the same period, the notion that government should distribute its benefits equally played an important role in the passage of general incorporation laws. In both national and state politics, the demand for equal treatment provided a rationale for extending internal improvements, such as canals and river and harbor improvements, into regions that otherwise might have claimed they were being treated less favorably than their neighbors.[21]

The second principle following from the concern for equal treatment was that government action not only must affect all citizens equally, but also must be the product of a political process in which all citizens participated equally. This principle required first that every white male citizen be given the right to vote without regard to wealth, education, or the like. It also lent support to the idea of majority rule.[22] In those situations where government acted, the premise of equal rights required that every individual have an equal right in determining the course of governmental action — that every individual have the same input into the governmental decision. One means of ensuring that every individual's choice be given equal weight was the principle of majority rule — the principle of counting the number of votes cast for each position, weighing each vote equally, and according victory to the side with the most votes.[23] For those who joined the Democratic party founded by Jackson and Van Buren, as well as for many of their opponents, the emphasis on equality, individualism, and ultimately majority rule became the dominant force in politics during the 1830s and 1840s.

The majoritarian ideal came to fruition at a time when power and authority in the United States remained fragmented, in large part as a result of the character of the federal system. Among the events of the 1830s that illustrated the limits of federal authority were Jackson's destruction of the second national bank, his opposition to federal funding of intrastate internal improvements, and South Carolina's nullification of the tariff of 1832, a move that resulted in something of a standoff between federal and state power. In the years that followed, state governments continued to pursue policies different from those of the federal government and of each other. The personal liberty laws of many mid-nineteenth-century northern states, for example, reflected a policy toward the return of fugitive slaves different from those of the federal government and of the southern states. Local governments also enjoyed significant freedom to pursue independent policies even though they were technically mere subdivisions of the states.[24]

Was there more than mere temporal coincidence between the fruition of the majoritarian ideal and the fragmentation of power and authority in mid-nineteenth-century America? It might be hypothesized that fragmentation of power facilitated easy resolution of social issues and acceptance of defeat by the losers. The crucial point is that, if a person in mid-nineteenth-century America lost a political contest in one forum, he could seek victory in another. Thus, if a person believed that government should charter banks or build roads to promote economic growth and lost an election on that issue on the federal level, he could easily seek to win a later election at the state level. Similarly, if he lost in one state, he could seek to win in another state or in some subdivision of a state. As even the Mormons ultimately learned, the nation's social structure remained in many ways similar to what it may have been in the eighteenth century: differences among localities persisted, yet ease of mobility usually enabled an individual to move to a new community. This fragmentation of authority was especially important for entrepreneurs and promoters; if a promoter seeking the aid of government for some project failed to obtain it at one level, he could almost invariably try another level of government or take his project to a new location, where he might meet with success. Both for people trying to experiment with ideas and for those trying to improve their economic lot, America's diversity and its fragmentation of power usually meant that, if a person failed to obtain the votes of a majority and thus failed to obtain governmental support for a project, it was easier to turn to another government and seek to persuade a different majority than to challenge the majoritarian foundation of the political system. Americans, in a sense, had a frontier not only in the West, but also in their diverse, federal political order, which nearly always offered a loser in one arena another in which to begin afresh.

Whatever the impact of federalism, it is plain that by the 1840s the majoritarian political tradition had matured. By then, divisive social issues and competing leadership elites in national and local politics had produced conflict and competition and forced political thinkers to redefine the concept of consent. Consent could no longer mean general community acquiescence in some public policy; something less — the approval of a majority — would have to suffice. For a brief period in the 1830s and 1840s, the diffusion of power through the federal system and the tendency to use power for allocative rather than regulatory ends may have made this new majoritarian tradition less of a threat to habits of pluralism than it would later become. Let us now examine how the new tradition led to a restructuring of government institutions to facilitate majoritarian rule.

The Legislature

In 1840 Robert M. T. Hunter, then Speaker of the House of Representatives, advanced the argument that the majority "party" in Congress "upon which it naturally devolved to propose a question ought to have the power to present its proposition in the shape for which it is willing to be responsible." By the time of Hunter's statement, majoritarian ideology had developed fully and had translated itself into a related but not identical idea that the majority party in Congress ought to control both the formulation and the ultimate enactment of legislation. The general acceptance of majoritarian ideology was manifested during the four decades between 1820 and 1860 in several subtle but important changes in the internal structure and procedures of Congress, changes that significantly increased the influence and power of majority political parties.[25]

One device by which a majority political party can attempt to control the operations of a legislature is a party caucus, in which the members of the party debate policy and bind themselves to abide by the caucus decision when a matter decided by the caucus reaches the legislative floor. The party caucus is a venerable institution in Congress, going back at least to 1796, when the Jeffersonian Republicans met to discuss policies and then to nominate Jefferson for the presidency. But although the party caucus is an old institution, the extent to which it has at various times sought to bind and succeeded in binding party members to the party's will is far from clear. The reason is that the caucus does not function publicly; although its influence on important issues can generally be traced, its influence on lesser issues is often hidden. Nevertheless, it seems likely that the caucus was not a powerful institution for enforcing party discipline in the closing years of the eighteenth and early decades of the nineteenth centuries. Recent scholarship indicates that in the earliest years of party formation, the majority Federalists, at least, did not constitute a cohesive organization capable of disciplining its members.[26] Similarly, during Madison's administration, Daniel Webster, then a young Federalist congressman, observed that there was "great diversity and schism, among the [majority Republican] party" so that the party could "not raise a Caucus, as yet, even, to agree what they will do"; another Federalist congressman, Alexander

Hanson, commented on a Republican caucus that broke up amidst "much dissention and wrangling."[27] Even during Jefferson's administration the Republican party was not always able to preserve discipline on important issues—a fact demonstrated by the ultimate failure of the attempt to remove Justice Samuel Chase from the Supreme Court bench through impeachment.[28]

By the mid-nineteenth century, however, the power of the caucus to bind party members on the legislative floor appears to have increased. In a statistical study done early in his career A. Lawrence Lowell concluded, though in a "cautious" way, that the influence of party on federal legislation "tend[ed] on the whole to increase" during the nineteenth century. Lowell found that in the Twenty-ninth Congress, which was elected in 1844, at least one party was able to obtain the votes of 90 percent or more of its members on an issue upon which the parties were divided in 61 percent of all Senate votes and 53 percent of all House votes.[29] More significant, perhaps, was Lowell's finding that the mid-nineteenth century was the one period in American history when party discipline was as effective in Congress as in the British Parliament, where "contentious legislation is in the main conducted by one party and opposed by the other." Lowell found that late in the century party unity was "decidedly less strictly" maintained in Congress than in Parliament.[30]

The caucus, however, is not the only instrument by which a majority party in Congress can control the course of legislation. Equally important is the capacity of the party leadership to control the work of congressional committees, which by the 1820s had already acquired significant control over the course of national legislation.[31]

One way party leaders increased party influence over committees was by concentrating important legislative work in the hands of a few committees, thereby limiting the number of separate bodies that had to be closely watched. In the Senate, the Committee on Finance became all powerful. Its power rested upon Senate Rule 30, enacted in 1850 at the behest of Robert M. T. Hunter, the committee's chairman. The rule effectively prohibited members of the Senate from adding amendments to any appropriations bill once it had reached the floor; amendments had to be added by the committee. The rule was important because Congress had already adopted the practice of enacting most legislation near the end of a session, when floor time was scarce; therefore, the best way to get a bill before the

Senate was to attach it as an amendment to an appropriations bill, which had priority over other legislation. By lodging in the Finance Committee exclusive power to add amendments, the Senate gave that committee effective control over its agenda and an effective veto over the substance of legislation. By their placement, in turn, on the Finance Committee and on important special committees such as the Joint Committee on Reconstruction, party leaders were able to dominate the Senate's proceedings as long as they retained their party's support.[32] In part, their ability to control the upper chamber stemmed from their capacity to drive legislation proposed by other senators from the floor by reporting a bill from a privileged committee like Finance, which had priority over other bills. The ultimate source of the leadership's power, however, lay in its capacity to cement a majority together by exchanges of favors and to compel senators who wished to enjoy the advantages of being part of the majority to retain the leaders' favor.

The power structure of the mid-nineteenth-century House roughly paralleled that of the Senate. In the House, there were two important committees. One was the Committee on Ways and Means, which had jurisdiction over the national debt, all banking and currency legislation, and all appropriations and revenue measures, including the tariff. Bills reported by this committee occupied most of the floor time of the House. The other powerful committee was the Rules Committee. An 1841 ruling of Speaker John White, who observed that "the rules" of the House must "conform to the will of the majority," gave a majority of the House power temporarily to suspend the regular rules by adopting a Rules Committee report in favor of suspension. In the same year, the Rules Committee received authority from the House to report at any time, and in 1853 its reports were given priority over other pending business. Given regular rules that did not facilitate the bringing of legislation to the House floor, the Rules Committee's power to bring legislation to the floor at any time through suspension of the rules gave it effective control over the agenda of the House and an effective veto over legislation. Together with the chairman of the Ways and Means Committee, the chairman of the Rules Committee, who after 1858 was always simultaneously the Speaker of the House, was the dominant figure in the chamber; as long as they executed their party's will, the Speaker and a few other members of the two committees were the leaders and masters of the House.[33]

Majority parties also kept control over congressional committees through power over the appointment and tenure of committee members. In the mid-nineteenth-century Senate, committees were elected, and elections were under the control of the majority party. In the House, on the other hand, committees were named by the Speaker, but as early as the 1820s it was "understood that the appointment of the committees in the House by the new Speaker . . . [was] to be settled by the leaders of the party," who would carry out the party's will. Indeed, in 1836 the House rejected a proposed rule that would have required a majority of each of its committees to consist of competent individuals chosen without respect to party; this move confirmed the relevance of party in the makeup of committees. As Senator Bayard later remarked, it was understood that "the political party having the majority . . . [would] necessarily control all the committees . . . because they . . . must, as a party, protect themselves against the chance of the control of the business of the body going into the hands of their opponents."[34]

More important was the majority party's control over committee chairmen. The most important fact about the selection of committee chairmen in the mid-nineteenth century was that a strict seniority system was not in effect. There was no requirement in either house of Congress that the member of the majority having served longest on a particular committee be made chairman; indeed, there was no prohibition against depriving a party member of a committee chairmanship and replacing him with another member of the same party. Leaders of a majority accordingly had considerable freedom to place on committees fellow members who would be most faithful and subservient to the majority's will, and independent-minded members would likely find themselves removed from positions of influence.[35]

In the Senate it became clear by the 1860s that committee chairmen could continue to serve only for as long as they agreed with their party's policies. Thus, William Allen, chairman of the Senate's Committee on Foreign Relations, asked to be relieved from further duty on the committee when he broke with the Polk administration over the treaty with Great Britain dividing the Oregon country; he told the Senate that, because he had "been unable to conform . . . [his] opinion to that which recent events . . . show to be the opinion of the Senate," he deemed it "proper . . . to afford the Senate an opportunity to reconstruct the committee, with a view to that coincidence of opinion between the Senate and its committee . . . which is essential to the unembarrassed action of the body." A decade later Hannibal Hamlin, who had been a Democrat, resigned his chairmanship of the Committee on Commerce when he broke with his party over the issue of slavery in the territories; Hamlin told the Senate that he recognized that he owed his chairmanship "to the dominant majority in the Senate" and that "when I cease to harmonize with the majority . . . I feel that I ought no longer to hold that respectable position."[36] During the next two decades no senator resigned a committee chairmanship because he disagreed with his party, but three were deprived of chairmanships. In 1859 Stephen Douglas was deprived of the chairmanship of the Committee on Territories after he had broken with the Buchanan administration on the issue of slavery in the territories. During the Civil War, John P. Hale lost the naval committe chairmanship after a lengthy feud with the Secretary of the Navy. Finally, Charles Sumner was removed from the chairmanship of the Foreign Relations Comittee when in 1871 he split with the Grant administration over the annexation of what is now the Dominican Republic.[37]

There was also support in the House for the position that a chairman of a committee ought to be in agreement with the views of the majority of the committee and of the House. In 1871, for example, Benjamin F. Butler refused to serve as chairman of a committee charged with investigating the Ku Klux Klan because it was "a parliamentary practice" that "the chairman of a committee should be in harmony with the majority who constitute it" and Butler did not feel himself to be so. Three decades before, when charged with being "possessed of a species of monomania on all subjects connected with people as dark as a Mexican," John Quincy Adams offered to resign as chairman of the Foreign Relations Committee if it deemed him ill suited to determine American relations with Mexico. Similarly, in December 1860 several southern congressmen refused to serve on the Committee of Thirty-Three charged with compromising differences between North and South, in part because they could not "consent to act with the majority of that committee" and would "be compelled to coincide with the minority."[38]

As a result of party control over the selection and tenure of members on committees and the concentration of jurisdiction in a small number of committees, control of mid-nineteenth-century legislative business was, in the words of one recent scholar, "removed from the committees and their chairmen, and placed in the hands of the party chieftains whose powers resulted not from committee chairmanships but from leadership of the party caucus." As late as 1879, President Rutherford B. Hayes observed that the House rules had resulted "in a consolidation of unchecked and despotic power in the House of Representatives," which tended to make a "bare majority of the House" into "the Government."[39] Unlike earlier Democratic leaders, however, President Hayes and other reformers of the 1870s were not pleased with this concentration of power, for it affected the very substance of the legislative process. It made legislation a product of a mutual exchange of favors in the interest of party unity — a process now called logrolling — rather than of reasoned consideration of the nation's needs. In turn, as vague criteria for distinguishing legitimate from illegitimate favoritism proved inadequate to maintain political honesty, the rights of minorities were made dependent on the will of the majority, and the entire political process was opened to the dangers of corruption.

The Executive

The idea that the institutions of government ought to respond to the will of the majority of the people also affected the functioning of the executive branch in the mid-nineteenth century. At the federal level, the effects were first felt with substantial force during the administration of Andrew Jackson. Jackson, who declared himself the agent of the democratic majority of the people, put the spoils system into effect. His announced objective in doing so, he told Congress in 1829, was to transform office from a "species of property" into "an instrument created solely for the service of the people."[40]

In fact, Jackson and his party had two interrelated objectives. The first, which the Jacksonians proclaimed repeatedly, was to put an end to the special privileges of the few and create a new structure of power that would give control of government to the people. Jackson contended that "offices were not established to give support to particular men at public expense" and that "in a country where offices . . . [w]ere created solely for the benefit of the people no one man ha[d] any more intrinsic right to official station than another."[41]

Office, of course, never came to be shared equally by all. When he came to power, Jackson was being pressed vigorously by men who wanted their share of power; at the beginning of his administration, thousands descended upon Washington seeking office. As Jesse Hoyt, who eventually became collector of the port of New York, informed Martin Van Buren, the incoming secretary of state:

> I take it for granted that all who do not support the present administration you will not consider your friends, and of course will lose your confidence. I have said from the commencement of the contest that I would not support any administration who would support men in power that had contributed to overthrow the democratic party in this State. I have preached this doctrine too long, and it has taken too [strong] a footing here, to be easily got rid of. This is not only the doctrine in theory, but we require it to be reduced to practice by the servants of the people to whom we have temporarily delegated the trust. I speak now the universal sentiments of the democracy of this city, and you may rely upon it no man can be sustained who aids or abets in the disappointment of the just expectations of the people on this subject—and all personal considerations and private friendships must yield to *political justice*.

It clearly seemed "right and politic to encourage and reward friends," and Jackson accordingly had little choice but to remove old officeholders from their jobs when "the public sentiment" in their locality "demand[ed] a change in the office."[42] But the result of removing traditional aristocratic officeholders and replacing them with others was not the equality that Jackson and "the democracy" sought. Once they had been in office for a time, most of the new Jacksonian leaders probably acquired whatever upperclass characteristics they had not already possessed when entering office. The end result of Jackson's new appointments thus may have been only the replacement of one elite by another, not the end of rule by the elite.

That result, however, was consistent with the other apparent objective of Jackson and his associates, which was to create new structures of order and authority to replace traditional ones that had deteriorated. The Jacksonians had watched centers of social power such as organized religion, professional associations, and informal business groupings collapse and thereby lose effective power to impose standards on their members. They expressed themselves on such matters as the "debased . . . standard of commercial honesty," "love of wealth," "corruption," and the need to return to the old republican "virtue."[43] They thus glimpsed the fact that the traditional social order inherited from the eighteenth century had disintegrated and that effective government could no longer rest on it. They may well have sensed as they tried to discharge the duties of office that they could no longer take advantage of old links with the old centers of social power to ensure uncoerced obedience, for those centers had become as weak as they themselves were.

But they were not without power of a different sort. Their capacity to bestow offices, contracts, and favors conferred real power on them if they required the recipients in return to give loyalty and render services on a continuing basis. The Jacksonians saw that they could bind "the mass of the parties" together "with the hope of office, and its honors and emoluments." More was at stake, however, than simply the winning of elections; indeed, William T. Barry, one of Jackson's appointees, denied "exercising . . . influence 'for political' or 'electioneering purposes.' " Dispensers of patronage could demand in return loyalty to and support of government programs as well as assistance in winning elections. As Barry informed S. L. Gouverneur, another appointee, he had "received the appt. . . . under the full impression that you were ready and willing to take upon yourself the entire responsibility of cooperating with the administration in its measures" and that those who "acted partially in their stations, ought not to expect to remain in office."[44] In sum, the Jacksonians commenced a reconstruction of the executive branch that was based on the willingness of people to enforce the will of a political majority in return for access to wealth and power.

The Jacksonian attempt to weld party and office into a new structure of authority was observable throughout the federal bureaucracy and in many states, notably New York and Pennsylvania. Detailed examination of three branches of the federal establishment — the post office, the customs service, and the land office — will illustrate how the new authority structure emerged.

In the Jacksonian era the post office was the largest branch of the federal establishment, with some eleven thousand local offices. Its size alone made it important, for by wisely distributing postal jobs an administration could gain power over a large number of employees and their families.[45] But postal jobs themselves explain only a small part of the post office's significance, for the department had special importance in two other ways. First, it did not ship mail by itself; instead mail was shipped by private contractors. Those contractors made a good deal of money; for example, the contract for the thirty-one-mile route between Hagerstown, Maryland and Mc-Connellstown, Pennsylvania was worth $1,400 per year, and the combined contracts from Baltimore to Washington and Baltimore to Wheeling, Virginia, were worth $57,000. Moreover, the number of contracts was large: by 1835, the number of contractors and their immediate dependents was over twenty thousand and they received almost $2 million from the post office.[46] Before the appointment of Amos Kendall as postmaster general in 1835, the department had let most contracts to its "old and faithful contractors" who had delivered the mail for long periods, through changes of administration, without regard to their politics. Kendall ceased favoring contractors who had carried the mail in the past and instead favored those whose politics were more acceptable to the administration.[47] Together with post office employees, these contractors and their employees constituted a sizable army whose economic interests ensured their loyalty to federal law and administration policy.

The post office gained added importance from the fact that its employees were "agents for disseminating information throughout the country." Jackson himself had noted of the post office that

> in a political point of view this Department is chiefly important as affording the means of diffusing knowledge. It is to the body politic what veins and arteries are to the natural — conveying rapidly and regularly to the remotest part of the system correct information of the operations of the Government, and bringing back to it the wishes and feelings of the people. Through its agency we have secured to ourselves the full enjoyment of the blessings of a free press.

Although control of the post office would by no means guarantee total control of the dissemination of news and political opinion, the post office could surely help to manipulate political opinion and maintain social order, as it did when it refused to deliver abolitionist tracts in the South. The franking privilege that local postmasters possessed until it was taken from them by statute in 1845 also aided in manipulating news and opinion: by distributing local postmasterships together with the right to send all one's personal mail free of charge to local editors, the Jacksonians cemented their relations with those editors and gained substantial control over the news and opinion printed for the public.[48] Each postmaster became "an electioneering outpost." By also requiring their opponents to pay postage for mailing opposition publications, they ensured that the opposition would function at a competitive disadvantage. In short, the postmasters, "when organized into a political corps . . . [could] give facilities to the circulation of newspapers, extras, etc., favorable to their views, and throw obstacles in the way of the circulation of those of an opposite character."[49] By making the circulation of opposition views expensive they could play upon the economic acquisitiveness of their contemporaries to encourage them to support rather than oppose the administration.

The customs office similarly relied on economic incentives as a means of exercising political control. Again, the potential for power in the service rested in part on the number of available places: by the 1850s the service in New York alone employed close to one thousand. Those thousand, however, were only the tip of the iceberg. The real power of the collector and his staff was their control of the speed with which imported goods cleared the port and the appraisal and classification of goods and hence the tax imposed on them.[50] In short, they controlled the profit of the merchants. As to the speed of clearance, there is evidence that by the 1850s some merchants were required to pay fictitious charges or wait indefinitely for port services.[51] In the classification and appraisal of goods, customs agents had significant discretion, particularly if goods were of an unusual sort, if they were purchased with foreign currencies of fluctuating value, or if they had been partially damaged.[52] Of course, if an agent refused to clear goods or imposed an excessive tax on them, a merchant possessed judicial and, after 1842, administrative remedies; but these were costly in terms of time and delay.[53] Thus, the customs service could erect significant obstacles in the path of a merchant who was in its disfavor. More important, though, were the benefits it could grant its friends. It could clear their goods with special dispatch and classify and assess them so that low taxes would be imposed. Within the existing state of customs administration there were no procedures for controlling such favoritism; in particular, undervaluations of individual shipments of goods could not be challenged by measuring them against an objective standard of value.[54]

The service accordingly had the power to give its merchant friends a special competitive advantage that their competitors lacked standing to challenge in either a judicial or an administrative proceeding. As one secretary of the treasury observed in the latter part of the century, even slight favoritism might "enable a successful evader of duties to outstrip and outsell all rivals in the same line of merchandise." By so organizing the customs service for political ends, an administration could place substantial pressure on merchants engaged in importing foreign goods, as did every administration from that of Jackson on.* Merchants could also be pressured into helping the administration obtain the support of businessmen and other individuals who dealt with them once the importation process had been completed. It was commonplace for a member of the party in power to proselytize someone with similar interests who had not voted for the party; on one occasion, for example, the Democratic leader of Hartford was urged to get one of his "mariners" to convince a fellow seaman to join the party.[55]

The land office was as politically significant in the newly emerging states of the West as the customs service was in the port cities of the East. As one Senate committee reported in 1840, "few places . . . afford[ed] such ready and certain means . . . of extending favors and accommodation to a large and influential portion of the community, as those attached to the land system." In part, the importance of the land office resulted from its size and from the public funds spent annually to maintain it. In 1833 there were fifty-three land districts throughout the West; in 1837, there were sixty-two. Each district had its own staff, and in addition there was a staff of 8 surveyors general and 126 deputy surveyors. By 1840 the cost of this administrative machinery was nearly $350,000 per year. Money paid out in salaries, however, accounted for only a small part of the land office's significance. Like officials in the post office and the customs service, those in the land office could do favors for many other citizens in their locality. As in the case of the post office, much work was contracted out to people who were not permanent employees of the gov-

---

*A merchant belonging to the party out of power could increase his leverage, however, by hiring a customs broker who was a member of the party in power. But, of course, this imposed an additional cost that his competitors avoided. See William J. Hartman, "Politics and Patronage: The New York Customs House, 1852–1902" (Ph.D. diss., Columbia University, 1952), p. 205.

ernment. Surveying, for example, was often contracted out to teams consisting not only of surveyors but of chainmen, foresters, and hunters as well; in 1819 Congress appropriated $237,000 for such surveying, and one surveyor during the second and third decades of the century received $450,000 from the government. Land office agents could also conduct public auctions on a basis favorable to local residents and act as real estate agents for favored clients. Local agents often held large amounts of federal money, which they could place on deposit in favored banks or lend to individuals. Finally, many agents bought and sold land on their own account and thereby became important economic figures in their localities.[56]

The land operations of the federal government gained added importance because they gave rise to disputes requiring administrative and sometimes congressional adjudication. Congress alone struggled during the century with between 30,000 and 35,000 claims covering some 45 million acres. These cases, along with land cases heard before the land office and even in the courts, were often highly political. Leading political figures like Daniel Webster, John M. Berrien, and Hugh Lawson White often served as attorneys for claimants — a sort of legal practice in which huge retainers could be earned; Edwin M. Stanton, for example, earned a fee of $25,000 in the 1850s representing the government in litigation contesting title to the center of San Francisco. Major land claimants also exercised influence on individual members of Congress. Major claimants in Missouri, for example, provided crucial support toward Thomas H. Benton's election to the Senate in 1820, and thereafter Benton persistently introduced legislation to enable his supporters to advance their claims. Even the judiciary was subjected to political pressure when the federal district judge for Missouri, an opponent of the large land claimants, was impeached for action unbecoming a judge when he entered into extrajudicial discussion of land cases pending before him. Even though he was not convicted by the Senate, this action against the federal judge was striking.[57] Obviously the land office, with far less political independence than a federal judge, could not avoid being subjected to political pressures.

The land office was central to the politics of several states and territories. When Arkansas became a state in 1836, the former surveyor general was elected governor and the former receiver at Little Rock became a congressman. In Michigan the Democratic party came to power through its control of the land office patronage. That patronage was also a valuable political lever in Indiana, and in Florida the land office faction dominated territorial politics for a decade. In the words of one Jacksonian politico, a position dealing with management of the public domain was simply "a very snug office."[58]

The post office, customs service, and land office were not the only branches of government that either employed large numbers or provided opportunities for profit for independent contractors dealing with government. At the federal level, there was also money to be made in War Department contracts, in the navy yards, and in the Bureau of Indian Affairs and the local agencies dealing with Indians.[59] What Jackson and his associates recognized was that this opportunity for profit could be used to weld party and office together at both the federal and state levels and thereby help solve the problem of declining authority structures.

This objective, however, often was not clearly seen as separate from the objective of ending the special privileges of aristocrats, and in fact the two were related. First, they were related in the rather obvious way that office could not be given to faithful political partisans until it had been taken away from its traditional aristocratic holders. When Jackson replaced the traditional officeholders with new men faithful to the party, that is, he solved both problems simultaneously. Second, the idea of rotation — "a leading principle in the republican creed" that sought to ensure access to office on the basis of equality rather than of privilege — increased the strength a party brought to office by increasing the number of those who could hope someday to hold it. The point is that men who expected to gain office within months or even a few years, whether by rotation of their own party members or by an electoral victory of the opposition party, would join with current officeholders to support and even increase official power; it would be better to support the exactions and impositions of the incumbent so that one could himself exact and impose in the future than to challenge the incumbent's power and find oneself assuming an office without prerogatives. "With a reasonable rotation," as William Dickson observed, "every citizen of political aspiration and experience who reach[ed] middle life and conduct[ed] himself well . . . [could] hope to crown his family with the reflected honor which office confer[red]. This prospect . . . [was] a motive to good work."[60]

Finally, the goal of eliminating aristocratic privilege and creating new power structures was related at least in theory to emerging concepts of majoritarian democracy. In a society that was to be democratic, power had to be held by the common man. This meant first that aristocrats had to be deprived of their special claim on office. It also meant that all official power, including the power of subordinate officials, had to be placed directly under the control of the people, preferably, as Frederick Grimke urged, by having all officials popularly elected or, where that proved impossible, by having them rotated in and out of office by those who were so elected. As Congressman John A. Logan told the House after the spoils system had been well established:[61]

> It is by having their agents constantly before them that their acts may be denounced or confirmed that the people maintain their supremacy and enforce their will. This, sir, is the theory and practice of our Government. Immediate responsibility we all incur, and speedy settlements we all must render. The appointment of subordinates or the nominations for appointments are just as much a part of our responsibility as any other which we have, and a share in those appointments and the right to become for a time a portion of the administrative force of the Government is one of the recognized rights of the people.

In short, the perception of office as political — as capable of determining the course of social change for the benefit of particular groups and interests — required, in a democratic state, that office be transformed into an instrument of a political majority. This transformation in turn required replacing aristocrats with what would later become known as spoilsmen and linking office with party in a way that ensured that the will of the majority party would be brought to bear upon the office holder. The latter would in turn acquire renewed strength to bring that will to bear upon a recalcitrant minority.

The Judiciary

The general mid-nineteenth-century perception of the political nature of all governmental activity also began to affect ideas about the nature of judge-made law. Most Americans who thought about law came to regard the task of the judge as an essentially political one in which the interests of some groups were often given preference over the interests of others. Although policy issues did not become explicit in many cases, most mid-nineteenth-century legal thinkers understood that all law is grounded in policy. This growing awareness of the political nature of the judicial process suggested to some that the judicial branch of government should be democratized so that the interests of the majority would prevail over those of the minority.

In the first third of the century members of the legal profession began to observe with frequency that all law, whether promulgated by a court or a legislature, was an essentially mutable and transitory product of sovereign command. There could be no doubt, as the author of one treatise observed, that "our reports are our law, and the publication of reports is, in fact, the enactment of laws."[62] Most of the legal profession also shared a conviction that the law's capacity for change was an instrument to be harnessed to promote economic growth. Although economic growth had been important throughout the nation's history, it reached spectacular proportions in the first half of the nineteenth century, as a predominantly agrarian economy substantially confined to the Atlantic coast began to develop into an industrialized economy of continental scope. This economic transformation was effectuated with much conscious effort: by the first third of the century economic success had become the preoccupation of many Americans.[63] Not surprisingly, the urge for economic development infected the legal profession. In states like Kentucky and Ohio, judges began to think that law should be "a practical system, adapted to the condition and business of society" and "suit[ed to] the local condition and . . . exigencies of every people." For much of the mid-century legal profession, the true glory of the common law was that its rules were "continually expanding with the progress of society, and adapting themselves to the gradual changes of trade and commerce, and the mechanic arts, and the exigencies and usages of the country."[64]

Courts from Massachusetts and New York to California frequently implemented such a philosophy, rejecting ancient authorities and looking instead to "the circumstances of the country," to "improvement in our commercial code," or to a rule's "inconvenience to holders of commercial paper" in order to justify their decisions.[65] In *Pynchon v. Stearns*, for example, an 1846 Massachusetts court failed to consider eighteenth-century American precedent and held, contrary to the English common law rule, that a life tenant's construction of a

house and an entryway thereto did not constitute waste. In its opinion the court cited only three cases, all dealing with the essentially
political question of the power of American courts to reject English
decisions, and then rejected the English rule on the ground that "the
ancient doctrine of waste, if universally adopted in this country,
would greatly impede the progress of improvement."[66] Similarly, in
M'Culloch v. *Eagle Insurance Co.*, an 1822 case that raised the question
whether a contract arose when an acceptance and a revocation of an
offer crossed in the mails, the court held that there was no contract,
arguing that its holding was "reasonable in mercantile contracts,
though it was decided otherwise in the [English] case of *Cooke* v. *Ox-
ley*."[67] Courts likewise demonstrated greater interest in the prospective consequences of their decisions than in common law precedent
when, in a series of cases, they abandoned the established English
doctrine of ancient lights, on the ground that the doctrine could not
"be applied in the growing cities and villages of this country, without
working the most mischievous consequences."[68] And in an analogous line of cases beginning with *Thurston* v. *Hancock*, early nineteenth-century courts undermined ancient property doctrine by rejecting the rule that neighbors must provide each others' buildings
with lateral support, for that rule too was seen as a threat to the
growth of the nation's cities.[69]

In implementing what recent scholarship has labeled an instrumental style of reasoning,[70] early nineteenth-century judges not only
refused to give effect to ancient English and American authorities;
they also rejected arguments that sought to deduce results in a formalistic style from fundamental premises about the inalienable
rights of man. The leading case in which an instrumental style of
reasoning triumphed over arguments based on concepts of inalienable human rights was *Charles River Bridge* v. *Warren Bridge*, decided
by the Supreme Court in 1837. The issue in the case was whether
the owners of a toll bridge built pursuant to a legislative charter
could enjoin the construction of a free bridge to be operated along a
parallel, proximate route by the state. Counsel for the plaintiff toll
bridge spoke often of "natural right[s]" and "fundamental principles,"
among them the rule prohibiting the taking of "private property for
public use, without compensation." In the lower court, one judge
agreed that the "fundamental principles . . . [on which plaintiff relied were] no longer considered disputable," and Justice Story, dis-

senting in the Supreme Court, observed that those principles had long "been held to be fundamental axioms in free governments like ours." But the majority of the Court, in an opinion by the newly appointed Jacksonian Chief Justice Roger B. Taney, took an instrumentalist approach and ruled in favor of the new state bridge, on the ground that "in a country like ours, free, active and enterprising, continually advancing in numbers and wealth, new channels of communication are daily found necessary, both for travel and trade."[71]

Instrumentalist arguments directed to the promotion of economic growth were triumphant between 1820 and 1850 in yet another line of cases, in which the Supreme Court discerned the importance of national economic unity in furthering economic growth. In the first case in the series, *Gibbons* v. *Ogden*, the Court in 1824 invalidated a New York grant of a monopoly over steamboat transporation on the Hudson River, because the monopoly threatened to obstruct the free flow of commerce among the states. As Chief Justice Marshall declared in his opinion, that free flow and the economic growth that would ensue were "primary objects for which the people of America adopted their government"; as Attorney General Wirt had argued, the free flow of commerce in a market potentially of continental scope provided a means "of exciting the energies of the people, of invoking the genius of invention, and of creating and diffusing the lights of science." Wirt later argued in *Brown* v. *Maryland* that the framers of the Constitution had perceived the power to regulate commerce as "a great source of national wealth and aggrandizement [;] . . . a great means of developing the agricultural and manufacturing resources of the country, and its general industry; . . . [and] an instrument by which the nation could be enriched." When another lawyer argued some years later that a free national market could not exist unless federal courts had power to declare "the common mercantile law of the respective States," the Supreme Court in *Swift* v. *Tyson* agreed and promulgated a uniform rule of commercial law "for the benefit and convenience of the commercial world." Still later, the Court in *Cooley* v. *Board of Wardens* reaffirmed the economic importance of unified national economic controls, "which the experience of more than half a century has taught us to value so highly."[72]

State courts in contracts cases similarly rejected arguments premised on an allegedly inalienable right not to be held to contractual liability to which one had not consented. For example, insurers were held liable for risks that they had never agreed to insure, such as additions to insured buildings, so that individuals would be encouraged to construct additions to buildings. Likewise, persons who had agreed to pay only for perfect performance of a contract were required to pay for substantial performance — a doctrine that enabled contractors to do more work by not requiring them to do it perfectly.[73] The early nineteenth century also saw increasing though not always successful attacks on the widespread eighteenth-century rule that money should not be lent at a usurious rate of interest; it was urged that, whereas the doctrine of usury meant that the community set the rate at which money could be lent, a better rule would be to permit individuals to make that choice for themselves. Even greater change occurred in other contract rules; doctrines that in the colonial period had permitted the law to fix prices at which goods were sold, to determine standards of quality, and to set other exchange terms were overruled and replaced by doctrines leaving such matters to the discretion of the individuals involved.[74] As a result of these and many similar sorts of cases, much of the judiciary, the legal profession, and ultimately the public at large was beginning by the 1820s to understand that "justice is regulated by no certain or fixed standard, so that the ablest and purest minds might sometimes differ with respect to it"[75] — in short, that the art of judging was often highly political.

The political character of the judicial process was emphatically illustrated in the increasingly common practice of judicial review, which assumed a more political cast in the late 1810s and 1820s. In part, judicial review of the constitutionality of legislation seemed more political because all judicial decisionmaking seemed more political. Beginning around 1815, however, courts further magnified the political character of judicial review by invalidating legislative acts resolving social conflicts between politically organized groups — something they had rarely done in the early years of the century.

One such case concerned the propriety of government aid to banks. Whether such aid was proper was a most divisive issue in the 1830s, but when the legislature of Tennessee granted aid to the state bank in the form of special remedies in suits against its defaulting debtors, the state's highest court made no attempt to avoid reconsidering the legislature's policy judgment; it implicitly rejected that judgment and invalidated the act. Another divisive social issue throughout the South in the 1820s and 1830s was whether to impose stricter legal controls on slaves and free blacks; but again, when one state legislature deprived manumitted slaves of equitable remedies to secure their freedom, the court ignored the legislature's resolution of the policy conflict and held the statute unconstitutional.[76] In the 1820s the scope of the power of eminent domain also became an issue productive of political division, but judges nonetheless continued to declare some legislative takings invalid. Finally, the constitutionality of debtor stay laws raised significant political questions, but courts nevertheless struck such laws down.[77]

The trend toward judicial reevaluation of legislative policy determinations intensified during the 1840s and 1850s. Three major issues on which organized political groups took stands and which sometimes influenced the outcome of elections during those decades concerned the authority of the states to prohibit the sale, ownership, or consumption of alcoholic beverages; the wisdom of granting state or municipal aid to railroads or other public works and appropriating tax money therefor; and the propriety of giving increased legal protection to property rights of married women.[78] On all three subjects, courts invalidated legislation in a number of cases.[79] The relationship between banks and state governments also remained controversial, and one state court ignored a legislative policy judgment and held unconstitutional a statute permitting incorporation of banks without legislative approval of individual charters.[78] In yet another case a court entered the political thicket when it held invalid a pardon to Thomas Dorr, a leader of the 1842 rebellion that temporarily overthrew the government of Rhode Island.[81]

In all such cases the courts could readily see "that . . . results of vast moment h[u]ng on . . . [their] decision." Even when passing upon the validity of private acts or of other legislation affecting only a small number of individuals, courts after 1820 were more aware of the public interest in and general significance of their decisions. Thus, the Supreme Court of Vermont noted "the interest which seem[ed] to have been excited in the publick mind" over its prospective invalidation of a private act releasing a debtor from imprisonment, while the Court of Appeals of Maryland recognized the "grave and delicate character . . . [and the importance] as respects the interests involved, and the results to the community" of a case challenging the constitutionality of a legislative revocation of the state university's charter. Similarly, the Virginia Court of Appeals observed that a case involving the power of a private corporation to raise subscriptions was "of great interest as regards the commonwealth and individual stockholders . . . and on principle . . . [was] deeply interesting to every citizen of the state."[82] In short, courts after 1820 frequently found they were being pressed to reopen social controversies that had tentatively been settled in a legislative forum.

Even with this increasingly political cast, judicial review might nonetheless have been justified as insurance against the danger that legislators would betray their trust and violate the Constitution but for the fact the legislative branch itself was becoming increasingly democratic. As it did so, the prospect of legislative betrayal seemed increasingly remote. In place of conflict and betrayal, courts like the Supreme Court of Alabama began after 1820 to assume that legislators were "in direct communication with the people, and responsible to them." The Supreme Court of Tennessee, like other American courts, had always "conceded that all power is inherent in the people," and its further concession that the "voice" of the people was "heard through the legislatures" pointed toward a conclusion, stated explicitly by the New York Court of Errors, that legislatures were "representatives of the sovereign power" and were therefore possessed of "the right to exercise sovereign power," which courts in turn ought not obstruct.[83]

Together, these three changes shifted judicial review into a new context. Courts could no longer conceive of review as the mere comparison of a legislative act with a fixed constitutional provision — a comparison involving neither exercise of political discretion nor opposition to the will of the people. Judges now acknowledged that most constitutional provisions were vague and pliable and that when they construed them so as to invalidate legislative acts, they often did so in order to further political, social, or economic doctrines that they endorsed but that the people had rejected in the more democratic legislative process. This new context made judicial review more difficult to justify, for it made plain the doctrine's antidemocratic tendencies. Awareness of the political and antidemocratic tendencies of judicial review, in turn, led to several challenges to the practice.

The earliest challenge occurred in Ohio as a result of an 1807 decision of the Ohio Supreme Court invalidating an act raising the jurisdictional limit of suits that could be heard without a jury by a justice of the peace. The Ohio legislature thereupon instituted impeachment proceedings against two of the judges. Supporters of the impeachment argued that the legislature had power to declare "what is or what is not law," whereas courts had the duty merely to say "what law is"; if the judges could declare what was not law, they would constitute themselves a legislative body superior to the legislature elected by the people. In short, the supporters of impeachment argued that judicial review was ultimately a political act by a court, but they failed by one vote to convict the two judges, who advanced arguments in their defense similar to those of Chief Justice Marshall in *Marbury* v. *Madison*.[84]

The next challenge to judicial review occurred after an 1815 conference of judges of the several Georgia superior courts expressed a view that legislation staying suits against soldiers and debtors was unconstitutional; the Georgia House of Representatives responded to this declaration with a resolution denying that the judges had any power to hold conferences, and for several years thereafter the judges held none.[85] Eight years later the Kentucky legislature responded even more sharply to two similar decisions invalidating an 1819 debtor stay law. The legislature, in urging the court to reverse its decision upon a petition for rehearing reminded the court that legislation "should, when it shall be thought expedient to do so, be repealed by the legislature, and not by the Appellate Court." When the court declined to reverse itself, the legislature, after failing to muster the two-thirds vote necessary to remove the judges from office, abolished the existing Kentucky Court of Appeals and created a new one, with new judges. This act divided the state into old-court and new-court parties that dominated state politics and received national attention for two years, until the old-court party won control of the legislative and executive branches of the state government in 1826 and voted the new Court of Appeals out of existence.[86]

This controversy in Kentucky may also have contributed to the final challenge to judicial review, put forward by John B. Gibson, a justice of the Pennsylvania Supreme Court. In his 1825 dissenting opinion in *Eakin* v. *Raub*, Gibson advocated abandonment of the doctrine and recited all the common arguments. He noted that "repugnance to the constitution is not always self-evident" and that because men "seldom . . . think exactly alike," "conflicts" in interpreting constitutional provisions would be "inevitable." Once the judiciary entered into considerations of unconstitutionality, Gibson wondered where it would stop. For Gibson there were no clear lines, particularly since review of the constitutionality of legislation required judges to make what he labeled "political" as distinguished from "civil" or legal determinations. He further argued that the legislature possessed "pre-eminence" in government; "the power of the legislature" is "the power of the people, and sovereign as far as it extends." Gibson could simply see no basis for courts to question political decisions made by the people; for him, judicial review denied "a *postulate* in the theory of our government, and the very basis of the superstructure, that the people are wise, virtuous, and competent to manage their own affairs."[87]

Others such as Justice Baldwin shared Justice Gibson's concern that decisions invalidating legislative acts would "not be . . . judgment[s] on what was the pre-existing law of the case, but on what it is after we shall have so amended and modified it so as to meet our ideas of justice, policy and wise legislation, by a direct usurpation of legislative powers." Other judges in Pennsylvania were well aware by the 1820s that "justice is regulated by no certain or fixed standard, so that the ablest and purest minds might sometimes differ with respect to it" and that the power of judicial review therefore gave judges a "latitudinarian authority" that was, in the language of one New York judge, "great and . . . undefined."[88] Nevertheless, despite this awareness of the political character of judicial review, courts continued at least in a narrow range of cases to strike down legislative acts as invalid, in part because of public acquiescence in the practice and in part because even thoughtful judges such as Gibson himself came to accept the occasional necessity of judicial review as a result of their experience that constitutions were "thoughtlessly but habitually violated" by the legislature.[89]

The democratic challenge to the practice of judicial review was not, however, the only effort in mid-century to democratize the judicial branch of government, and the general acceptance of judicial review did not signal the end of other efforts. Many Americans continued to perceive the judiciary in political terms, and their perception led to the most successful effort at democratization. This occurred in the 1840s and 1850s, when most states subjected the judiciary to greater control by popular majorities by altering the tenure and method of selecting judges.

In the state constitutions adopted during the revolutionary era, judges obtained office by one of two methods — election by the legislature or appointment by the governor, with the majority of states favoring election. In Connecticut and Rhode Island the colonial charters, which became the new state constitutions, provided for annual legislative election of the judges, and as a result the tenure of judges in those states was only one year; when Connecticut adopted a new constitution in 1818, it moved to tenure during good behavior. New Jersey's constitution of 1776 provided that judges would hold office for terms of five to seven years. In Pennsylvania the 1776 constitution provided for seven-year terms, but the constitution of 1790 changed judicial tenure to good behavior. In Georgia, lower court judges enjoyed tenure during good behavior as superior court judges had prior to 1787; thereafter judges of the superior court had three-year terms. The remaining eight of the original states provided for tenure during good behavior in their eighteenth-century constitutions.[90]

Of course, as the legislative and executive branches of government became increasingly politicized in the nineteenth century, appointments to the bench came to be reserved increasingly for lawyers who believed in the program of the party in power and had rendered party services. By naming faithful party members to the bench, the two other branches thereby made the judiciary more responsive to the will of the people than it might otherwise have been. But the judiciary's responsiveness was imperfect: when the electorate transferred control of the legislature or the executive from one party to another, judges who had been appointed for life remained in office although their programs were no longer in accord with the majority's will. Moreover, judges were never subject to the will of the people directly, but only indirectly through the medium of the party organization.[91]

Democrats of the 1840s and 1850s sought to remove party intermediaries and subject judges to direct popular control by requiring election of judges by the people. They also sought by shortening terms of office to ensure that judges would not long remain on the bench after the people's political preferences had changed. At first their program of short terms for elected judges made little headway, but beginning in the late 1840s it achieved dramatic success at the state level.[92]

As of 1845, only Mississippi provided for the popular election of all judges for short terms, although four other states had made some provisions for popular election. In 1846, however, New York after prolonged debate provided for the popular election of all judges for short terms. Within a decade, fifteen of the twenty-nine states existing in 1846 had provided for popular election of their judges, with seven states alone acting in the year 1850. Moreover, every state entering the Union between 1846 and 1860 provided that most, if not all, judges should be popularly elected for terms of years.[93] Only the difficulties of amending the federal Constitution insulated the federal bench from this movement to render judges—and hence, judge-made law—accountable at frequent elections to the will of the majority of the people.

In sum, majoritarian democracy had affected the entire body politic by the middle of the nineteenth century. All institutions of government—legislative, executive, and judicial—had come to be perceived at bottom as political institutions making inevitable policy choices as a matter of will. One consequence of this perception was to blur distinctions among the ways in which different governmental institutions functioned—distinctions that had been important to the revolutionary and Jeffersonian generations and that underlay the doctrine of separation of powers. The other, more visible and more important consequence was to subject all governmental institutions, except the few that, like the federal courts, fortuitously escaped, to control of the political party placed in office by a majority of the people.

2

The Antislavery Movement and Moralistic Objections to Majoritarian Democracy

It is not clear whether Jacksonian democracy, by rendering all three branches of government more susceptible to control by a majority political party, also made government more responsive to the will of the common people. The traditional view was that Jacksonian democracy did result in greater power for the common people, but more recently historians have expressed reservations. One fact, though, is clear: however well the institutions of majoritarian democracy may have worked in the 1830s, they had become oppressive to some by the 1850s if not long before. Once slavery became the central issue in national politics in that decade, a number of groups, including the least elite of all — the slaves — found that a majoritarian political process failed to provide adequate protection even for the most basic rights.

Three positions developed with regard to the issue of how the federal government should resolve those disputes about slavery over which the Constitution gave it jurisdiction. The first position, the majoritarian one that came to be associated with Senator Stephen Douglas and the northern wing of the Democratic party, was popular sovereignty — the idea that the way to resolve the disputes was to submit them to the people concerned and to be bound by the majority's rule.[1] This position has been discussed at length in the preceding chapter.

The second view, which prevailed in the South, was that the federal government was a mere trustee of the states, which were the ultimate possessors of sovereignty and the ultimate protectors of the rights of the people. Two constitutional principles followed from the assumption that the federal government was the mere trustee of states' rights. One, given effect by Chief Justice Roger Taney in *Scott v. Sandford*, was that Congress lacked power to legislate in violation of rights reserved to the states in the original federal compact. The other was that state governments had the right to interpose their power against the execution of the national, majoritarian will.[2]

In one sense, the South's program for decentralization looked back to the era of the American Revolution, when local communities were in significant ways independent of larger geographic entities; many southerners, in fact, saw the War between the States as their own War of Independence, waged to preserve their local autonomy against an increasingly centralized authority that had proved unresponsive to their needs. The ideal of local self-rule was also a response to the emergence in the United States of what the South Carolina secession address labeled "a consolidated Democracy," which was "no longer a free Government, but a despotism." As John C. Calhoun had elaborated the position favored by most of the white South, local and state power were needed to interpose the will of a local majority against that of the national majority so as to ensure that no nationwide law could be made that was unacceptable to both majorities and hence to a broad base of the population as a whole. But although this principle admirably fitted the needs of a minority section, the alternative it offered to majority rule was essentially obstructive rather than affirmative and has had little relevance during the past century of active social legislation at all levels of government.[3]

A third position was developed by politically oriented antislavery leaders who coalesced in 1854 to form the Republican party. The essence of this position was that all people, even a national political majority, must obey a higher law than mere legislation enacted by human political majorities — namely, the law of human freedom. Because this ideology resulted through a circuitous process in the emergence of bureaucratic institutions, this chapter describes that ideology in detail. The remaining chapters then trace the steps by which the antislavery position was transformed into an early variant of the modern bureaucratic state.

The mid-nineteenth-century notion that politics must function in a manner consistent with a higher law was an amalgam of three strands of American thought. One strand was religion, particularly radical evangelical religion, which contributed the ancient notion that there exist ultimate principles of morality from which all human law is derived and with which all human law must be consistent. Western religion rests upon faith in the existence of immutable principles, and when religious emotions are deep and strong, as in early nineteenth-century America, a faith in transcendent principles of right and wrong is likely to be equally deep and strong. For example, the Reverend William Ellery Channing, a leading Unitarian minister of the time, extolled the "lofty strength in moral principle which all the power of the outward universe cannot overcome." Theodore Parker, another Boston minister and later an antislavery activist, urged people to recognize "the eternal nature of Truth" and to see that "what is of absolute value never changes." Addressing the relation between politics and higher law, Parker warned that a "nation, like a man, is amenable to the law of God; suffers for its sin, and must suffer till it ends the sin." For religious enthusiasts such as Charles G. Finney, truth was a fixed, permanent law that a person accepted when God worked a revelation in his soul and "the spirit" aroused his "conscience and . . . [made] it pierce like an arrow." As Lyman Beecher wrote, the person who trusted thus in his own commission as the Creator's agent knew "certainly that he . . . [was] right exactly, and that all men . . . were wrong in proportion as they differ[ed] from him." He also knew that rules enacted by human institutions that were not in accord with his understanding of eternal law were not law, "for none but the Law-giver himself . . . [could] make exceptions to his own laws." For the righteous the sin of slavery was not difficult to discern.[4]

A second strand of antislavery political thought was American transcendentalism. Like religious leaders, the transcendentalists rarely concerned themselves with questions of human law and jurisprudence. However, some of them did articulate a moral philosophy that was inconsistent with the premises of nineteenth-century majoritarian thought and on occasion recognized the inconsistency. Transcendentalists like Orestes Brownson objected to the world they saw around them, in which "the great strife . . . [was] for temporal goods, fame or pleasure"; "Right yield[ed] to Expediency, and Duty . . .[was] measured by Utility." Another transcendentalist, George Ripley, found regrettable the "tendency . . . among a great number of benevolent and philanthropic men . . . to forget the eternal distinctions of right and wrong, and to substitute in their place, as the criterion of actions . . . merely empirical considerations, derived from an exaggerated sense of public utility." Ripley denied that "utility [was] the sole and ultimate ground upon which . . . obligation rests"; the ultimate ground was "conformity to our moral relations" as perceived "by the moral faculty." James Marsh, believing in "universal truths" and "a law of moral rectitude," wished America to enjoy what Frederic Hedge saw as not only "a perpetual increase of prosperity and glory" but also "an equal increase of intellectual prosperity and moral glory." In short, the transcendentalists sought a moral rebirth of America—a rebirth that would occur, in the words of Ralph Waldo Emerson, when men began to "obey no law less than the eternal law."[5]

Because both evangelical religion and transcendentalism had a substantial impact on subsequent nineteenth-century reform movements, particularly the antislavery movement, they infused law and politics with higher-law principles. The impact occurred in several ways. First, a number of clergymen and transcendentalists became active leaders in political antislavery. Second, religious and intellectual leaders often influenced political leaders. In the early 1840s, for example, Theodore Weld served as counselor and speechwriter for John Quincy Adams while that elder statesman led the abolitionist fight on the floor of Congress.[6] Other prominent political advocates of higher law during the 1840s and 1850s were, like Adams, strongly and openly influenced by the clergy or by their own religious experiences. Charles Sumner, for one, was deeply moved by William Ellery Channing's "pleading trumpet-tongued for humanity, for right, for truth" and by a faith in "great principles of justice and charity." John P. Hale, a New Hampshire senator who, when confronted with moral questions such as slavery, would ask "what . . . Jesus [would] have done in precisely similar situations," was likewise influenced by his clergyman, the Reverend John Parkman. And Gerritt Smith, a New York philanthropist and antislavery reformer, "fell easily and thoughtlessly into the common modes of religious terminology" when discussing legal questions; according to his biographer, Smith refused to recognize any "distinction between higher law and lower." For Smith, "all law . . . had its seat in the bosom of God; all law was high; if low things, policies, expediencies, devices, utilities took the name of law, they usurped it."[7] Third, evangelicalism played a vital role in preparing the common people for the coming of later reform movements. Throughout the first third of the nineteenth century much of New England, upstate New York, and the Great Lakes states was burned over by evangelical revivals; it was precisely in localities where revivalism had had its greatest impact that political antislavery would have its greatest strength.[8]

The third strand in antislavery political thought is found in eighteenth-century traditions about human rights. According to those traditions, which had been particularly strong during and after the American Revolution, all individuals possessed certain rights that neither government nor other individuals could infringe.[9] In the area of criminal procedure, for example, postrevolutionary courts in Massachusetts grew increasingly concerned about "the legal rights of the subject" and accordingly held that rules that had been "established in arbitrary times" and were "expedient under a government of prerogative . . . [but] not suited to the spirit of our free institutions" would have to be changed.[10] Rhetoric about human rights had also been important in the postrevolutionary abolition movement, which had resulted in the emancipation of slaves throughout the North. As soon as the Revolution had begun, many Americans had recognized that slavery was inconsistent with the ideals of the Declaration of Independence. As early as 1777, one group of slaves in New Hampshire had noted that "the God of nature gave them life and freedom, upon the terms of the most perfect equality with other men" and that their freedom was "an inherent right of the human species, not to be surrendered, but by consent." When Massachusetts several years later held slavery to be inconsistent with its state constitution, its highest court declared in similar language "that all men are born free and equal; and that every subject is entitled to liberty, and to have it guarded by the laws as well as his life and property. In short, without resorting to implication in construing the Constitution, slavery is as effectively abolished as it can be by the granting of rights and privileges wholly incompatible and repugnant to its existence." Twenty years later, St. George Tucker, campaigning for emancipation in Virginia, similarly argued "that a people who have declared, 'That *all* men are by nature *equally free* and *independent*,' and have made this declaration the first article in the foundation of their government," could not tolerate slavery.[11]

A particularly important aspect of the human-rights tradition was the legal profession's longstanding concern for individual property rights. James Kent, for example, long believed in the "natural, inherent and inalienable" rights of man and in "natural equity or reason" as a legitimate basis for judicial construction of legislation. He implemented those beliefs in a leading eminent domain case, construing a statute so that it would not authorize a seizure of property that would have violated the "clear principle of natural equity, that the individual, whose property is thus sacrificed, must be indemnified." Similarly, Joseph Story maintained that the idea of private property was "consonant with the common sense of mankind and the maxims of eternal justice" and that legislative interference with private property would violate "the principles of natural justice . . . [and] the fundamental laws of every free government."[12]

Kent's and Story's concerns were given effect in a series of early cases, most involving seizures of property, which declared that courts could invalidate legislative acts that transgressed natural rights, even if the acts violated no written constitutional rule. The cases in which courts actually held that they possessed such power were not numerous,[13] but the courts frequently asserted the power in dictum and then bolstered their attack on the particular legislation at hand with references to relevant constitutional provisions or judicial precedents.

The power of the judiciary to invalidate legislation without relying on an explicit constitutional provision was first adumbrated in the Supreme Court in *Calder* v. *Bull*. In an opinion concurring in the disposition of the case, Justice Chase wrote that "an act of the legislature (for I cannot call it a law), contrary to the great first principles of the social compact, cannot be considered a rightful exercise of legislative authority." Less than two decades later, in *Terret* v. *Taylor*, the Court struck down Virginia legislation interfering with corporate property rights, because violation of those rights would be "utterly inconsistent with a great and fundamental principle of a republican government" and with "the spirit and the letter of the constitution of the United States, and . . . the decisions of most respectable judicial tribunals." Still later, in *Wilkinson* v. *Leland*, the Court explained itself more fully:

The fundamental maxims of a free government seem to require, that the rights of personal liberty and private property

should be held sacred. At least no Court of Justice in this country would be warranted in assuming, that the power to violate
and disregard them—a power so repugnant to the common
principles of justice and civil liberty—lurked under any general
grant of legislative authority, or ought to be implied from any
general expressions of the will of the people. The people ought
not to be presumed to part with rights so vital to their security
and well-being.[14]

Similar themes were echoed in state court opinions. In *Taylor* v.
Porter, for instance, a New York court struck down legislation authorizing the laying out of private roads because it found a taking of
private property for private purposes. After citing the language in
Wilkinson quoted above but before turning to detailed examination
of state constitutional provisions, the majority explained that "security of life, liberty and property [lay] at the foundation of the social
compact." The Supreme Court of Maryland, reluctant to rest solely
on the constitutional provision against impairment of contractual
obligations, also invalidated legislation in reliance on "a fundamental principle of right and justice, inherent in the nature and spirit of
the social compact (in this country at least) . . . that rises above and
restrains and sets bounds to the power of legislation." In the same
vein, a Connecticut judge rejected the concept of legislative omnipo-
tence and argued that the judiciary was obliged to guard against pal-
pably unjust enactments violative of the social compact. And the
Vermont Supreme Court explained that legislative power was confined both by the constitution and by limits "resulting from the nature and principles of right and wrong, which must stand as boundaries to the sphere of every legislative operation."[15]

By the 1830s, however, the tradition that judges could invalidate
legislation interfering with property rights on the ground that such
legislation deprived people of their natural rights was waning. As the
instrumental style of reasoning discussed in chapter 1 became increasingly dominant, it seemed increasingly clear to judges that
there was "no paramount and supreme law which define[d] the law
of nature, or settle[d] those great principles" of legislation from
which property was derived.[16] The rise of antislavery, however, rescued the waning tradition,[17] for economic rights of property and
contract probably ranked next to the right of personal liberty as the
most important rights of which slaves were deprived. In fighting that

deprivation, the advocates of antislavery argued that the old natural rights doctrines were inconsistent with slavery and by giving those doctrines wide publicity reinvigorated them.

The inconsistency between slavery and the natural rights foundation of the new republic was not at first universally acknowledged. It was possible to argue, for example, from the eighteenth-century concept of the right to own property and to dispose of it at will, to the right to own and dispose of slaves. Indeed, some abolitionists believed that the Constitution itself encouraged slavery and hence that the only way to end slavery was to condemn the Constitution and eschew political activity under it. Perhaps because of ambiguities in antislavery thought, but more likely because of the power of majoritarian thought, antislavery ideology did not immediately become a staple of American political rhetoric.[18]

It was only in the 1830s and 1840s, when southerners and their sympathizers gagged congressional discussion of antislavery petitions,[19] barred the federal mail to abolitionists, assaulted abolitionist editors (killing one of them), annexed Texas to the Union, and brought about a war with Mexico seemingly for the purpose of extending slave territory[20] that many northerners who feared the loss of their own civil liberties became aware of the inconsistency between slavery and the rights of man secured during the Revolution. To men like John Quincy Adams, who had been raised in the human-rights tradition of the revolutionary era, the congressional resolutions of the 1830s prohibiting discussion of antislavery petitions were "a direct violation of the Constitution of the United States . . . and the rights of [his] constituents." Other antislavery apologists feared that the gag placed upon petitions related to slavery could "hereafter be drawn into a precedent to justify attempts to suppress the popular voice on other subjects" and that encroachment, gathering strength, might continue "until it shall sweep away . . . all the guarantees of popular rights." "The next step," claimed Adams, would "be to inquire into the political beliefs of the petitioners."[21]

Identical values were at stake in the analogous controversy over the use of the mails. There, too "the next step" would be "to stop the circulation of all antimasonic papers, then those that are opposed to the administration"; ultimately, lynch laws would "be enforced against any who dare to utter sentiments not in accordance with those of their masters." The Constitution, according to the Cincinnati *Philanthropist*, could not "at the same time secure liberty to you, and expose us to oppression — give you freedom of speech, and lock our lips — respect your right of petition, and treat ours with contempt." Either "all [must] be free, or all slaves together."[22]

Mob attacks on editors likewise brought many new converts to antislavery, among them Salmon P. Chase, the future Chief Justice, who was convinced that "Freedom of the Press and Constitutional Liberty must live or perish together." Most important, perhaps, the attacks on editors, which occurred almost simultaneously with the imposition of the gag rule in the House and the attempt to bar abolitionist publications from the mails, left many northerners, in the words of the *Cincinnati Daily Gazette*, without "any doubt that there exist[ed] . . . a secret confederacy, whose bond of union [was] a covenant to put down the liberty of the press and the freedom of speech." They feared, according to the *St. Louis Observer*, that if people let a public meeting "today . . . declare . . . that you shall not discuss slavery," then another meeting would "tomorrow . . . decide . . . it is against the peace of society that the principle of popery be discussed." Next, "speaking against distilleries, dram shops, and drunkenness" would be forbidden, "and so on to the end of the chapter." In "the great trial" that the Massachusetts Anti-Slavery Society thought "pending between LIBERTY and DESPOTISM," it appeared that if the people gave "ground a single inch, there . . . [would be] no stopping place."[23]

There were thus two great elements in the political attack on slavery: ideas about the higher law of God or some such transcendent force, and ideas about principles of human rights either conferred by God or inherent in a republican form of government. The first body of ideas was a product of the religious or transcendental faith of many early antislavery advocates. The second was a product of the struggle for individual and minority rights, particularly the constitutional liberties of speech and press — that is, the struggle to preserve a pluralistic society.

These two elements were not at first conjoined. A number of spokesmen of the political antislavery movement stressed only the divine origins of human law and human liberty. Lysander Spooner, for one, argued that law was "simply the rule, principle, obligation, or requirement of natural justice"; William E. Channing saw human rights as "the gifts of God . . . inseparable from human nature"; and

William Swain argued "that God ha[d] made no difference in this respect between the white and the black." Similarly, the American Anti-Slavery Society declared that to destroy another's "right to enjoy liberty" was "to usurp the prerogative of Jehovah." Others emphasized human rights. The Michigan Anti-Slavery Society, for example, resolved that free men had "certain inalienable rights, which no being in the universe, not even God himself, can have a right to infringe, among which are life, liberty, and the pursuit of happiness." The Declaration of Independence, in particular, assumed a central role in antislavery thought. Thus, John Quincy Adams argued that the Declaration "embodie[d] the fundamental elements and principles of American constitutional law" and was a "solemn deed of acquittance of all rightful power to violate the natural and inalienable rights of man." "By the affirmation in it of 'the existence of certain great fundamental principles,' the people," according to Joel Tiffany, " 'estopped themselves' from ever 'rightfully' trampling upon them." In contrast, the Constitution was in Adams's view merely a vehicle "for the adjustment and proper application of these great principles of constitutional law."[24]

But ultimately the moral and political elements of antislavery thought merged into a single body of political thought. The merger occurred whenever antislavery thinkers sought to spell out the relationship among higher law, human rights granted by God, and human rights derived from the very meaning of republicanism. They would then explain, as did Salmon P. Chase, that the doctrine of "natural rights, derived . . . from the constitution of human nature and the code of Heaven . . . the same in all ages . . . and destined to no change, [had been] proclaimed by our fathers in the Declaration of Independence to be self-evident" and had been "reiterated in our state constitution as its fundamental axiom." "Master and slave," Chase told the Senate, were thus free and equal both "according to the principles of the Declaration of Independence, and by the law of nature," and abolitionism itself was "embodied in the self-evident truths of the Declaration of Independence . . . and in the Golden Rule of the Gospel — nothing more, nothing less." In the words of Theodore Parker, "the idea of freedom" rested "on the immutable laws of God . . . [and] the natural religion of mankind . . . [and] demand[ed] a government after natural justice."[25]

By the time antislavery had become politically prominent in the mid-1840s, its advocates had gone beyond merely stating the premises on which their jurisprudence rested. They had also begun to list, albeit in an imprecise way, the core rights that were defined by the characteristics of the slave system; by the deprivations that antislavery leaders suffered during the course of their struggle; and by older, inherited definitions of human rights.

The foremost contention of antislavery advocates was that all men were entitled to personal liberty. The concept of personal liberty included many of the liberties protected by the Bill of Rights and infringed during the abolitionists' struggle for civil liberties. Foremost among these were the rights to freedom of speech, press, and assembly. "Freedom of speech and the liberty of the press" were referred to as "the palladium of our rights." William Cullen Bryant, for one, maintained that "the right to discuss freely and openly, by speech, by the press, by the pen, all political questions, and to examine and animadvert upon all political institutions . . . [was] a right as clear and certain, so interwoven with our other liberties, so necessary, in fact, to their existence, that without it we must fall at once into despotism and anarchy." Other constitutionally protected rights that antislavery advocates included in the concept of personal liberty were "religious liberty," "trials by jury," and " 'the right of the people to be secure' . . . against 'unreasonable searches and seizures.' "[26]

But the crucial element of personal liberty was the right to protection of the laws, and it was precisely this right that slaves were denied. All antislavery advocates agreed that "the slave should be legally protected in life and limb — in his earnings, his family and social relations, and his conscience"; in the words of Joshua Giddings, "he who murders a black man shall be hanged . . . he who robs the black man of his liberty or his property shall be punished like other criminals." Notions of legal protection inevitably led to notions of legal equality. The antislavery position, as expressed by Charles Olcott, was "that the benefit and protection of these just laws [should] be extended to all human beings *alike* . . . and that all mankind [should] be allowed the *same* legal rights and protection without regard to color or other physical peculiarities." All people, according to Henry B. Stanton, should be given "impartial legal protection." In the words of William H. Seward, the Republican party, the final political arm of antislavery, stood above all for "one idea . . . the equality of all men before human tribunals and human laws . . ."[27]

Antislavery advocates also gave great attention to property and contract rights, urging that these economic rights be extended to all individuals, including slaves. One of "the primary and essential rights of humanity [was] the right to occupy a portion of the earth's surface." Ownership of land, as Schuyler Colfax argued, would turn the dependent poor, such as slaves, into independent yeomen; "giving them independent freeholds [would] incite them . . . to rear families in habits of industry and frugality, which form the real elements of national greatness and power." To deny people land, on the other hand, was to keep them dependent, and "to be dependent . . . [was] to be degraded."[28]

Of course, the right to own land also included, as Lincoln said, the "natural right to eat the bread" earned from the land "with [one's] own hands without asking leave of anyone else." The right of property "include[d], of necessity, [the] right to the products of [a man's] own industry, and his consequent right to dispose of those products, by barter or sale." All individuals were entitled to "the inalienable right of unrestricted free trade"; hence, "all commercial restriction . . . except the wise and needful prohibition of immoral and criminal traffic" and "all monopolies, class legislations, and exclusive privileges" were "unequal, unjust, morally wrong, and subversive of the ends of civil government." And, just as it was inappropriate for government to regulate lawful commerce, so too it was wrong, according to Samuel Gridley Howe, to regulate the conditions of labor; "it emasculated people to be protected in this way," for they ought to "be used to protecting themselves."[29]

Just as majoritarianism was a powerful political idea because it was consistent with the competitive social ethic that prevailed in much of antebellum America, so too the listing by antislavery politicians of core rights to which all people were entitled by virtue of some higher law was an emotionally attractive one in vast areas of the North. One reason was that the list of core rights accurately described social and economic realities in the egalitarian, mid-nineteenth-century rural North, where small property owners and small businessmen contracted with one another on a free and equal basis, spoke freely about their political views, and tolerated one another's differing religious beliefs.[30] The second reason for the success of antislavery ideas was that they explained to people who believed deeply in God and in a divinely ordained moral law why majoritarian decisions that violated their moral codes were wrong and either need not be obeyed or, even if they ought to be obeyed temporarily, would ultimately have to be changed. Although the political thought of many antislavery leaders was elitist in the sense that it did not value all opinions equally but gave greater weight to those it deemed true, the heart of antislavery political and social theory was the equality of all before God and the law. Antislavery doctrine, like the evangelical revivalism to which it was akin, sought to raise the humblest person to the level of the greatest aristocrat, at least in regard to legal rights; moreover, antislavery was often preached by leaders like Lincoln, Chase, and Seward who came from quite humble backgrounds. In short, the elitism of the antebellum antislavery movement was a moral rather than economic or social elitism, and one entirely consistent with the moral elitism that revivalism had brought to much of the antebellum North.

By the mid-1850s, the emergence of antislavery thought as a significant force in American politics brought it into sharp conflict with democratic majoritarian thought. This conflict manifested itself most clearly in that decade in the debates over the program of popular sovereignty. Beginning in 1848, when the extension of slavery to the trans-Mississippi West first became a major issue in a presidential campaign, many Democratic thinkers and orators developed the position that the question whether slavery should exist in any territory should be decided by a majority of the voters of that territory, because the majority of the people were ultimately sovereign. This position gained strength throughout the late 1840s and early 1850s until it was enacted into law in the Kansas-Nebraska Act of 1854. For Stephen A. Douglas, the sponsor of the act, the principle of majority rule was particularly appropriate for the resolution of the most basic constitutional issues for which accepted constitutional principles did not exist.[31] Douglas developed his position with greatest thoroughness in his 1858 campaign against Abraham Lincoln for re-election to his Senate seat. In one speech in Chicago, for example, he explained why he denied

the right of Congress . . . to force a good thing upon a people who are unwilling to receive it. The great principle is the right of every community to judge and decide for itself whether a thing is right or wrong, whether it would be good or evil for them to adopt it . . . It is no answer to this argument to say that slavery is an evil, and hence should not be tolerated. You must allow the people to decide for themselves whether it is a good or an evil . . . Whenever you put a limitation upon the right of any people to decide what laws they want, you have destroyed the fundamental principle of self-government.[32]

Organized in 1854 in response to the Kansas-Nebraska Act,[33] the Republican party rejected the view that the people, through a majority vote, must always be allowed to decide whether a law is good or bad. Lincoln, in the same 1858 campaign against Douglas, was a typical Republican spokesman. Generally, Lincoln indicated that he would not follow the wishes of a political majority if, in his judgment, that majority sought to take a course of action that he believed was morally wrong. As Lincoln said of Douglas on one occasion, "When he invites any people, willing to have slavery, to establish it, he is blowing out the moral lights around us. When he says he 'cares not whether slavery is voted down or up,'—that it is a sacred right of self-government.—he is, in my judgment, penetrating the human soul and eradicating the light of reason and the love of liberty in this American people."[34] In short, although he was willing to allow some tolerance of slavery as an existing institution, Lincoln and his fellow Republicans did not view slavery as a morally indifferent matter that popular majorities could be left free to accept or reject. For Lincoln and the Republican party, slavery was a moral wrong and the people could not be permitted forever to countenance such wrong; they could be allowed in the end only to do right.

As slavery became the preeminent issue in national politics during the 1840s and 1850s, a series of nationally prominent cases also brought majoritarian and antislavery jurisprudential styles into open conflict in the courts. The advocates of antislavery lost nearly all these cases, for judges steeped in the instrumental style of reasoning associated with democratic majoritarianism continued to give effect to the related objectives of economic growth and national unity. But antislavery advocates were able to set before the public at large a coherent critique of instrumentalism based on the antislavery jurisprudence they had already developed.

The first Supreme Court decision on slavery to arouse national controversy was *Prigg* v. *Pennsylvania*, in which the Court in 1842 upheld the constitutionality of the Fugitive Slave Act of 1793. The white appellant, Edward Prigg, had been indicted under a state statute prohibiting the capture of any black in Pennsylvania and his subsequent transportation across state lines into slavery. The jury had found Prigg guilty as charged, but had simultaneously returned a special verdict that the black taken out of Pennsylvania was a slave under Maryland law who had fled to Pennsylvania several years earlier to escape from slavery. After the highest court of Pennsylvania had affirmed the verdict, Prigg appealed to the Supreme Court. Justice Story, writing for the majority of the Court, overturned Prigg's conviction. Story's opinion rested on an instrumentalist concern for national unity, which can best be seen in his depiction of the fugitive-slave clause of the Constitution as "so vital to the preservation of [the] . . . domestic interests and institutions [of the South] that it cannot be doubted that it constituted a fundamental article, without the adoption of which the Union could not have been formed" and could not continue to exist. Of course, as Story might have added, preservation of the Union was vital to the central instrumentalist objective of "prosperity of the community" announced by Chief Justice Taney in the *Charles River Bridge* case.[35]

Shortly after the *Prigg* case, Chief Justice Lemuel Shaw of Massachusetts was asked to grant a writ of habeas corpus to one George Latimer, allegedly a fugitive slave from Virginia. Latimer, who had been seized pursuant to the 1793 federal act, had sought the writ in order to obtain a trial of his status before a Massachusetts court jury, pursuant to the commonwealth's Personal Liberty Law of 1837. Shaw, however, relying on *Prigg*, held the state personal liberty law preempted by the Fugitive Slave Act insofar as it applied to slaves and denied Latimer relief. Shaw thought "the duty of returning runaway slaves . . . imperative on the free states, and . . . that on no other terms could a union have been formed between the North and South"; implicit in his reasoning was a judgment that the Union could be preserved only on the same terms. Because of his overriding concern with the preservation of the Union, Shaw considered Latimer's "a case in which an appeal to natural rights and the paramount law of liberty was not pertinent."[36]

Several years later, in *Jones* v. *Van Zandt*, the Supreme Court again faced issues arising under the Fugitive Slave Act. The action was one for a penalty under the act for concealing and harboring a fugitive slave; it came to the Court on numerous technical grounds and on the issue of the constitutionality of the act. Reaffirming its recent holding in *Prigg*, the Court observed that the fugitive-slave clause "was undoubtedly introduced into the constitution, as one of its compromises," without which the Union could not endure. Thus, as in the past, the Court directed its reasoning toward the vital objective of preserving national unity.[37]

The advocates of antislavery, however, viewed the issue of the constitutionality of the Fugitive Slave Act differently. The *Liberator* labeled Story's decision in *Prigg* as "unjust and unreasonable" and one that "establish[ed] . . . horrid doctrines." It particularly complained about "the manifest injustice of deciding whether a man is free or a slave . . . by . . . a summary process, and without the intervention of a jury." It concluded that the decision was simply "*not law* — for the entire system of slavery [was] at war with the rights of man." The *Law Reporter* accused Justice Story and Justice Shaw "of using their offices to oppress their fellow men", and the *Liberator* accused them of "act[ing] the part of Pilate in the Crucifixion of the Son of God," and of being as morally reprehensible as a "slave pirate on the African coast." The antislavery commentators likewise condemned the *Van Zandt* Court as violating "the law of the Creator, which invests every human being with an inalienable title to freedom," and "the provisions of the Constitution," which "were mainly designed to establish as written law certain great principles of natural right and justice."[38]

The debate over fugitive slaves became even more heated following passage of the Fugitive Slave Act of 1850, part of the Compromise of 1850. On the one hand, the advocates of antislavery argued that the new Fugitive Slave Act was "incompatible with the power of [free Negroes to enjoy,] in safety and tranquility, their natural rights" and, further, "violate[d] the golden rule of Christianity, of doing unto others as we would have them do to us." They condemned the act as "revolting to our moral sense, and an outrage upon our feelings of justice and humanity, because it disregard[ed] all the securities which the Constitution and laws ha[d] thrown around personal liberty." In short, the new act was seen as contrary to "the higher law of every man's own conscience." The judiciary, on the other hand, found enforcement of the act essential to the continued preservation of the nation. Judges evinced concern for "the peace, prosperity, and happiness of the citizens of these United States" and took the position that it was "well known that our Southern brethren would not have consented to become parties to a constitution under which the United States have enjoyed so much prosperity unless their property in slaves had been secured." The fugitive-slave clause of the Constitution was thus an "essential element" in the formation and preservation of the Union, "necessary to the peace, happiness and highest prosperity of all the states."[39]

The line of fugitive-slave cases culminated in 1859 with *Ableman* v. *Booth*. The case was a consolidation of two appeals by federal authorities from decisions of the Wisconsin Supreme Court. In the first of the two Wisconsin cases, Booth, an antislavery agitator, had obtained a writ of habeas corpus from a judge of the state court after having been charged before a U.S. commissioner with aiding and abetting a fugitive slave to escape from a federal deputy marshal. In the second of the cases, the Wisconsin court had again released Booth on a writ of habeas corpus after he had been duly indicted and convicted of the offense charged.[40]

The Wisconsin judges first analyzed the relation of the state and federal judiciaries in a manner consistent with the instrumental style. But they then disclosed their antislavery beliefs in holding the Fugitive Slave Act of 1850 unconstitutional. They found particularly objectionable the provision of the 1850 act authorizing the return of alleged fugitives without any appearance in court. They thought that even "without the express guaranty of the Constitution," the right of an individual to "his 'day in court' would be implied as a fundamental condition of all civil governments"; for the Wisconsin judges, the Bill of Rights merely confirmed what was otherwise "in accordance with the first principles of natural law." The Wisconsin judges were unimpressed by the government's reliance on *Prigg* v. *Pennsylvania* as a controlling precedent; their position was that when "duty and obligation require a departure from such precedent and authority, in obedience to a paramount law—the *fundamental law*, to which each and all are equally bound," they were compelled so to depart.[41]

In reversing the Wisconsin court, Chief Justice Taney affirmed the constitutionality of the 1850 act in less than one sentence and devoted the remainder of his opinion to an instrumentalist analysis of the need for national unity. He argued that "no one . . . [would] suppose that a Government . . . preserving the union of the States, could have lasted a single year . . . if offenses against its laws could not have been punished without the consent of the State in which the culprit was found." He found that, "unless there was a common arbiter" between the states "armed with power enough to protect and guard the rights of all, by appropriate laws, to be carried into execution peacefully by its judicial tribunals," government and, indeed, all social order would fall prey to "local interests, local passions or prejudices" and "to acts of aggression and injustice by one State upon the rights of another, which would ultimately terminate in violence and force."[42]

Twentieth-century historians have tended to view the conflict during the 1850s between proslavery and antislavery forces as an essentially political one fought over fundamentally economic objectives.[43] The fugitive-slave cases suggest, however, that the conflict had another important dimension. Those cases could have been contested by both sides entirely on instrumentalist, higher law, or natural rights grounds. But the fact is that the advocates of compromise with slavery rested their case upon arguments about what was politically wise and economically expedient, whereas opponents of slavery made essentially moralistic arguments about the law of God and the rights of man. At least in the courts, the conflict between slavery and antislavery was not only a struggle for political power, but also a conflict between groups possessing differing views about the proper role of law and government—between a group that believed that courts should explicitly pursue socially expedient policy goals and a group that believed that courts should decide cases consistently with standards of what, in some ultimate sense, was right and wrong.

This conflict came to a head in the 1857 case of *Scott* v. *Sandford*,[44] in which the Supreme Court held that Congress lacked power to bar slavery from the territories. The plaintiff, Dred Scott, claiming to be a citizen of Missouri, had brought suit in a federal circuit court for an assault upon himself, his wife, and his children. The defendant, John Sandford, a citizen of New York, claimed, first that because Scott was a black, he could not be a citizen of a state for the purpose of conferring diversity jurisdiction and, second, that the assaults were justified because Scott and his family were Sandford's slaves. Scott replied that free blacks were citizens and that he had become free when a previous master had taken him first to Illinois and subsequently to Fort Snelling in the Territory of Upper Louisiana, which had been declared free territory by the Missouri Compromise of 1820.

The Court, in an opinion by Chief Justice Taney, rejected Scott's replication. First, Taney held that Scott was not a citizen of Missouri for diversity purposes. Missouri did not recognize Scott as a citizen, and Taney, citing both precedent and legislative history, held that the Constitution did not make him a citizen either. Though couched in historical terms, Taney's rationale reflected his concern for national unity. Taney would not presume that slaveholding states regarded blacks as citizens, for a contrary holding might throw southern society into turmoil and force the South to leave the Union. The Court also rejected Scott's claim that he had been made free by virtue of his sojourn in either Illinois or Upper Louisiana. To support its rejection of the claim concerning the effect of Scott's stay in Illinois, the Court relied on its earlier decision in *Strader* v. *Graham*,[45] in which it had held that temporary residence in a free state did not make a slave free if the law of the state to which he subsequently returned still deemed him a slave. Although the Court might have used analogous reasoning to reject Scott's claim of freedom based on a stay in Upper Louisiana, it instead reached the much broader conclusion that the Missouri Compromise of 1820, which had declared Upper Louisiana free, was unconstitutional. Rejecting the argument that the provision in the Northwest Ordinance of 1787 prohibiting slavery provided a precedent for congressional prohibition of slavery in other territories, the Court held that Congress had a constitutional obligation to keep all territories open for settlement and development by citizens of all states, including slaveowners. Although there is no evidence that the Court expected its decision to promote directly the economic development of the territories, it probably expected its appeasement of the South to promote national unity by preserving "the peace and harmony of the country" through "the settlement . . . by judicial decision" of the sectional crisis.[46]

The decision infuriated many northerners. Antislavery leaders regarded the denial of Scott's citizenship as "a violation of the sacred principles announced in our Declaration of Independence, [and] hostile to the spirit of our institutions." More disturbing was the holding that the Missouri Compromise was unconstitutional. Like the holding that a sojourn in a free state did not make a slave free, the invalidation of the Missouri Compromise was "contrary to . . . the fundamental principle . . . that every man has an inalienable right to his liberty, and that it can only be taken from him by a statute of the State in which he lives." Liberty, according to the advocates of antislavery, was the natural state of man, whereas slavery could occur only when local police regulations altered that natural state. The point of this argument was that, because Congress could not take away liberty without due process of law, Congress could not enact any law protective of slavery. The Court, however, had undercut that argument, holding, in effect, that the federal government was obliged to protect not liberty but slavery. As a result, antislavery advocates began to fear that slavery would be made legal throughout the nation — "that some future decision of the Pro-Slavery majority of the Supreme Court will authorize a slave driver, as threatened by the devotees of Slavery, to call the roll of his manacled gang at the foot of the monument on Bunker Hill, reared and consecrated to freedom." They feared that nothing could stop a proslavery Supreme Court, unconcerned with human rights, from legalizing slavery in the North.[47]

The worst apprehensions of the antislavery advocates were aroused by the case of *Lemmon* v. *People*, decided by the New York Court of Appeals early in 1860 and pending on appeal to the Supreme Court during the fall elections of that year. The case arose when Mrs. Lemmon, in transit by sea from Virginia to Texas, disembarked with her slaves briefly in New York City to change vessels; immediately a writ of habeas corpus was taken out to obtain freedom for Mrs. Lemmon's slaves on the ground that they had been brought into a free state. The lower New York courts granted the writ, and in March 1860 the New York Court of Appeals affirmed, with three judges dissenting.

Judge Wright, speaking for himself and three of the other four judges in the Court of Appeals majority, called "slavery repugnant to natural justice and right . . . [and] antagonistic to the genius and spirit of republican government." Wright also ruled that there was "no grant of power to the Federal Government, and no provision of the Constitution from which any can be implied, over the subject of slavery in the States, except in the single case of a fugitive from service." Judge Clerke, in dissent, opined, however, that the Constitution had sought to create "one nation, not only in its character as a member of the great family of nations, but also in the internal, moral, social and political effect of the Union upon the people themselves." He thought it "essential to this grand design that there should be . . . free and . . . uninterrupted . . . intercommunication between the inhabitants and citizens of the different States." Of course, such intercommunication would be facilitated if southerners could bring their slaves with them to the North.[48]

Although this instrumentalist point of view lost in the New York courts, the advocates of antislavery feared greatly that it would prevail in the Supreme Court. Within a year of *Scott*, Lincoln had warned that the Court's next step would be to decide that a state could not exclude slavery from its borders, and Horace Greeley's *New York Tribune* was predicting that New Yorkers would soon "see men buying slaves for the New York market" with "no legal power to prevent it."[49] The accuracy of these prophecies, however, was never tested, for Mrs. Lemmon's appeal, which was expected to be argued before the Supreme Court during the December 1860 term, was never heard.[50] On the contrary, the conflict of which the *Lemmon* case constituted only a small part began to move toward resolution when the forces of antislavery gained control of the political branches of the federal government in the election of 1860[51] and was brought to final resolution upon the battlefields of the Civil War.

3

The Triumph and Failure
of Antislavery and the
Transformation of Federalism

THE REPUBLICAN VICTORY of 1860 and the subsequent triumphs of
Unionists both at the polls and on the battlefields made the moral
precepts that had been associated with the antislavery movement
seem more important than ever. With their assumption of power,
many people politically associated with antislavery decided that the
time had come to restore morality throughout government. They
hoped the war would serve as "an ordeal of purification rather than
destruction" that would "reinvigorate and recover the republic, its institutions and functions of civil government, and its political and social character, from the decay and degeneracy of national virtue,
and . . . replenish the life of the nation with increased moral vigor
and purity." For both Charles Eliot Norton and Charles Sumner the
war demonstrated "politics" to be "a subordinate branch of morals" —
"the application of morals to the administration of public affairs."
Likewise, the future Harvard historian Albert Bushnell Hart, deliv-
ering his high school valedictory address in 1870, thought that
"right" had "triumphed" in the Civil War and that the war had again
set Americans moving forward on the path "toward moral improvement."[1]

After the war, reform leaders like E. L. Godkin and Carl Schurz
continued urging their fellow citizens to restore to their proper place
the "fundamental virtues of our civilization" and thereby "reestablish
the moral character of our government." Godkin argued that "the
diminution of political corruption, . . . the general raising of the
tone of public men, and the recognition of character as the greatest
and most valuable of political forces . . . [was] the great question of

our time." Samuel Bowles, the moral-minded editor of the *Springfield Republican*, similarly pleaded that "all hands fall to work to clean out and disinfect the national premises"; and George William Curtis, the civil service reformer, urged his associates to drive from power mere party politicians who commanded "the rings, the demagogues . . . the pretorian guards, all the minions of prejudice, passion, and selfish interest." "The curse of our politics," all reformers acknowledged, was "the yoke of party discipline." Charles Francis Adams, Jr., warned that if American politics were not cleansed of mere partisanship, America's democratic system was "apt . . . to degenerate into government by the politicians and the caucus" and ultimately "into jobbery."[2]

Even some Democratic party figures who before the Civil War had been strong supporters of the majoritarian ideal, especially the doctrine of popular sovereignty, abandoned their old ideology and began to talk about the importance of moral principles in politics. For example, Orestes A. Brownson, who had been a prominent supporter of both Andrew Jackson and Martin Van Buren, concluded in the 1860's that "experience prove[d] that the ballot . . . [was] far less effective in securing the freedom and independence of the individual citizen than is commonly pretended," for "the power of the ballot . . . may be rendered ineffective by the tyranny of party." Brownson concluded, instead, that "the reliance for the wisdom and justice of the state must after all be on moral guarantees."[3] Other Democrats also saw soon after 1860 that they could not use majoritarianism successfully to criticize the programs of the majority Republican party. As early as the war itself, Peace Democrats like Congressman Valadingham of Ohio had found it necessary to argue about the essential wrongness of the majority's position — to argue, that is, on legalistic and moralistic rather than on democratic grounds. The end of the war brought no change in the Democrats' position: they could oppose Reconstruction only on antimajoritarian grounds. Although the rhetoric of opposition was the old eighteenth-century argument about the need to keep power decentralized in order to check despotism, the despot now to be feared was not some king or dictator, but a popular majority.[4]

The decade of the Civil War and Reconstruction witnessed not only increased challenges to the core democratic ideal that government ought to respond to the will of the majority of the people, but also new attacks upon related concepts, such as the instrumentalist jurisprudence of many antebellum judges. Perhaps the heaviest criticism of all was directed at Chief Justice Roger Taney and the Taney Court. Much of this criticism resulted from the Court's decision in *Scott* v. *Sandford*, but more was involved than an attack on the result of a single case. More important, critics denounced the reasoning style of Taney and judges like him. The newly triumphant forces of antislavery, it is important to note, did not condemn the federal judiciary as a whole, the Supreme Court as an institution, or its power of judicial review. Nor did they deride the Taney Court for its ultimate objectives of economic growth and national unity, for antislavery forces also valued those objectives highly. Their criticism was directed only at the Taney Court's style of reasoning. The *Atlantic Monthly*, for example, censured Taney because he had "not hesitate[d] to embody his political principles in judicial decisions" and criticized his Court for forgetting "the maxim, 'Judicis est jus dicere, non dare' " and for "declaring . . . rule[s] of government" rather than "rule[s] of Law." As one senator noted, it was not surprising that the Supreme Court should give effect to its own views of policy rather than to the rules of law, for men were appointed to the Court not "because they [were] lawyers, but rather because they [were] not lawyers" and because they "entertained sound views on . . . transcendent [political] question[s]." For the remainder of the century, the reputation of the Taney Court remained clouded by the charge that, as a result "of political appointments to the bench," its decisions "read like a collection of old stump speeches."[5]

Reformers of the Civil War era were not content merely to criticize the system of majoritarian democracy that had dominated midcentury American politics or to speak of the importance of morality in government. They also made many determined, practical efforts to apply antislavery moral precepts to political life. Perhaps their most prominent effort was the movement for civil service reform (to be discussed in chapter 5), but that effort was not their only one. At the municipal level, reformers sought to improve the quality of local government through the development of "more Christian character." Likewise, Carl Schurz, a leading reformer who served in the Senate during the Grant administration and as secretary of the interior in the Hayes administration, later supported Grover Cleveland for the presidency because he viewed him as a man of "incorruptible integ-

rity" who possessed "a high sense of official honor" and "a keen in-
stinct of justice"; similarly, the *Nation* praised Cleveland's "firm and
pronounced stand against paternalism in government" for recalling
"the nation to its senses, and reviv[ing] that 'sturdiness of our national character' which appeared to be dangerously weakening."[6]

Moral principles derived largely from the antislavery movement
soon proved incapable, however, of providing clearcut answers to
many of the novel political and constitutional questions that arose in
the 1860s as a consequence of the Civil War. One issue on which antislavery ideology provided little explicit guidance was whether
former slaves and other blacks ought to possess the right to vote. Before the war, antislavery advocates had never had power to determine whether slaves, once freed, would be entitled to the vote, and
differences in their responses to this hypothetical question were unimportant. But once slaves were freed and Republicans had power
to give them the vote, disagreements became an important political
issue. For a minority in the old antislavery movement, such as
Charles Sumner, the right to freedom plainly entailed the right to
vote; both as a practical matter and as a moral matter, Sumner
argued that no man could be truly free unless he possessed the right
to protect his interests in the political process. At the other extreme
stood Republicans like Secretary of State William H. Seward, who
maintained that voting was a mere political rather than a civil or
natural right; political rights, which were mere constructs of government, could in the view of Republicans like Seward be granted or
withheld at the whim of government.[7] A third possible view within
the party, to which moderates like John A. Bingham may have
adhered, was that although government was not compelled to grant
anyone the right to vote, government did have to distribute the right
equally once it granted it to some; hence the right to vote could be
withheld only if there was a rational basis for distinguishing those
denied the right from others to whom it was given.[8]

Black suffrage was not the only issue on which former antislavery
ideologues were not in full agreement. Another was the status of the
states that had seceded from the Union in 1861 to form the Confederacy. Radicals like Thaddeus Stevens were prepared to treat them
as conquered provinces, subject to full congressional government
and able to obtain readmission to the Union only when Congress
was willing to grant it. At the other pole stood President Andrew

Johnson and his supporters in the Republican party, whose understanding was that various state acts of secession were unlawful and
hence were nullities and that, as a result, the eleven allegedly seced-
ing states had never left the Union and were entitled to their full
rights and status as states as soon as they reconstituted their governments at the war's end. As in the case of black suffrage, there were
middle positions to which other former antislavery advocates adhered consistently with their old ideology.[9]

On these and other issues, Lincoln's Union party began soon after
the Civil War to dissolve. Former comrades like Salmon P. Chase,
William Seward, and Charles Sumner found themselves at odds not
only because of their conflicting political ambitions but also because
the moral precepts on which they had once agreed no longer provided adequate guidance in the new circumstances they confronted.
The very bitterness of their divisions suggests that not only personal
rivalry but also issues of principle stemming from competing visions
of their old ideology lay beneath the factional divisions within the
Republican party during Reconstruction.

The impeachment of President Johnson and its aftermath provided contemporaries with perhaps the most disturbing example of
Republican factionalism. The impeachment was disturbing, first,
because it occurred: the fact that a president placed in office by the
Republicans had to be brought to trial at the bar of the Senate was
itself evidence of distressing divisions within the old antislavery co-
alition. The impeachment proceedings were also disturbing because
Senate Republicans were unable to close ranks sufficiently to bring
about Johnson's conviction; the president was acquitted only because seven Republicans, out of a principled belief that he was guilty
of no crime, broke party ranks to vote in his favor. But most disturbing of all to political moralists was the aftermath of impeachment,
when a torrent of abuse was directed at the Republican Senators
who had supported the president. Although the abuse was only
temporary and the seven Republicans regained their standing in the
party in the first year of Grant's administration, even the brief period
of abuse demonstrated to some that the party of principle no longer
had a sufficient respect for the principles of longtime members.[10]

Despite the divisions that characterized Reconstruction, many old
antislavery advocates continued to hope that their moral precepts
could be applied to the conduct of government. Henry Adams, for

one, later recalled that "the task of bringing the Government back to regular practices, and of restoring moral and mechanical order to administration" did not appear "very difficult" even as late as 1868, when the majority of voters "united in the election of General Grant to the Presidency . . . probably . . . more or less affected in their choice by the parallel they felt between Grant and Washington." "No one doubted that Grant's intention had been one of reform; that his aim had been to place his administration above politics." Grant, however, was an immense disappointment to those concerned with political morality, and his "administration marked the avowal" of the fact that "the moral law had expired."[11]

"The result . . . [was] a kind of moral anarchy" in which "hardly anybody live[d] by tradition, or authority, or under the dominion of habits acquired in youth." "The American layman," according to Adams, "had lost sight of ideals; the American priest had lost sight of faith"; "the American people . . . had lost the sense of worship." The next presidential election, in 1872, wrote Charles Eliot Norton, marked a further "decline in public morality," and within a few years, by the time of James Russell Lowell's 1876 ode commemorating the nation's centennial, many Americans were wondering if theirs was still the nation of which they had "dreamed in youth / Where wisdom and not numbers should have weight." To Adams it seemed apparent that "the system of 1789 had broken down, and with it the eighteenth-century fabric of *a priori*, or moral, principles," as "truths *a priori* held their own against truths purely relative" and "no one could surely say where the real authority, or the real law, lay."[12]

"The moral disorganization of . . . [the] day"[13] was apparent not only in the realm of politics but also in that of constitutional law. The jurisprudential precepts of a movement that had essentially one goal — freeing the slaves — were simply inadequate to meet all the demands placed on the legal system of the late nineteenth century. Concepts of human rights provide guidance only in the narrow range of cases in which human rights are arrayed against competing values; they are of little help in deciding the great mass of cases in which two or more possible results are equally consistent with the enjoyment of "natural rights." This fact was brought home powerfully both to the legal profession and to the general public by two of the leading constitutional controversies of the late nineteenth century.

The first controversy was resolved in the *Legal Tender Cases*, which passed upon the constitutionality of congressional legislation making paper currency issued during the Civil War legal tender for the payment of debts. In its first decision, *Hepburn* v. *Griswold* , which was handed down in 1870 by a vote of five to three, the Court held the legislation unconstitutional as applied to debts contracted before its passage. However, with the appointment of two new justices in 1871, the Court overruled itself in the *Legal Tender Cases* and by a vote of five to four held the legislation constitutional in all respects.[14]

Few observers doubted the significance of the Court's actions. "Great anxiety" was "felt in reference to these decisions"; in the colorful language of Henry Adams, the issue of legal tender "grew in interest till it threatened to become something more serious than a block; it fell on one's head like a plaster ceiling, and could not be escaped." As the Court itself observed, "it would be difficult to overestimate the consequences which must follow our decision," which "will affect the entire business of the country, and take hold of the possible continued existence of the government." In fact, major business decisions were contingent upon the outcome of the cases: state governments, railroads, and all other debtors who were required to pay principle or interest on debts contracted prior to 1862 were in doubt during 1870–1871 whether to make those payments in coin or currency.[15]

The *Legal Tender Cases* also had great divisive political significance. Before *Hepburn* v. *Griswold*, there was an "expectation that the decision adverse to these Acts would irritate the Radicals in Congress," who were the principal supporters of the legislation. When *Hepburn* was announced, many "senators," according to the *Nation*, "expressed their opinion that the decision would be reversed; Congressmen . . . furiously denounced it as rivalling the Dred Scott decision in bad pre-eminence." Nonetheless, Chief Justice Salmon P. Chase, perhaps the most prominent Republican radical in the late 1850s and early 1860s, wrote the main opinions holding legal tender unconstitutional largely on the basis of moralistic jurisprudential precepts that lay at the core of radical antislavery thought. Chase wrote for the majority in *Hepburn* that the legal tender acts were not "consistent with the spirit of the Constitution" and resulted in deprivation "of property without due process of law." He stated his views at greater length in the *Legal Tender Cases* in a dissent joined by Justices Clifford and Field; there Chase wrote that the legal tender acts violated "that fundamental principal of all just legislation that the legislature shall not take the property of A. and give it to B." and, further, that because the acts were " 'contrary to the great first principles of the social compact,' " they could " 'not be considered a rightful exercise of legislative authority.' " In a separate dissent, Justice Stephen J. Field, another strong exponent of the moralistic precepts of antislavery jurisprudence whom congressional radicals had viewed as a reliable ally at the time of his appointment in 1863, suggested that the legal tender acts were "acts of flagrant injustice" for which "there is no authority in any legislative body, even though not restrained by any express constitutional prohibition." Moreover, Field continued, "there are unchangeable principles of right and morality, without which society would be impossible, and men would be but wild beasts preying upon each other." He concluded by referring to "fundamental principles of eternal justice, upon the existence of which all constitutional government is founded, and without which government would be an intolerable and hateful tyranny."[16]

The difficulty in the *Legal Tender Cases* was that the moralistic precepts of antislavery jurisprudence were equally serviceable to the justices voting to uphold the congressional legislation. Justice Joseph P. Bradley, who like Field frequently cited antislavery jurisprudential precepts, invoked their egalitarian aspects in affirming the constitutionality of legal tender. After noting that "the sovereign power, by its right of eminent domain, may . . . take private property for the public use and give government certificates therefor," Bradley continued:

> Can the poor man's cattle, and horses, and corn be thus taken by the government when the public exigency requires it, and cannot the rich man's bonds and notes be in like manner taken to reach the same end? If the government enacts that the certificates of indebtedness which it gives to the farmer for his cattle and provender shall be receivable by the farmer's creditors in payment of his bonds and notes, is it anything more than transferring the government loan from the hands of one man to the hands of another—perhaps far more able to advance it? Is it anything more than putting the securities of the capitalist on the same platform as the farmer's stock?

Similarly, Justice William Strong, who provided the fifth vote for the *Legal Tender* majority, noted that legal tender had been essential to "the vast body of men in the military service . . . composed of citizens who had left their farms, their workshops, and their business with families and debts to be provided for." These men could not be paid "with ordinary treasury notes, nor could they discharge their debts with such a currency." For the Court majority, as Justice Bradley observed, it was only fair that "the creditor interest . . . lose some of its gold" so that "the debtor interest of the country"—those small, free laborers who "represent[ed] its bone and sinew"—would "be encouraged to pursue its avocations."[17]

The moralistic precepts of antislavery jurisprudence gave equally divided guidance a decade later in the *Civil Rights Cases*, which invalidated 1875 legislation barring racial discrimination in public accommodations. Justice John M. Harlan made the obvious argument in dissent that the Reconstruction amendments sought "by a change in the fundamental law" to establish "universal *civil freedom* throughout the United States" and to prohibit "discriminations . . . in the enjoyment of those fundamental rights which by universal concession, inhere in a state of freedom." However, as Harlan himself recognized, the issue was much more complex. He conceded that the 1875 legislation would be unconstitutional insofar as it sought to prohibit purely private discrimination. But, citing *Munn* v. *Illinois*, Harlan argued that the discrimination involved was not purely private, because the 1875 legislation dealt with public accommodations, in which all members of "the public have rights." Access to those accommodations was "consequently not a matter purely of private concern." The majority, however, which included such old antislavery stalwarts as Justices Bradley and Field, reached the opposite conclusion, that the congressional legislation sought to control merely the "acts of individuals, unsupported by State authority in the shape of laws, customs, or judicial or executive proceedings," that Congress was therefore seeking to regulate "the *private property of individual citizens*," and hence that the 1875 act was unconstitutional.[18]

Why did Justices Field and Bradley, who until the 1880s had been strong proponents of the antislavery position, hold unconstitutional in the *Civil Rights Cases* an act of Congress designed to confer rights on former slaves? The received view is that the two justices, along with others, had grown conservative and had retreated from the pro-civil-rights views that they had expressed in the 1870s in decisions like the *Slaughter-House Cases*. It is unnecessary, however, to hypothesize any change or retreat to explain why Field and Bradley disagreed with Harlan in the *Civil Rights Cases*. It is necessary only to note that the antislavery movement of the 1840s and 1850s, to which all three justices owed their ideology, was itself a child of classic nineteenth-century liberalism, complete with all its assumptions about the limited power of government and the autonomy of individuals from government. Before the Civil War it was possible to be both a classic liberal and an advocate of antislavery because no one had any idea how extensively the government would have to use its power to enable former slaves to participate equally in American government and society. It was equally possible, when the *Civil Rights Cases* demonstrated how intrusively governmental power would need to be used to legislate equality, for men like Field and Bradley to conclude that classic liberal values were at least as important as a specific antislavery result.* Thus did one of the central precepts of antislavery jurisprudence — that government ought not interfere in purely private, individual concerns — frustrate the most important antislavery goal, equality for blacks. Antislavery had again failed as a moral force.

Another element, perhaps, in the postwar failure of moral principles in politics was a series of intellectual changes, not directly related to politics, that undermined the revivalistic underpinnings of higher-law political and legal thought. Revivalism had rested on faith that the moral law of God consisted of a body of absolute, fixed, and immutable precepts made known to man chiefly through divine revelation in the Bible. After the Civil War that faith was badly shaken. Perhaps the most important movement challenging the

---

*Perhaps the conflict between classic liberalism and a specific antislavery result could have been avoided in the *Civil Rights Cases* if the majority of the Court a decade earlier in the *Slaughter-House Cases* had adopted the position of Justice Bradley in dissent. Bradley had argued in *Slaughter-House* that all people should be protected in their natural rights, perhaps even against infringement by other private individuals; if his position had been adopted, the Supreme Court would have been required to delineate protected and nonprotected rights. The Court, however, rejected Bradley's view. Instead, both the majority opinion of Justice Miller and the dissenting opinion of Justice Field in *Slaughter-House* appear to have taken the position that, with a few exceptions, all rights are created by law and may be granted or taken away by the states at will, provided the states act equally with reference to all citizens. Construing the Fourteenth Amendment to require only that the states treat all citizens equally raised the issue ultimately of the boundary between state and private action — precisely the issue before the Court in the *Civil Rights Cases*.

older orthodoxy was evolutionary thought, associated with Charles Darwin's *Origin of Species*. Although many Americans rejected Darwin's theory of natural selection, they responded more favorably to his theory of evolution.[19] With their response, the conception of a universe governed by immutable divine laws was impaired, for the one immutable law that evolutionary theory dictated was the law of change.*

On those occasions when moral principles failed to provide answers to the pressing legal and political issues of the Reconstruction era, government gave the appearance of functioning, as it had often seemed to do earlier in the nineteenth century, purely in response to the will of the politicians who controlled it. The appearance was strengthened by the survival of the majoritarian ideal and of majoritarian rhetoric. Many Republicans and Democrats clung to the concept of government of the people, by the people, and for the people and to the related concepts of majority and, ultimately, party rule. Those concepts, never wholly discredited or outmoded, remained powerful after the Civil War; Lincoln's choice at Gettysburg of the language of democracy demonstrates their persistence. Their persistence is also apparent in the remarks of opponents of civil service reform, like Benjamin F. Butler, who criticized "growing aristocratic tendencies to a caste of life officers"; and John A. Logan and William Williams, who objected that the entire civil service plan was taken "without disguise from monarchical Governments" and was "totally anti-republican, and subversive of elective Government."[20]

---

*Only those who accepted both the theories of natural selection and of evolution could have other immutable scientific laws in which to believe, but those laws gave little comfort to the orthodox. Nor could the orthodox simply fall back upon the word of God as revealed in the Bible, for the new science of biblical criticism was undermining the validity of that text. Though initially rejected by most Americans, the new scholarship continued to gain adherents throughout the last third of the nineteenth century, and the literal truth of the Bible came increasingly to be questioned. See Francis P. Weisenburger, *Ordeal of Faith: The Crisis of Church-Going America, 1865-1900* (New York: Philosophical Library, 1959), pp. 80-109. Finally, the orthodox belief that salvation could occur only through a single true church was undercut by a third development—increasing contacts with nonchristians throughout the world and an increasing awareness that all religions shared in proclaiming the truth of God. See ibid., pp. 109-116. The result was that by the 1880s the revivalistic, evangelical Protestantism of the antebellum period had been replaced by a tolerant Protestantism that lacked clear doctrinal beliefs and tended to regard any churchgoer as a true believer. See ibid., pp. 1-20. This habit of accepting all beliefs as equally true inevitably spread from religion into law and politics.

Every failure of antislavery morality thus brought to the fore a renewed threat of government by partisan will and a renewed danger of majoritarian tyranny. Every such failure thereby jeopardized the pluralistic character of American society.

The dangers of tyranny by the majority and the threats to pluralism in the postwar era were exacerbated by dramatic changes in the structure of American federalism during the 1860s and 1870s. The Civil War and Reconstruction resulted in unprecedented centralization in American institutions. Although postwar centralization was far less than exists today and proved insufficient to bring about major social changes, people accustomed to antebellum federalism found the new power of the national government frightening. As Hamilton had written in *The Federalist*, antebellum Americans had assumed that "the State governments . . . [would], in all possible contingencies, afford complete security against invasions of the public liberty by the national authority."[21] Before 1860, state political leaders had on occasion obstructed law enforcement at the federal level, most notably during the nullification controversy in 1833, which resulted in something of a standoff between state and federal power and led to a modification in the tariff. State courts had also served as a check upon tyrannical enforcement of federal law. Before 1833, when Congress passed legislation in response to the nullification crisis permitting most federal officials to remove actions against them into federal court, state courts could hear actions against officials to the effect that the federal policies they were enforcing were unlawful.[22] And until the Supreme Court decided the case of *Ableman* v. *Booth* on the eve of the Civil War, state courts had unquestioned jurisdiction to issue writs of habeas corpus to liberate people held in federal custody for violations of federal law.[23] Indeed, even the Republican antislavery advocates who would do so much after 1860 to centralize power in the federal government had used the state courts in the litigation leading up to *Ableman* in order to impede the execution of what they considered to be a tyrannical federal policy of returning fugitive slaves to their masters.

Secession represented the ultimate effort of states to secure local liberty against invasion by the federal government, and the failure of secession made clear the latter's supremacy. By 1865 no one could doubt what had been uncertain only four years earlier: that the military forces of the United States had power to suppress insurrection anywhere in the nation, even if state governments led the insurrectionary movement. The success of Union arms gave federal authorities a degree of real power unimaginable to antebellum Americans.

The Reconstruction Congress exercised the new power of the federal government in dramatic ways. First, between 1866 and 1875 it passed a series of civil rights acts providing that black people throughout the United States should be protected in their property and contract rights and in their right to the enjoyment of public accommodations and conveyances, that masked groups would not ride on the highways in an effort to deprive people of their rights, and that no one would be deprived of any federally protected right by another person acting under color of state law. The acts also created civil remedies for injured individuals, specified a number of criminal offenses, authorized the appointment of federal officials in every county to provide enforcement assistance, and stated the conditions under which the president had authority to use military force. Although the Supreme Court declared some of this legislation unconstitutional and none of it was enforced nationwide or for any extended period until the mid-twentieth century, these acts marked a sharp break with antebellum patterns of federalism.[24]

An even more striking departure from prewar norms was the creation of the Freedmen's Bureau. Though initially created in 1865, the bureau did not receive its full powers until legislation of 1866. After guaranteeing blacks essentially the same rights protected by the Civil Rights Act of 1866 and further stipulating that blacks should be subject to the same criminal law as whites, Congress gave the Freedmen's Bureau jurisdiction "over all cases and questions concerning the free enjoyment of such immunities and rights" provided by the act. The bureau's commissioner, General Oliver O. Howard, construed this statute to authorize local bureau agents working in southern localities to try minor civil and criminal cases. In serious criminal cases, Howard directed bureau subordinates that the statute authorized them to turn offenders over either to federal or state courts; alternatively, he suggested that offenders might be turned over to the army for trial before military commissions.[25]

Recent scholarship has shown that the Freedmen's Bureau did not have a transforming effect on race relations in the South and, in fact, that it did a great deal to preserve white supremacy and white control over the region's black labor force. The bureau ultimately failed because it was never provided with sufficient manpower and resources to do its job of ensuring that blacks were treated equally and fairly, because an unsympathetic president interfered with General Howard's effective use of the machinery that Congress did provide, and ultimately because few, if any, mid-nineteenth-century Americans understood just how radical Reconstruction would have to be if it were to change southern society significantly. Yet the failure of the Freedmen's Bureau should not mask its truly revolutionary effect on federal-state relations. According to General Howard, the bureau adjudicated some hundred thousand complaints per year, most of them involving common-law matters of contract, tort, and property that were traditionally the preserve of the state courts. Moreover, there is evidence that bureau officials often decided cases differently than state courts would have — in favor of rather than against blacks. In short, the Freedmen's Bureau strengthened federal power in the South sufficiently to frighten anyone who perceived the traditional balance between state and federal authority as a potential obstacle to the tyranny of a national political majority.[26]

But the most striking of all congressional policies during Reconstruction was that providing for governance of the South. The policy had two aspects. First was Congress's delay in readmitting representatives and senators from the seceded states until the governments of those states had met prescribed conditions. Second was the Military Reconstruction Act of 1867, which established military governments in ten of the seceded states and subordinated existing civil authority to that of the general in command. For several years Congress thereby denied to the people of ten states what had always been among the most basic of states' rights in the federal system: the rights to local self-governance and to representation in Congress. Although these policies for governing the South were neither as extreme as many congressmen wanted nor sufficient to accomplish the objectives of Reconstruction,[27] they nevertheless constituted a significant departure from all antebellum models of federalism.

While Congress was legislating in novel ways to enhance federal power, the jurisdiction of the federal courts was also expanding, largely as a result of other legislation. One of the first expansionary acts, passed in 1863, granted a federal court hearing to any federal official who was sued for making an arrest under color of authority derived from an act of Congress or from the president. Next came the Habeas Corpus Act of 1867, which gave federal judges power to release prisoners held in state custody. Civil rights legislation between 1866 and 1875 also significantly increased the range of federal jurisdiction. In addition, an 1864 act gave jurisdiction to the federal courts over any suit against a national bank, and one in 1868 permitted any federally chartered corporation to remove cases brought against it into federal court. This expansionary movement culminated in the Judiciary Act of 1875, which conferred jurisdiction over all civil actions arising under federal law.[28]

The increasing power of the federal courts over the lives of individuals was not, however, entirely a product of legislated changes. Government prosecutors and the courts themselves also made decisions that augmented the judiciary's power. During the Civil War, federal courts throughout the North were called upon to decide cases involving disloyal individuals: in New York, for example, the circuit court heard cases involving persons arrested by presidential order, as well as a case involving an alleged conspiracy by southern sympathizers to burn New York City.[29]

After the war, federal prosecutors and courts became active in the suppression of such criminal activity as peonage, voting fraud, and use of the mail for immoral purposes. The federal criminal process thereby became a tool for federal intervention in fundamental social issues previously within the domain of the states. One such case was a prosecution brought in 1873 against Susan B. Anthony for violating federal voting laws.[30] While they were bringing new sorts of proceedings, federal prosecutors were also showing less concern for defendants' civil liberties, most notably in a series of cases in which they sought to compel businessmen to give testimony or produce records in order to convict those businessmen of crimes or to recover penalties against them. Meanwhile the Supreme Court in *Ableman* v. *Booth* and in *Tarble's Case* was also prohibiting state courts from issuing writs of habeas corpus on behalf of prisoners in federal custody and was thereby depriving the states of an important weapon for protecting individual liberty against further federal encroachment.[31]

One must not, of course, exaggerate the growing role of the federal courts in the postwar years. Suppression of crime, for example, remained largely a state concern in the late nineteenth century just as it does today. Nonetheless changes in the jurisdiction and practices of the federal courts enabled the government to bring legal proceedings different in kind from those brought in federal courts in the antebellum period.

Perhaps the most telling example of the new way in which the federal government used its courts was a case brought against Samuel J. Tilden in 1877, one year after he had lost the presidency to Rutherford B. Hayes, to recover income taxes allegedly due during the period 1862–1872.[32] Such use of the internal revenue laws and the federal judicial process against a widely respected political opponent of the prosecutor was novel enough, but even more novel were the efforts the government made to prove its case. In the belief that Tilden might own stock in the Chicago & Northwestern Railroad, it sought to compel a vice president of the railroad to produce its stock transfer books; the latter was excused only because he was not the custodian of the books. It also sought to compel Tilden's stock-brokerage firm to produce all its books and records for the preceding ten years. Tilden's lawyer claimed "that the suit . . . [was] a mere fishing suit, brought here for a general inquisition into the private affairs of the defendant," and the government's request to unseal and thereby permit publication of some of its evidence even before trial suggests that its true aim may have been not tax collection but Tilden's embarrassment.[33] It is impossible to be certain whether Tilden had evaded taxes or what the government's motives were in proceeding against him; what matters is that in the 1870s the federal government used its power to attack its political opponents in the courts — a power that before the Civil War no one had even dreamed it possessed.

The new power of the federal government in the postwar period also became increasingly concentrated in Congress. The power of the presidency declined markedly during the administration of Andrew Johnson and remained low during that of Grant. The statutes and other highly public events of the period reflect this decline. Two acts of March 2, 1867 were of greatest importance. One was the Tenure of Office Act, which prohibited the president from removing subordinates from office without the consent of the Senate; the other was a rider to an army appropriations bill that prohibited the president from issuing orders to the army except through the general of the army, General Grant, who was understood to be sympathetic to the dominant forces in Congress, and forbade the president to relieve the general of command without prior approval from the Senate. These bills were important both for their substantive content and for their assertion of legislative power over the personnel of the executive branch and over the transmission of presidential commands to subordinates. Even more important in restricting the chief executive was the 1868 impeachment of President Johnson, whose acquittal by the Senate by no means returned the presidency to any height of power.[34]

The presidency remained weak during the Grant administration. As members of Congress had stated a few years earlier, "the authority of Congress" was "paramount." "Congress," Gideon Welles recalled, "was the supreme department of the Government": it "control[led] the action of the Government, prescribe[d] its policy, its measures, and dictate[d] appointments to the executive, or subordinate, department." In Grant's time, according to Henry Adams, it was considered "the duty of the President to follow without hesitation the wishes of the people as expressed by Congress."[35]

The dominance of Congress was based upon its formulation of policy and its control of appointments and appropriations. In the words of Henry Adams, "so far as the President's initiative was concerned," his "recommendations were uniformly disregarded." President Grant agreed that the chief executive "must be in sympathy with Congress." Senator Hoar similarly observed that "eminent Senators . . . would have received as a personal affront a private message from the White House expressing a desire that they should adopt any course" of policy other than their own; "if they visited the White House, it was to give, not to receive advice." In regard to appointments, Senator Sherman noted in 1871 that "members of Congress, especially of the House of Representatives, claim[ed] the right to dictate local appointments"; and Grant himself noted that it had "become the habit of Congressmen to share with the Executive in the responsibility of appointments . . . The President very rarely appoints, he merely registers the appointments of members of Congress."[36] A final source of congressional dominance was its practice of making detailed, itemized appropriations, thus requiring all executive agencies to come to Congress for money and giving the legislators a means of ensuring that the money was spent as it desired.[37]

The concentration of power in the federal government and ultimately in its legislative branch exacerbated the consequences that flowed from the failure of antislavery morality. The moralistic political style of the mid-nineteenth century had developed in response to the threat that a political group in control of the entire federal government might use its powers to tyrannize the people. If no changes had occurred in the power and structure of the federal government between the 1830s and the 1870s, the failure of the moralistic style would simply have left those who were worried about the possible tyranny of party with the same intellectual problem they had faced in the 1830s. The changes in government, however, augmented the threat of party tyranny by giving the majority party in the federal legislature far greater power than it would ever have had before the Civil War.

The 1872 case of *Blyew* v. *United States* provides one final illustration of the way in which the rise of federal power combined with the collapse of antislavery morality to make governmental decisionmaking appear to be purely a matter of power and will. Blyew and another were indicted in federal court for the murder of Lucy Armstrong, a blind black woman over ninety years old who was found in her cabin with "her head cut open as with a broad-axe." The prosecution was brought in federal court because in Kentucky, where the murder was committed, blacks were barred by statute from giving testimony in state court; in view of the fact that the only witnesses were black, it appeared unlikely that a prosecution could be maintained in state court. The issue in *Blyew* was whether any basis existed for the federal court's assumption of jurisdiction over a crime, committed within the boundaries of a state, that was normally a matter for state jurisdiction. Attorney General Akerman sought to rest jurisdiction on section 3 of the Civil Rights Act of 1866. This section gave the federal courts power to hear civil and criminal cases "affecting persons who are denied, or cannot enforce in the courts or judicial tribunals of the State, or locality, where they may be, any of the rights secured to them by the first section" of the 1866 act, including the right to testify and the right to the benefit of all laws protecting personal security.[38]

If there ever was a case in which the precepts of antislavery morality—indeed, the precepts of any morality—justified an assumption of jurisdiction, *Blyew* was the case. Federal assumption of jurisdiction, however, would have obliterated the federal system. As the Supreme Court noted, it could not hold that the federal courts had jurisdiction in any case in which a black person was denied the right to testify, for such a holding would enable any litigant to have his case heard in federal court merely by producing a black person who was prepared to give testimony about any point at issue, no matter how insignificant. Such a holding would have given the federal courts jurisdiction over all litigation, civil or criminal, and would have left the state courts to hear only matters in which no one desired to have a federal forum. Nor could the Supreme Court easily hold, as Justice Bradley suggested, that federal jurisdiction was appropriate "on the ground that the cause is one affecting the person murdered, as well as the whole class of persons to which she belonged." An earlier precedent, *United States* v. *Ortega*, had ruled that in a criminal prosecution only the government and the defendant, not the victim of the crime, were persons affected by the case, and that ruling made sense analytically.[39] A judgment in a criminal case binds only the government and the defendant and has a direct effect only upon their rights and duties. Of course, the victim of a crime and other similarly situated persons for or against whom no judgment runs are indirectly affected by the outcome of a prosecution, but so is the whole world. The success or failure of government in enforcing the criminal law affects all citizens, as does the outcome of much civil litigation. Blacks, in particular, were adversely affected by the entire legal system of the Reconstruction South, and to have upheld federal jurisdiction in *Blyew* on the ground that blacks in general were adversely affected by Kentucky's failure to permit blacks to testify would have granted federal courts power to nullify operation of the state's entire legal system.

Whether *Blyew* was examined from the perspective of antislavery moral beliefs or from the perspective of traditional notions of federalism, there was simply no middle ground. Protection of the rights of black citizens would mean obliteration of state judiciaries and of state legislative independence; protection of the states, on the other hand, ultimately meant that black people would have no rights. Moreover, there was no principled basis for choosing whether to protect the rights of southern states or the rights of blacks. This basic choice, which had to be made before the nation could be fully reconstructed, could be made only in accordance with the will of whoever happened to hold power in Congress, in the federal executive, and on the federal bench.

The trials of Reconstruction thus showed that antislavery morality, linked as it was to the ideal of a transcendent morality, could not preserve American pluralism and protect all individuals and minorities against the tyranny of the majority. Indeed, the efforts of antislavery moralists to protect one minority, the freedmen, seriously undercut one of the main bulwarks of pluralism in antebellum America, the federal system. Thus, the same fears and concerns that had given rise in the 1830s to the moralistic political style of the antislavery movement remained even stronger four decades later. The renowned constitutional scholar John Norton Pomeroy, for one, still saw "a pure democracy" as "the most terrible of tyrannies" and consequently favored "limit[s] upon the exercise of authority." Some years later another commentator similarly noted that the period after the Civil War was marked by a "passionate desire" on the part of the American people "to control and limit . . . government . . . in strong contrast with the deferential and implicit confidence which the common people reposed in their representatives, those especially of their legislatures, a century ago."[40]

In the last three decades of the nineteenth century, concerns like these would generate a new approach to preventing the tyranny of party, protecting individual and minority rights, and thereby preserving the traditional pluralistic social order of the nation.

4

The Quest for
a Scientific Morality

ONCE IT BECAME CLEAR that neither the federal system nor the principles of antislavery moralists would protect all individuals and minorities from the tyranny of the majority, a crisis of sorts existed. Those concerned with preserving the pluralistic character of American society recognized that new "machinery of some sort had to be invented" and "new standard[s] . . . created"[1] if those in power were to be kept from imposing their will on all. But what new machinery and standards could they use to re-form and re-construct the American political system?

Reformers in the last third of the nineteenth century turned to science to accomplish their reconstructive task. Thus, E. L. Godkin hoped that the nation would be rescued from its "moral anarchy" by "mental . . . culture" and that "the next great political revolution in the Western world" would give "scientific expression to the popular will, or, in other words . . . place men's relations in society where they never yet have been placed, under the control of trained human reason." This new scientific spirit permeated every discipline related to the art of government. In economics, for example, the data-oriented "inductive" method of the historical economists challenged the "purely deductive" method of the classical economists. Under the leadership of Richard T. Ely, a group of economists in 1885 founded the American Economic Association, declaring their belief "that political economy as a science . . . [was] still in an early stage of its development" and that they "look[ed] not so much to speculation as to the historical and statistical study of actual conditions of economic life for the satisfactory accomplishment of that development." The new science of economics would not be entirely divorced from ethical concerns, however; the charter of the new economics association announced that its members would direct their research toward the "solution" of "social problems" through "the united efforts, each in its own sphere, of the church, of the state, and of science."[2]

Likewise, A. Lawrence Lowell, a future president of Harvard, told political scientists that "the first effort of the student of government to-day must be to discover the facts, in the faith that any light thrown upon political conditions can not fail to help toward a wise solution of the problems they involve." John W. Burgess, the founder of Columbia's Department of Political Science, cautioned his colleagues that "political science must be studied historically . . . in order to secure a correct comprehension"; and at least one early psychologist, James M. Baldwin, believed that his was a more useful field of study than theology simply because it was scientific.[3]

The new scientific spirit also affected the study of history. According to Herbert L. Osgood, "American historians" learned that they must "cease the attempt to defend a dogma," while John W. Burgess consciously strove to stop writing "American history as written by Puritan clergyman and fanatical abolitionists." Under Herbert B. Adams at Johns Hopkins, the history seminar "evolved from a nursery of dogma into a laboratory of scientific truth." Adams began

> to cultivate more and more the laboratory method of work and to treat its book collections as material for laboratory use. The old tables which had once been used for the dissection of cats and turtles were planed down, covered with green baize, and converted into desks for the dissection of government documents and other materials for American institutional history. Instead of cupboards for microscopes, instruments, and apparatus—instead of show-cases for bottled snakes and monkey-skeletons, the visitor now beholds book-cases full of books, pamphlets, manuscripts and coins under glass, a growing museum of prehistoric, Egyptian, and classical art. These collections are frequently used for purposes of historical illustration. The idea that the sources of history are more extensive than all literature, begins to dawn upon the student as he explores the environment of this seminary library which is also a seminary-museum.

Adams was not alone in believing that "what the laboratory is to physical science . . . the library must be to moral science" and that the nation needed what Albert B. Hart called "a genuinely scientific school of history, which shall remorselessly examine the sources and separate the wheat from the chaff; which shall critically balance evidence; which shall dispassionately and moderately set forth results . . . [pursuant to] the fortunate analogy of the physical sciences."[4]

The legal profession also aspired to the scientific ideal. One professor at the Yale Law School asserted that "the law [was], after all, the science of justice." "Law, considered as a science," wrote Christopher Columbus Langdell, "consist[ed] of certain principles or doctrines," the mastery of which so "as to be able to apply them with constant . . . certainty . . . [was] what constitute[d] a true lawyer." As it had in other disciplines, the scientific ideal led to a revolution in legal education — the introduction of the case system, which, according to William Keener, "proceed[ed] on the theory that law is a science" and that "only by regarding [it] as a science [could] one . . . justify its being taught in a university." Ephraim W. Gurney wrote to Charles W. Eliot that "the whole tendency of the [case] system would be, to build up a great school of law as an exact science."[5]

When they turned to science in search of principles by which to govern society, the late nineteenth-century reformers betrayed a simplistic conception of the scientific method, one at odds with more sophisticated concepts that contemporary scientists were already beginning to develop. Whereas professional scientists perceived a need for theory in order to give order and structure to their empirical data, laymen tended to look upon science as simple empiricism concerned almost entirely with direct observation of surface appearances.[6] Most intellectuals of the post–Civil War generation defined the scientific method as the abandonment of abstract principles derived from divine revelation or individual intuition; in their place, scientists by "classification of facts" substituted "judgments independent of the idiosyncrasies of the individual mind."[7] Late nineteenth-century laymen believed that scientists simply took "note of all that comes within the range of sensuous experience, and declare[d] whatever may be derived therefrom by careful induction. As a philosopher," a late nineteenth-century scientist could "not go farther."[8] Historians, economists, political scientists, and lawyers all assumed that if they could successfully use neutral and objective scientific methods to ascertain the facts, their knowledge of those facts would guide them to proper solutions of the problems the nation faced.*

This assumption was not outlandish. Judges, political leaders, and intellectuals in the late nineteenth century possessed few reliable empirical data on which to base decisionmaking; before they had accumulated the mass of data that we possess today, they could not know of the ambiguity and complexity lurking within it and of the need for sophisticated methods of analysis. It seemed entirely possible that a decisionmaker who examined the facts thoroughly and impartially might find data suggesting an appropriate course of action, at least in the absence of strong countervailing reasons of moral principle or social policy.

The assumption that knowledge of facts would provide answers to problems was confirmed by the experience of business organizers, whose new data collection processes were providing valuable information for making business decisions. As American businesses became national in scope, they often did not possess the most rudimentary data. In the early 1850s, for example, rolling stock of the Erie Railroad "in perfect order" often stood during "the greatest press of business . . . for months upon switches without being put to least service, and without its being known where they were." Later in the decade, however, new data collection procedures enabled the Erie management to "tell at any hour in the day, the precise location of every car and engine on the line of the road, and the duty it is per-

---

*Given these intellectual trends in the closing years of the century, judges might have been expected to turn to principles associated with social Darwinism. But although the judges may have had Darwinian notions about the survival of the fittest, see *Lochner* v. *New York*, 198 U.S. 45, 74–76 (1905) (Holmes, J., dissenting), they do not appear to have expressed them in their opinions. I have found no opinion in which judges referred to Darwinian as distinguished from laissez-faire ideas that rested, in turn, upon the same classical liberal tradition from which many antislavery ideas about the rights of the individual emerged. The closest approximation I have found to Darwinian language is in *State* v. *Goodwill*, 33 W. Va. 179, 10 S.E. 285 (1889), where the courts observed that "the natural law of supply and demand is the best law of trade." 33 W. Va. at 184, 10 S.E. at 287. This language, however, is not truly Darwinian; rather, it reflects the influence of classical economic theory, which was related to but nonetheless distinct from and antecedent to social Darwinism. See Richard Hofstadter, *Social Darwinism in American Thought, 1860–1915* (Philadelphia: University of Pennsylvania Press, 1945), pp. 121–124. Moreover, this quotation is merely a single sentence in an eight-page opinion that discusses at great length the rights of individuals in a free and republican society.

forming," with the result that the railroad put its capital equipment to greater use at a greater profit than it would otherwise have earned.[9]

Similarly, government officials and political thinkers often lacked even basic data in the post–Civil War years. A stark example of the lack of data came to the attention of Richard Ely as late as 1891, when he was attempting to ascertain the number of paupers in the United States; he discovered that neither the states nor the federal government had accurate records showing the approximate number of persons in public institutions or receiving outdoor relief.[10] Given such gaps in social information, it is not surprising that many people hoped that an apparently simple process of gathering facts could be as valuable to American society as it had been to American business.

Unlike scientists today, late nineteenth-century laymen had no conception that scientific inquiry requires initial determination of relevant questions and puzzles, and that the selection of the questions and puzzles lends structure and even substance to the principles and conclusions abstracted from facts.[11] We understand, for example, that the Erie Railroad found data that made its operations more efficient because its managers were seeking data that would promote its efficiency. We also understand that so-called scientific analysis of facts cannot yield answers to legal, political, and ultimately moral questions that require difficult value choices. Late nineteenth-century reformers, on the other hand, did not believe that in the social or even the physical sciences knowledge is necessarily a product of human choice and cognition as well as of raw natural data.

Because our view of the nature of scientific inquiry differs from the view held by late nineteenth-century reformers, we seek to discuss explicitly matters with which the reformers dealt only by implication. We want to know the puzzles that late nineteenth-century social scientists sought to solve and the questions that they asked. Although people in the late nineteenth century would have found this focus upon puzzles and questions — that is, upon the intuitionistic elements of science — unscientific, we must so focus if we are to comprehend their mode of thought in depth.

Accordingly, the remainder of this chapter will show how, in exploring the sciences of law, government, and society, the reformers pursued two courses of inquiry. First, they studied periods in the American past when the nation had seemed to possess moral values, in an effort to identify the social foundations on which those values had rested. Second, they sought to develop systems that would enable them to classify legal and governmental problems in categories that would dictate the solution or proper outcome.

Morality, Aristocracy, and Community in History

The quest for a scientific morality thus led reformers and intellectuals to turn their attention to the past. But they did not direct their efforts indiscriminately; on the contrary, they studied "the teaching of the past" in conjunction with the "trial in the present."[12] Their historical researches were informed by what they perceived to be the great political question of their time: how to replace a governmental structure in which political majorities enriched themselves and enhanced their power at the expense of minorities with an order in which all citizens readily abided by accepted moral values. In their effort to supersede the essentially Jacksonian forms of government that remained dominant in their own time, the reformers looked back beyond the Age of Jackson to the eighteenth- and early nineteenth-century American past.

E. L. Godkin, for one, often recalled the attractions of that idyllic, pre-Jacksonian past when "stern, simple, enduring, self-reliant, self-respecting men" had been the backbone of the nation. Writing in sympathy with Godkin and other American reformers, Lord Bryce similarly found that America's early leaders had been men of unbending integrity and sturdy independence in comparison with the mere party managers of the late nineteenth century. In a like vein, Abram Hewitt, one of the managers of Samuel J. Tilden's 1876 presidential campaign, hoped that the electorate would choose Tilden and thereby "bring back that better era of the republic in which, when men consecrated themselves to the public service, they utterly abnegated all selfish purposes."[13]

The preeminent figure striding across the American past was, not surprisingly, George Washington. The historian Henry Adams described him as "the Pole Star," who "amid the endless restless motion of every other visible point in space . . . alone remained steady, in the mind of Henry Adams, to the end." Adams's George Washington was part of a larger constellation, which included "his Constitution of 1789," "his Quincy," "his Plymouth Pilgrims," and ultimately "his eighteenth century"; at the opposite "end of the vista" stood "Tammany Hall." As a result of his professional interest in the history of the early national period, Adams devoted a decade to writing about the administrations of Jefferson and Madison; however, "all the[se] other points"—"John Adams, Jefferson, Madison, Franklin, even John Marshall"—assumed "their bearings" in relation to Washington and the eighteenth century.[14] Washington and the nation's other early leaders were similarly important to other reformers, including Rutherford B. Hayes, who campaigned for the presidency by promising "the restoration of the civil service to the system established by Washington," and his opponent, Samuel J. Tilden, who promised to restore the "high standards of political morality" that he associated with the administration of Jefferson.[15]

What made the early years of the republic so attractive was the fact, noted with pride by Henry Adams, that among the great leaders of early nineteenth-century politics—"Jefferson, Madison, Gallatin, Marshall,—not one was dishonest." Jefferson "might occasionally make misstatements of fact; yet he was true to the faith of his life, and would rather have abdicated his office and foregone his honors than have compassed even an imaginary wrong against the principles he professed." Jefferson removed some Federalists from office and made political appointments in their place, Adams claimed, only because "he could not follow his true instincts; for the pressure upon him, although trifling when compared with what he thus helped to bring on his successors, was more than he could bear." Meanwhile Jefferson's "associates, like Madison, Gallatin, and Monroe, were men upon whose reputations no breath of scandal rested." Adams wrote that Madison, indeed, removed no one from office "except in cases of misbehavior," in the belief that "the wanton removal of meritorious officers" would render the president "subject . . . to impeachment."[16]

Others looked back, as Adams had suggested they should, to the eighteenth-century roots of early nineteenth-century politics, and were deeply impressed by moral standards firmly ingrained in the "ideal hearth and fireplace of olden times" and by "the simple virtues of industry, frugality and clean living." G. S. Hall, the president of Clark University, regarded the eighteenth-century moral code as "the one and the only one that represents the ideal basis of a state of citizen voters as contemplated by the framers of our institutions," and E. L. Godkin commented that "one of the very valuable social features of Puritanism was the weight of its moral yoke," which "made right living so stern and hard, so full of self-denial, that the cheats fled from it."[17]

The search through the pre-Jacksonian past thus provided the reformers with examples of the moral values whose restoration they deemed essential in late nineteenth-century political life. More important, in the course of their historical inquiry reform-minded intellectuals identified other aspects of the eighteenth- and early nineteenth-century American polity that had then served as preconditions to the practice of morality in government. They were especially attracted to two such aspects of early American government — its reliance on aristocratic leadership and its communitarian structure, for several of them glimpsed how aristocracy and community were related and perhaps essential to their central goal of restoring morality.

Those who were seeking to alter the democratic structure of authority that existed in mid-nineteenth-century America preferred a system in which men gained office on account of their wisdom and virtue rather than on account of their political skills or electoral support. The reformers wanted, in the words of Henry Cabot Lodge, to place "honest men of moderate intelligence . . . in office" and to create "an independent party composed exclusively of good men." According to Carl Schurz, they admired a leader who " 'interpose[d] educated intelligence and assert[ed] the worth of self-reliance' " and who was always "true to his principles, his convictions of right and the commands of his conscience even against the behests of his party." Even Woodrow Wilson, who was not notably disturbed by the democratic qualities of American government, concluded that "the size of the modern democracy necessitate[d] the exercise of persuasive power by dominant minds."[18]

Thus, the reformers of the late nineteenth century found their ideal political world, in which talent was rewarded by office, in the early American past. Just as Grover Cleveland wanted government to employ "the best men possible," so Henry Adams found that Thomas Jefferson, in removing Federalists from office, had sought to act in a way calculated to "injure the best men least." Indeed, Adams quoted Jefferson as declaring that the only questions a president should ask about a candidate for office were "Is he honest? Is he capable? Is he faithful to the Constitution?" Jefferson's beliefs, Adams claimed, were reflective of an "organized social system . . . admirably adapted for the uses of the eighteenth century." That system, which still existed in 1800, at least in New England, had been created by a "cordial union between the clergy, the magistracy, the bench and bar, and respectable society" and "supported by the convictions of the people." Adams was not alone in regretting the loss of influence by respectable society; others were also troubled by the increasing difficulty of "mak[ing] out what people mean when they speak of a gentleman."[19]

One reason the reformers wanted respectable society to lead the nation was that leaders drawn from the upper class would be most likely to possess "those qualities of mind and character which the stern task of genuine reform requires." Only the aristocracy, wrote John W. Burgess, possessed the "intelligence, skill, and fidelity" essential for the application of scientific morality to public affairs. Many reformers believed that they themselves constituted precisely the sort of aristocracy needed in government. Richard T. Ely, for example, declared himself "an aristocrat rather than a democrat"; and Henry Adams told his brother Charles Francis Adams, Jr., that the nation needed leadership from a "set of young men like ourselves or better." Like antislavery moralists, these reformers envisioned not an aristocracy of the rich that would use its power to enhance its wealth, but what Ely called "a natural aristocracy . . . which lives for the fulfillment of special service."[20]

The other reason respectable society should be entrusted with political leadership, in the reformers' eyes, was the upper class's unparalleled opportunity "to acquire an excellent education" — a crucial ingredient in the quest for a scientific morality. It was clear to men like John W. Burgess that government "demand[ed] the finest training, as well as the finest talent, for the successful management of its affairs;" even Woodrow Wilson thought that a "technically schooled civil service" was "indispensable." Reformers of the late nineteenth century believed it essential that the nation be taught to "respect . . . trained expert opinion" and "to consider highly educated officials as representative."[21] Through their program of civil service reform, which emphasized merit as the basis for appointment to government office, and their program of educational reform, which emphasized advanced, professional training in graduate schools for future government officials, the reformers sought to achieve their ideal: government by those best fitted to govern.

In the search for a scientific morality, late nineteenth-century reformers discovered not only the importance of elite leadership to a wise and moral government, but also the communitarian roots of morality and wisdom. The communitarian ideal powerfully influenced the reformers. Wendell Phillips, the veteran antislavery agitator who turned to other reform movements after the Civil War, illustrates its attraction. His "ideal of a civilization" was a "New England town of some two thousand inhabitants, with no rich man and no poor man in it, all mingling in the same society, every child at the same school, no poorhouse, no beggar, opportunities equal, nobody too proud to stand aloof, nobody too humble to be shut out." Phillips was not alone in his love of small communities. According to the *Nation*, "the object of our political system is to form a genuine community." Historian Herbert B. Adams betrayed similar views by encouraging his students to write two volumes of monographic essays on life in early New England towns, while Henry Adams found an analogue to the early New England community in eighteenth-century Virginia, where "every plantation was attached to a parish" and the two together formed a community; he was convinced that these prototypical eighteenth-century American communities persisted into the opening years of the nineteenth century, when "the same bad roads and difficult rivers . . . connect[ed] the same small towns." G. S. Hall was entranced by what he labeled the "best educational environment . . . ever realized in history," which had existed in early nineteenth-century towns in western Massachusetts, and he "lamented [the] decay of these little old towns," where relationships were built on face-to-face daily contact. Edward A. Ross maintained that to avoid a "grand crash" the nation had to develop new institutions that would replace the "local solidarity" of the small community. Josiah Royce, the Harvard philosopher, suggested recreating this solidarity by dividing the country into a series of provinces, such as New England and the Pacific Coast.[22]

Late nineteenth-century reform-minded thinkers had inklings of a possible direct relationship between morality and community. Indeed, for G. S. Hall, "the whole of morality" could "be well-defined as life in the interest" of the community or of "the race." Those who lived in small towns went "back to sources" and made contact with the "fresh primary thoughts, feelings, beliefs, modes of life of simple, homely, genuine, men." James M. Baldwin argued that every society needed techniques for "socializing" its residents, "inculcating reverence for the common ideals," and "substituting its collective will for the private wills of its constituents." Nearly all late nineteenth-century American social scientists endorsed solidarism in preference to individualism; they agreed that the individual was a creature of society and was shaped by it in fundamental ways; they no longer viewed society as a mere aggregate of individuals. Thinkers such as E. L. Godkin turned to the small community as a device for controlling individual behavior, because they opposed the use by majorities of coercive governmental power; they recognized that people living in small towns would act morally not because they were compelled by law, but because they did not want to "assume the burden [of] giv[ing] up all claim to the good opinion of their neighbors."[23]

Unfortunately for reform thinkers, the concentration of population in some geographic areas, the economic interdependence between different areas, and the ease of sustained communication rendered impossible a return to an idyllic past of geographically compact communities inhabited by small numbers of people well acquainted with one another. Too many people had profit to make, and even fewer were willing to relinquish the high level of material comfort resulting from expansion of the nation's interdependent economy. Too many others had abandoned tilling the soil for the nation to return to the agrarian economy that had been the foundation of the eighteenth-century communitarian order. Intellectually oriented reformers themselves were not then, as they are not now, prepared to relinquish the comforts of urban life and return to the soil. Although some reformers strove to preserve intact existing small communities, it was unrealistic to think the clock could be turned back.

However, the same advances in transportation and communication that made a return to eighteenth-century agrarian communities unthinkable made new sorts of communitarian authority structures possible. These advances enabled people to associate on the basis of their common interests rather than on that of the mere accident of their place of residence. In the view of Simon Sterne, a New York attorney active in civil service reform and in the founding of the Association of the Bar of the City of New York, communities could be organized and then take their place in the larger polity on the basis of "intellectual affinities, instead of mere geographical propinquity." Josiah Royce, the Harvard philosopher, agreed with Sterne that only "men who take counsel together in small groups" could be "safe rulers . . . who [would] wisely think and rightly guide." Edward Ross, the sociologist from Princeton University and the University of Nebraska, similarly took note of "communions . . . founded on affinity and selective choice," such as the "Baptists or Odd Fellows or Railway Mail Clerks."[24]

E. L. Godkin summarized the contribution that communities of affinity could make to political reform in an 1870 article, "The Prospects of the Political Art." To put an end to the enactment of legislation by "multifarious conflicting interests," which was becoming "a positive hindrance [rather] than a help to healthy progress," Godkin recommended "the appointment of committees or commissions for the examination of questions that it would be too outrageous and too ridiculous to treat off-hand by general debate." Each such group would "form . . . a kind of intellectual state" or "community of ideas" that would have a great "effect . . . on manners." Others used similar language. Francis E. Abbot, a close acquaintance of many late nineteenth-century reformers, spoke of the "community of the competent," and Herbert B. Adams, the historian at Johns Hopkins, noted "the importance" in late nineteenth-century America "of corporate influences, of associations of men and money."[25]

The two thinkers who pursued most deeply the possibility of organizing American society into communities of affinity were Henry Adams and Charles Sanders Peirce. Both understood that scientific inquiry—and hence scientific morality—could exist only within communities of scientific inquirers and that, because such communities did not exist, they would need to be created artifically.

Adams began his professional career as a historian committed to "the severest process of stating, with the least possible comment, such facts as seemed sure, in such order as seemed rigorously consequent." But the "result had satisfied him . . . little," for "where he saw sequence, other men saw something quite different, and no one saw the same unit of measure." By the end of the century, Adams had concluded that "chaos was the law of nature" and that " 'chaos' " was " 'all that science' " could " 'logically assert.' " " 'Order and reason, beauty and benevolence,' " were " 'characteristics and conceptions . . . solely associated with the mind of man' " and honored only " 'so that science shall not become impossible.' " Adams's ultimate conclusion was that scientists "had reduced their universe to a series of relations to themselves."[26]

From this it followed that a group of men could have a similar understanding of the universe only if they investigated it from a similar perspective — that is, only if they were part of a community committed to inquiring into reality from a shared point of view. Adams never drew this conclusion explicitly, but Charles Sanders Peirce, a scion of Harvard, of Cambridge, and of Massachusetts with whom Adams was acquainted, did. Peirce, the son of a Harvard mathematician, possessed an extraordinary insight into the workings of science; he concluded that solitary individuals seeking knowledge of truth would find only "ignorance and error," that scientific truth and hence reality itself were accessible only to a "*community* of philosophers," and that the very notion "of the conception of reality . . . essentially involves the notion of COMMUNITY." Indeed, Peirce defined truth itself as that "opinion which is fated to be ultimately agreed to by all who investigate."[27]

Adams and Peirce, however, though among the most clever, were not among the most influential men of their age. Although some of their contemporaries spoke of the need for subordinating individual endeavor to communitarian control,[28] none spoke as explicitly about the dependence of scientific inquiry and morality upon the existence of communities of scientific inquirers. Indeed, few recognized that moral standards in general were dependent upon communal assertion of the standards. Most political reformers and reform-minded intellectuals of the late nineteenth century knew only that they wanted a polity that gave due weight to morality, aristocracy, and community; they may have suspected, but they did not state clearly, how those values were intertwined.

However unclear their ideas may have been, reformers nevertheless implemented them as they founded a series of new organizations based on intellectual affinity. One of the first communities of affinity organized after the Civil War was the American Social Science Association, in 1865. Its aim was similar to those embraced by earlier communities of propinquity: to give members "the advantage of each other's knowledge" so that "doubts" could be "removed, conflicting opinions harmonized, and a common ground afforded for treating wisely the great social problems of the day." Later, the American Social Science Association gave birth to more tightly knit groups, notably the American Historical Association in 1884 and the American Economic Association in 1885. Also founded in this era was the American Bar Association.[29]

In addition to founding new organizations, late nineteenth-century reformers also put their ideas to work in efforts to solve some of the major political and social problems of their time. One such problem concerned the rights and obligations of laborers in large industrial and transportation firms. Various solutions were proposed for dealing with this problem. One — that of the National Labor Union in the 1860s and the Knights of Labor in the 1870s and 1880s — was to organize labor for the purpose of political education and ultimately political action through the normal processes of majoritarian democracy. In view of their suspicion of majoritarian governmental processes, it is not surprising that the elite reformers gave little support to either the National Labor Union or the Knights of Labor.

A second solution — an approach that would survive into the twentieth century and set the pattern for labor-management relations during the New Deal — was propounded by the trade unions and, after 1886, by the American Federation of Labor. The trade union movement urged laborers to unite in order to maximize their economic power and then to use that power not through the political process, but through collective bargaining and ultimately the strike. The elite reformers, however, opposed this approach, too. Thomas M. Cooley, for example, compared the activities of trade unions with those of predatory railroads: "organized laborers" used "strikes," "boycotts," and "kindred means" to "force compliance with their demands" just as railroads used "their own methods . . . of like nature." Although Cooley recognized that railroad methods had "been employed with greater skill and power" and hence had "been generally more effective and mischievous," the crucial similarity was the use of concentrations of private economic power to bring about a significant redistribution of wealth for the benefit of the wielders of power rather than for society as a whole.[30] A similar objection could apply to the program of the Knights of Labor, which, like the trade unions, wanted to redistribute wealth; the difference was that the Knights sought to use public rather than private power to attain that objective.

Those elite reformers who recognized the existence of a labor problem but opposed solving it through a substantial redistribution of wealth offered another general solution. Their approach was consistent with efforts of reformers in other areas to preserve the moral and communitarian traditions of an earlier era under the guidance of a trained corps of elite leaders; it sought to induce workers to join with one another and, at times, with their employers as well, for the purpose of improving their material and moral well-being without diverting their employers' wealth to their own use. Their premise was that, whereas a laborer in Europe was "a member of a distinct order in society, engaged in a sort of legal war with the other orders, and . . . bound to his fellows, not simply by community of material interest, but by sentiments of caste pride and fidelity," most American "laborers" could "reasonably hope . . . to become employers," for most "successful employers" had "begun by being laborers themselves." In America, "the social line between the laborer and the capitalist" was "very faintly drawn."[31]

It is noteworthy that advocates of this third approach usually were not members of the laboring class, but middle- and upper-class thinkers with close ties to other reform interests. Two such men were Carroll D. Wright, a reform-minded Republican politician who served for nearly two decades as the first U.S. commissioner of labor, and Franklin H. Giddings, the editor of the *Springfield Union*. For a time, Wright became interested in and wrote in support of schemes for profit sharing; Giddings was an advocate of worker cooperatives in both the production and retail distribution of goods. Giddings argued that the advantage of the cooperative movement was that it did "not ask the State to take possession of all capital, and manage all industry, and order all men in their industrial life"; instead, it relied "on the vitality, adaptability and growing power of voluntary association." He further maintained that, by putting an end to specific "evils associated with competition" that had grown excessive "through the shameful neglect of the government to fulfill its primary functions of protecting equal rights and enforcing justice," government could open the way "for the realization of the co-operative ideals."[32]

Wright advanced a more significant suggestion in an 1882 study of why labor unrest was greater in Fall River than in the two other Massachusetts towns of Lawrence and Lowell. His conclusion was that the greater power of trade unions in Fall River resulted in the intensification of labor strife, leading both employers and employees to be concerned only with their self-interest and to resort more frequently to coercive tactics to advance it. In Lawrence and Lowell, on the other hand, managers treated employee grievances with concern and made provision for certain employee needs, such as housing. The remedy for Fall River, according to Wright, was "an awakening of honest public sentiment" in the community that would lead to improvement in living quarters and in the educational and recreational facilities offered to the workers.[33]

Meanwhile, George M. Pullman was maturing his plans for the model industrial town of Pullman, Illinois, to be built and governed on the principles that had attracted Wright. Pullman hoped that his town would introduce "a new era . . . in the history of labor." As economist Richard H. Ely wrote in an article about the town, "part of the design of Pullman" was "to surround laborers as far as possible with all the privileges of large wealth." Workers reported that contrary to conditions in Chicago, where "there was mud on all sides . . . , clouds of soft coal, poor sewerage, villainous water, and everything else that was bad and disagreeable," they had in the town of Pullman "a clean and comfortable house and plenty of pure air," other "comforts and luxuries," "money in the savings bank, our children . . . getting a good education, [and] everything . . . peaceful and hopeful." In short, as Ely observed, George Pullman had "partially solved one of the great problems of the immediate present, which is a diffusion of the benefits of concentrated wealth among wealth-creators."[34]

Pullman had even larger aims than the diffusion of his existing wealth and the comfort and contentment of his workers. He sought also to promote the "moral and intellectual growth" of his community and its residents by inculcating "habits of respectability," "propriety and good manners." He hoped to eliminate "agitators" and other "baneful influences," especially taverns, from his model town.[35] Pullman went to great lengths, reminiscent of those of seventeenth-century Puritan magistrates, to achieve his goal of moral improvement. For example, he refused to sell homes to workers who preferred to buy rather than rent, because the sale of homes would force him to "run the risk of seeing families settle who are not sufficiently accustomed to the habits" he wished "to develop"; then, "all the good of my work would have been compromised by their presence." Like the leaders of colonial New England towns, Pullman thus sought to achieve moral conformity in part by excluding potential noncomformists. When newcomers moved into town, the Woman's Union took special pains to instruct them in taste and values, and, if it was later discovered that families "accustomed to filth and squalor . . . would not mend their ways" and present a proper public appearance, company inspectors gave them warnings and even threatened to impose fines. The result, in the words of one resident, was that the company "exercise[d] a surveillance over the movement and habits of the people in a way to lead one to suppose that it ha[d] a proprietary interest in [their] souls and bodies."[36]

George Pullman undoubtedly hoped, as a student of his town's history has written, that his model community would produce a "practical recognition of interlocking self-interest" among his managers and employees living together in the town — a recognition of mutual self-interest that might be instrumental in resolving general issues of labor-management relations. Carroll Wright, an enthusiastic suporter of the model town, undoubtedly agreed;[37] as Wright had noted, unionization in Fall River had hurt both labor and management, whereas cooperation in Lawrence and Lowell had benefited both. Wright explained in his *Outline of Practical Sociology* that the recognition by management and labor of their mutual self-interest would permit them "to come to an understanding" through "the powers of reasoning and the exposition of facts" before "a rupture" took place. Wright's friend Charles Francis Adams, Jr. agreed. Like Wright, Adams argued that impartial inquiry into the facts followed by "an appeal thereon to the reason and . . . enlightened sense of right of all concerned" was "in the long run" more "effective" than "force" in resolving "differences between the corporations and their employees." In America, Adams contended, "the final appeal must always be to reason" grounded in the mutual self-interest of management and labor rather than "to the sheriff or the soldier."[38]

When examined from the perspective of 1890, the moralistic and communitarian approach to the labor problem advanced by men such as Charles Francis Adams, Franklin Giddings, George Pullman, and Carroll Wright did not seem absurd. The residents of Pullman, Illinois, for example, lived in a style that was outwardly more respectable and moral than the life-style of many Chicago residents. Initially the town also brought greater stability to labor-management relations. As George Pullman learned somewhat to his chagrin during the 1893 depression, he could not lay off workers as demand for his sleeping cars declined, because his rental income from the town would also thereupon decline; his town, as it had been designed to do, made Pullman responsible for the well-being of his workers.[39]

For men like Adams, Giddings, Pullman, and Wright, whose own material well-being may have made them insensitive to working-class desires for a redistribution of wealth, values of community, morality, and stability were important. Their schemes for labor reform furthered these values. By the early twentieth century, however, those schemes had failed, primarily because most wage laborers preferred redistribution of the nation's industrial wealth to the communal moral solidarity offered by the elite reformers. As labor and management began to think increasingly in distributional terms, the essential antagonism of their interests became more apparent and the communal goal of the elite reformers appeared increasingly chimerical. In the area of labor-management relations, the demand of workers for sufficient wealth to enable them to enjoy practical freedom destroyed reform hopes of industrial governance by means of moral standards derived from a community of interest.

The Effort at Categorization

The labor problem was not the only one that late nineteenth-century reformers failed to solve by recourse to ideas about the governance of communities in accordance with principles of morality. Other problems also escaped solution. The difficulty was not merely that opposition existed to many reform proposals for restructuring society along moralistic and communitarian lines; a more fundamental problem was that such proposals, derived from analysis of the past, often bore no relation to contemporary problems created by rapid technological change. As one railroad executive commented, late nineteenth-century Americans at times did not "have . . . any precedent or experience upon which . . . [to] rely."[40] At such times, reformers turned to processes of categorization as a problem-solving technique.

In eighteenth- and early nineteenth-century America, figures of authority such as the local magistrate had possessed a broad and general mandate to deal with the myriad problems brought before them. Although these local figures generally could not exercise their mandate except in accordance with moral values acceptable to their communities, they rarely had to share authority with competing power centers. In most eighteenth-century localities a small, closely knit group was likely to have full possession of whatever power existed for solving whatever sorts of problems arose. Late nineteenth-century ideas about categorization, on the other hand, presupposed a governmental structure that differed from that of the eighteenth century in two related but distinct respects. Late nineteenth-century reformers rarely entrusted any single person or small group of people with comprehensive authority; instead, they authorized a large number of distinct institutions to deal separately with narrow, discrete, well-defined categories of problems. Nor did they leave these institutions free to approach the specific problems over which they possessed jurisdiction by giving them a broad and general mandate to act justly and morally; on the contrary, the structure and character of each institution and the nature of the problems with which it dealt severely constrained the ways in which it could approach a problem and the considerations it could take into account in solving it.

By creating a series of institutions, each with a well-defined role, the reformers categorized problems in ways that affected not only who would resolve any given problem but also how it would be resolved. As a result of this specialization of function, institutions received distinct, generally narrow jurisdictions and assumed roles or operational styles that largely determined the results they would obtain for the particular problems they confronted. Contemporary notions of categorization entailed more, however, than mere specialization of institutional function. A second way in which the method of categorization worked was to identify factual characteristics typically associated with problems that mandated their resolution in a specific manner. Problem-solving institutions were thus directed not only to limit the sorts of problems they approached and to approach them from a particular role perspective; they often were further directed to subdivide the problems they faced into still more narrowly defined categories that, in turn, often dictated the specific way in which a problem would be solved.

One example of how the categorical thinking of late nineteenth-century Americans differed from the thinking of earlier times is the manner in which disputes between individuals were resolved. In a typical eighteenth-century New England town, there was little specialization of function among the institutions to which disputes might be presented and little evidence of categorical thinking within any institution. If a dispute were submitted to either a church or a court — the two main eighteenth-century institutions for resolving disputes — it would be adjudicated by a group of neighbors sitting either as a congregation or as a jury in accordance with a single, transcendent set of moral or ethical customs or norms. If a disputant chose, instead, to have his dispute arbitrated, the arbitrators would typically be neighbors so deeply imbued with the same substantive values as a congregation or jury that they probably would have recourse to those values in resolving the case.[41]

By the end of the nineteenth century, all this had changed. Choice of institution now had a significant effect on the substantive rules that would be applied to determination of a dispute: arbitrators would be likely to apply business custom; a church would adjudicate a case in accordance with moral or religious values; and a court would apply common law or statutory law. Specialization of function had also occurred within the judiciary. Few eighteenth-century colonies had possessed equity courts that met frequently,[42] but a century later most states had busy equity jurisdictions that applied a body of law different from that applied in common-law courts. Even after a case had gone to a particular court, notions of categorization influenced its outcome. Much depended, for example, on whether a court concluded that a case belonged to the category of tort or of contract, and lawyers like Oliver Wendell Holmes, Jr., spent great energy refining the boundary between the two.[43] The distinction was important, for the rules for establishing liability in each category differed, as did the available remedies. The use of categories thus was important in the late nineteenth century in two respects: the category to which a dispute belonged helped determine not only which decisionmakers — and hence, which perspective — would be involved in its resolution, but also which substantive decisional standards would be used.

Widespread use of categorization processes initially emerged in large-scale businesses, particularly railroads, in the 1850s. The size of a few of the major railroads — the Baltimore & Ohio, the Erie, the

New York Central, and the Pennsylvania—made routinization of decisionmaking unavoidable, and the need for routinization in turn generated a need for categorization. It became obvious quite early that a single executive or small group of executives could not make all managerial decisions involved in the operation of a large railroad, and that different types of decisions would have to be delegated to different officials, each with a limited, specialized jurisdiction. Thus, railroads found it necessary through "a judicious subdivision of labor" and "a proper division of responsibilities"[44] to create complex bureaucracies, each segment of which was responsible for a different aspect of railroad management. In the late 1850s, for instance, the Erie Railroad was directed by a general superintendent, who was the chief executive officer; a general freight agent, in charge of transportation of freight; a general ticket agent, in charge of passenger transportation; a general wood agent, in charge of fuel supply; a superintendent of telegraph, in charge of communications; a foreman of bridge repairs; and a department of engine and car repairs. In addition, operating directly under the general superintendent were four division superintendents, each of whom was responsible for operations on one of the four divisions of the railroad's main line; and two branch superintendents, with jurisdiction over each of the railroad's two branch lines. Finally, in addition to these operating departments, most railroads also possessed entirely independent financial departments charged with collecting and disbursing funds and with auditing the corporation's accounts.[45] Over time, the head of each department undoubtedly developed a unique conception of role, determined by the segment of the railroad's activities within his jurisdiction; the role of the freight agent, for example, must have come to be the maximization of freight revenues, even when maximization required the use of equipment and facilities not in perfect repair, whereas the role of repair officials was to ensure proper maintenance of all track and equipment in use. The emergence of these specialized roles inevitably produced conflict between various departments, but such conflict led to clarification both of the role of top executives—that role being the resolution of conflict—and of the jurisdictional boundaries between the departments.

In short, during the 1850s and afterward the Erie and other major railroads developed complex categorization schemes that identified the discrete, different sorts of activities performed by railroad managers, assigned each activity to a specific executive or department, and gradually produced an espirit de corps within each department that dictated its general approach to the matters assigned it. These bureaucratized structures were far different from the management patterns of small, early railroads, in which, as in nearly all other antebellum businesses, the chief executive of the company could "give its business his personal attention, and . . . be almost constantly upon the line engaged in the direction of its details," acting upon "all questions in relation to its business" that were presented to him.[46]

Systems of categorization emerged in mid-nineteenth-century railroads not only in regard to the assignment of management tasks to executives but also in regard to the assignment of railroad costs to various social classes and groups. For example, early railroads set freight rates in accordance with supply and demand or on the basis of estimates derived from either their own experience or that of canals as to what the market would bear. As volume increased and markets became more complex, however, a need emerged for more systematic rate structures. In the 1850s the Pennsylvania devised the basic rate structure eventually adopted by most railroads, classifying more than two hundred articles according to four basic categories, with low-weight, high-value goods like clocks and woolens carried at a higher rate per ton than heavy, low-value goods like coal and lumber.[47] Thus, the Pennsylvania developed and other railroads later ratified a rate classification structure that arguably subsidized some industries and consumers at the expense of others.

Railroad accounting practices systematized in the 1870s had a similar impact. New methods of accounting, pioneered by Albert Fink, involved complex schemes for classifying expenses. These methods significantly affected the social distribution of the costs and profits associated with railroading. One important question was whether costs associated with the replacement and repair of roadbed and equipment should be categorized as an operating cost or a capital cost. By 1880 all railroads categorized such maintenance expenses as operating costs, a practice that probably led to higher rates as the railroads sought both to cover those expenses and to secure a profit. Charging such rates in effect compelled users to make a contribution to capital for which they received no direct dividends. If categorized as capital costs, on the other hand, maintenance expenses would have required the raising of additional capital. Although the need to pay dividends to holders of new capital might in the long run and in a perfect market have produced rates identical to those charged when maintenance expenses were considered as operating costs, there can be little doubt that new accounting schemes had short-run distributional consequences unfavorable to railroad users and, to the extent that markets were imperfect, may also have had similar long-run consequences.[48]

As other businesses expanded during the last three decades of the century and routinization of their operations became necessary, they similarly began to subdivide management responsibilities among executives with limited jurisdictions and to make business decisions on the basis of fixed, often categorical, standards. For example, the I. M. Singer Company, which became the world's leading manufacturer of sewing machines, created a complex organization of twenty-five regional offices in the United States reporting to a central office in New York, fifty-three regional offices in continental Europe reporting to headquarters in Hamburg, and thirty-five offices in Great Britain and much of the rest of the world reporting to a London office. Within these offices employees had specialized responsibilities; some dealt with marketing and sales, others with credit and collections, and still others with service and repairs. The McCormick Harvesting Machine Company established a similar organization in the 1880s, as did other firms in subsequent years. Other businesses also emulated the railroads in their pricing and accounting practices: the Singer Company financed much of what might otherwise have been considered capital improvements out of its current earnings — a policy that kept prices high, dividends low, and ownership of the company more concentrated than it might otherwise have been. Like the railroads, newly organized department stores adopted a policy of selling goods only at fixed prices rather than permitting bargaining over price. This policy required the store management to allocate various categories of fixed expenses among the different departments; in short, management had to decide, in effect, to subsidize some lines of retail trade at the expense of others, just as railroads subsidized the shippers of heavy, low-value freight at the expense of others.[49]

As already suggested, it appears that two factors led to division and specialization of management functions and to the rise of new pricing and accounting categories in various American businesses.

One factor was the growth in the size of enterprise: when a single executive or small executive group could no longer decide business questions in response to *ad hoc* bargaining or on other *ad hoc* bases, it became necessary to delegate decisionmaking authority to a large number of managers, often in different localities, and the development of fixed categories and standards became the only means of coordinating operations and ensuring that they functioned in accordance with the general will of top managers. A second factor may have been a series of decisions by managers of large firms possessing vast economic power to aid one or another economic class or group at the expense of others. Although it is doubtful that this second factor led to the bureaucratization of management or induced management bureaucrats to establish standardized pricing and accounting practices, it is entirely possible that certain specific standards were formulated with full awareness of their distributional effect upon those outside the firm.

Neither factor can explain, however, the growing division of labor and specialization of function in late nineteenth-century universities or the unusual emphasis on processes of categorization in late nineteenth-century academic thought. Universities were not then so large as to preclude their being controlled by a single man; Charles W. Eliot, for one, was able as Harvard's president to participate directly in the management of each of its schools and departments. Nor does it seem likely that thinkers in fields like psychology emphasized processes of categorization in order to alter the distribution of social wealth and power. Nevertheless specialization and categorization were central features in the transformation of the American academic world in the late nineteenth century.

The first step in that transformation was to separate clearly the university from the state. Most institutions of higher learning in mid-century had been chartered by state legislatures, and all had retained connections of various sorts with state governments. As late as the 1850s Harvard, for example, was seeking and obtaining financial support from the Massachusetts legislature, which in turn elected all but a few ex officio members of Harvard's Board of Overseers. Although specific ties between state and college varied among colleges and among states, in nearly all cases significant ties persisted until the 1860s.[50]

Although the nation's two wealthiest universities — Columbia and

Harvard — and a few other colleges had gained independence from state control by 1865, no ideology yet existed in support of the private, independent university as distinguished from the public, state-supported one. That ideology apparently was born in an 1873 debate about whether to create a national university supported by a $20 million federal endowment. The leading opponent of the new university was Harvard's President Eliot. Motivated in part, perhaps, by a concern that Harvard not face competition from a new, well-endowed institution, Eliot argued his case on the grounds, first, that public support of higher education "sap[ped] the foundations of public liberty," and, second, that a national university would become a partisan pawn staffed by incompetent professors appointed by transient political majorities. Another leading reformer of the time, John W. Burgess, seconded Eliot in this position a decade later, asserting that "the partisanship which, as the rule, dominates all appointments here renders any governmental agent unfit to tamper with . . . [universities,] for partisanship seeks to manipulate every thing for personal or party advantage and does nothing, intentionally, for such abstractions as civilization and culture."[51]

Having separated the university from the state in order to avoid popular, majoritarian control, reformers like Burgess and Eliot next sought to restructure university government along scientific lines. This initially required a more precise delineation of the roles of various entities within the university's governance structure. At the beginning of the nineteenth century, what would later emerge as three distinct entities — the faculty, the administration, and the trustees — had often overlapped. At Yale, for example, the president of the college remained a regular instructor of students as late as the 1820s; during the same decade the Harvard faculty made a determined argument that its members, rather than outsiders, should constitute the college's principal governing board. It was also commonplace throughout the first two-thirds of the century for college trustees to shape the curriculum, prescribe classroom work, and otherwise regulate and interfere in even the smallest details of academic life.[52]

In the last third of the century, new patterns of governance slowly emerged, and by 1900 there was a new ideal: trustees would hold the property and regulate the finances of the university, including professorial salaries, and the president and faculty would govern and instruct the students and make academic appointments. At a few universities, notably Harvard, even the functions of the president and the faculty became differentiated as academic decisions and appointments were delegated to the faculty and the president's primary task became the resolution of interdepartmental conflicts.[53]

Of course, the trustees did not always respect the newly differentiated functions of the president and faculty. The trustees of Cornell, for example, dismissed William C. Russel, a professor and vice-president, without apparent cause, and those of Ohio State dismissed university president Walter Quincy Scott, in part because the son of the board's president had been dropped from the university for academic reasons and a son-in-law of the board's secretary had not been appointed an assistant professor of Latin.[54] But such actions produced much unfavorable publicity, both inside and outside the university. Russel, for one, commented publicly that professors "must be free" and could not be treated as "clerks or servants, nor have trustees any right to look down on them . . . or treat them summarily." In a similar vein, the eminent historian Herbert B. Adams, when offered the presidency of Ohio State after Scott's dismissal, expressed concern about the "unstable tenure of your president and all the faculty" and about the president's lack of "power and influence with reference to the appointment and tenure of professors." Likewise, when Yale's president Noah Porter directed William Graham Sumner to cease using Herbert Spencer's *Study of Sociology* as a textbook in his course because the book "attack[ed] every Theistic Philosophy of society," Sumner responded in a public letter that he considered "Spencer's religious opinions . . . of very little importance" in comparison with "the question whether it was a good or available book in a scientific point of view." Sumner further declared that he "would not submit to a restraint the motive of which was consideration for metaphysical and theological interests."[55] Although Sumner later withdrew Spencer's text, he nonetheless struck an important blow for academic independence of faculties from presidents and trustees.[56]

While the jurisdiction and role of trustees, administrators, and faculties were being differentiated, categorization and differentiation were also occurring in the form of "specialization of instruction." Whereas scientists in early nineteenth-century American colleges had often taught subjects such as moral philosophy as well as science, the pattern late in the century was one of increasing departmentalization of knowledge. There was, of course, no complete agreement as to what constituted the "main divisions of knowledge." Charles W. Eliot, for example, believed there were four—language, history, natural science, and mathematics—whereas W. T. Harris, U.S. commissioner of education at the turn of the century, contended there were five—mathematics and physics, biology, literature and art, grammar and language, and history and political and social science. But few late nineteenth-century scientific reformers would have doubted that what distinguished the categories of knowledge and hence of instruction was the fact that "their study calls into activity different methods of observation and different trains of thought—different categories of the mind, so to speak."[57]

Reformers like Eliot at times suggested that increased specialization in research and teaching was essential because even brilliant men could not master all knowledge; he cited as an example Oliver Wendell Holmes, Sr., who as professor of anatomy and physiology at Harvard also taught histology and pathology and "described himself as occupying, not a chair, but a settee." But expansion of knowledge, unlike expansion of business, did not inevitably lead to division and specialization of labor, for the sum of human knowledge did not expand with unusual rapidity in late nineteenth-century America. What led to specialization was less an expansion of knowledge than a change in Americans' conception of knowledge. American academics in the first half of the century had often assumed that an idea was warranted and verified by proof of its moral advantages; one Princeton professor, for example, in reviewing a book adumbrating portions of Darwin's theory of evolution, wrote that "it would be deemed an ample refutation of any system to show clearly that it was atheistic in its essential character." In expressing such a view, this professor showed himself to be part of a culture in which Jacksonian democrats tested the worth of an idea by counting the number of men who believed in it and in which antislavery advocates tested an idea by examining its moral pedigree. In antebellum America both scientific experimentation and moral inquiry were integrated by a single set of moral ideals that gave intelligibility to all human endeavor. A moral theorist who had internalized a set of transcendant values could use them equally well in the role of statesman, priest, or scientist and could indulge what Eliot would later label "the vulgar conceit that a Yankee can turn his hand to anything."[58] In the new epistemological world of the late nineteenth century, however, theories were tested—as William

Graham Sumner reminded Yale President Porter in their debate over Sumner's use of the Spencer text—on the basis not of their moral worth but of their consistency with evidence. In this new world, the immense quantity of evidence yet to be unearthed and the existence of various methodologies for unearthing it precluded any one person from having expertise in more than a small portion of the sum of human endeavor. The new concern for evidence required that knowledge be compartmentalized.

What merits repetition, however, is that categorization did not come to the academic world—as it had, perhaps, to the business world—as an inevitable product of expansion. It came because leading educators, acting for what might be called reasons of state, imposed a new conception of knowledge upon the academic world. As Eliot observed, the problem with the "vulgar conceit" of Yankees was that Americans "insensibly carr[ied it] into high places, where it . . . [was] preposterous and criminal." In his view, the failure of Americans to demand "knowledge and experience . . . of our lawgivers" or to require "special training . . . for our diplomatists . . . amount [ed] to a national danger."[59] It was the need to move beyond old moral precepts to a new scientific morality that brought about the late nineteenth-century transformation of American education.

If attaining knowledge by studying facts without the aid of a priori theories required compartmentalization of the branches of knowledge, it also required researchers within a single branch to classify and categorize facts. Here too processes of categorization moved beyond specialization of function as students of the human condition strove to apprehend its true nature.

Much late nineteenth-century scientific and scholarly thought resulted from the efforts of academics to apply to their own fields the methodology of Charles Darwin, the great scientist of the mid-century English-speaking world. Darwin had an impact on late nineteenth-century thought in several significant ways. But notions of categorization were most deeply affected by Darwin's contribution to taxonomy.

People had been classifying animals for thousands of years, but by the nineteenth century ancient taxonomic schemes had come to seem arbitrary. Eighteenth-century taxonomists, especially Carolus Linnaeus, had begun to develop new ones, but those schemes too had an arbitrary cast and appeared to be a priori products of scientists' minds rather than inherent in nature. Darwin's *Origin of Species*, however, provided a rationale for the new taxonomic schemes by demonstrating that animals that happened to fit within a single category belonged there because they enjoyed a common ancestry. Darwin thereby seemed to prove that post-Linnaean categories were genuine schemes of nature and not merely figments of particular scientists' imaginations.[60]

Scientists in other fields similarly searched for classification schemes that were inherent in nature. William Graham Sumner noted this trend in the new science of sociology. The sociologist, according to Sumner, "need[ed] to arrange his facts" and required a scheme of "classification so as to take up the facts in a certain order." If the sociologist failed to "do this he . . . [would] be overwhelmed in the mass of his material so that he never . . . [could] master it." Thus, Sumner in 1882 called for "adequate criteria by which to make the necessary tests and classifications, and appropriate canons of procedure, or the adaptation of universal canons to the special tasks of sociology." Two decades later, Sumner quoting Karl Pearson, was even more specific, stating that " 'the classification of facts and the formation of absolute judgments upon the basis of this classification . . . is peculiarly the scope and method of modern science' " and, further, that " 'the classification of facts, the recognition of their sequence and relative significance is the function of science.' " Indeed, in *Folkways*, published in 1906, Sumner developed a population curve with which he classified all people as geniuses, people of talent, mediocrities, proletariat, dependent, defective, and delinquent.[61]

Other disciplines also recognized the need for new schemes of classification. As early as 1879, G. S. Hall commented upon the need in psychology for "a radically new classification of mental faculties more fundamental than the almost mythic . . . one of feeling, intellect, [and] will," and in subsequent years new categories were introduced, largely imported from Germany. As in sociology, schemes of categorization made immense progress in the early years of the twentieth century, with, for example, the development by 1910 of modern intelligence testing. In political science, "a political constitution" came to be viewed as "a specimen to be studied, classified, and labeled, as a building or an animal is studied, classified, and labeled by those to whom buildings or animals are objects of study." Categorization was also popularized through racist speeches of politicians like Senator John W. Daniel of Virginia, who argued that "you will never change the different qualities of the races which God has created in order that they may fulfill separate and distinct missions in the cultivation and civilization of the world."[62]

Speeches like those of Senator Daniel reveal what was at stake in the late nineteenth century's categorization effort. One crucial question that Americans then faced was how the nation's white majority should treat its black minority. Before 1860, slavery had been justified on the grounds that it comported with the will of the white majority or that it constituted the foundation of an idealized southern way of life. On the other hand, it was attacked as inconsistent with a higher-than-human law handed down by God or some such transcendent force. The failure of these various appeals to political and moral values to solve the problem of American race relations led to a bloody civil war. Moreover, even when one of the value systems emerged victorious from the battlefields it proved incapable of solving many of the novel race relations issues that its victory had generated.

At that point, intellectuals began to suggest that if problems were investigated only neutrally and empirically rather than from some a priori perspective, the factual knowledge gained might well suggest desirable public policies. When they confronted the facts, however, late nineteenth-century intellectuals were overwhelmed until they began to subdivide their inquiries into distinct fields of research and to classify and categorize facts even within those fields. Given the novelty of the taxonomic methodology, it is not surprising that many late-century categories, like the racial and ethnic ones, were unoriginal and superficial. Still, the effort seemed useful. By subdividing Americans into racial and ethnic groups and analyzing the characteristics of people within each group, intellectuals probably felt better able to explain why most blacks occupied a socioeconomic position inferior to that of most whites. Moreover, the capacity to explain and understand the nation's existing social structure in all its elaborate complexity reconfirmed what had been, perhaps, the main lesson of the Civil War—that the costs of fundamental social change are so high that they almost inevitably seem to exceed the benefits. And that lesson came to constitute a powerful justification in support of the status quo.

The tendency to support the status quo was, I believe, implicit in the reformers' effort at categorization, just as it was in their attempt to locate the communal and aristocratic roots of morality in the past. Empirical inquiries that are not consciously designed to see facts from a new perspective will normally report upon facts in common and familiar ways; for, once a researcher makes a "neutral and objective" decision not to impose a novel and idiosyncratic perspective on his data, he necessarily abandons all effort at creative synthesis of the data and becomes unable to describe and characterize it except by recourse to familiar, commonplace categories. And, when public policy is formulated through reliance on those categories, government becomes incapable of fundamentally altering the status quo.

It is not surprising that late nineteenth-century reformers invented forms of policy analysis supportive of the status quo. They were, after all, striving to replace two forms of analysis—policymaking by majority will and policymaking on the basis of moral principle—capable of revolutionizing a social order. The efforts of Jacksonian democrats and antislavery moralists to revolutionize American society had had immense costs in governmental instability and ultimately in human blood. Having paid those costs, late nineteenth-century reformers wanted a government that brought peace and stability by slowing the pace of change. In the bureaucracy they created they achieved their aim.

5

Building Bureaucratic
Authority Structures

BY THE CLOSING YEARS of the nineteenth century, four approaches to governmental organization were available to Americans. One was that of majoritarian democracy, inherited from the Jacksonians and still robust despite its failures and critics. A second was the application of antislavery moral precepts; although these principles addressed many late nineteenth-century problems either ambiguously or not at all, they did provide guidance for some problems, and former antislavery advocates who found themselves in positions of power after the war were eager to implement them. A third approach, generated by reformers and intellectuals who were aware of the inadequacies of both majoritarian democracy and antislavery morality, was the study of history to identify the social preconditions of moral government; once those preconditions were adequately understood, reformers hoped to reestablish them and thereby restore morality to government. The fourth approach, also generated by those dissatisfied with the first two, allocated narrowly defined problems to various institutions, each of which was to resolve those problems by expert analysis and categorization of the facts.

In the last third of the century, proponents of the last three approaches frequently made suggestions for altering the majoritarian system of government inherited from the antebellum period. Often they suggested schemes that combined two or more of the approaches. Political leaders who still believed in the rhetoric of majoritarian democracy usually opposed these suggestions, with varying success. The result by 1900 was the emergence of a new governmental structure that was an amalgam of all four approaches. The same structure, somewhat modified and elaborated, endures today.

The Reorganization of Congress

As we discussed in chapter 1, from 1840 to 1880 effective legislative power in Congress rested with party chieftains who derived their power from the support of the party caucus. Party leaders were able to supervise the work of congressional committees closely by concentrating important business in a small number of committees and by controlling the appointment and tenure of commiteee chairmen. By the turn of the century, however, committees were increasingly becoming "little legislatures," each of which went "its own way at its own pace," did "not consult and concur [with other committees] in the adoption of homogeneous and mutually helpful measures," and had "no thought of acting in concert." "The chairmen of the Standing Committees," Woodrow Wilson observed, no longer "constitute[d] a cooperative body like a ministry;" each chairman was responsible not to a central party committee, but to the other members — including the minority members — of his own committee and to a broader, often nationwide constituency of interest groups routinely concerned in the matters considered by his committee.[1]

This transformation in the role of the committees was a product of two changes in the structure and processes of each house of Congress. First, in accordance with schemes for categorization, important legislative work was divided among a larger number of committees by the end of the century than it had been earlier. Second, committee chairmen came increasingly to hold their posts by virtue of their expertise and seniority rather than their loyalty to party programs.

The changes began during Reconstruction, when committee work associated with appropriation of funds was separated from that associated with raising revenue. The House acted first, creating in 1865 a separate Appropriations Committee, which thereafter became the legislative clearinghouse of the lower chamber even though it never enjoyed the full powers of the old Ways and Means Committee. In 1867 the Senate likewise separated the Committee on Appropriations from the Committee on Finance and made the Appropriations Committee the main clearinghouse for legislation. The separation of revenue-raising from revenue-appropriating functions did not, however, significantly affect the power of majority leaders to control the Congress; the number of important committees remained few, their work was easily coordinated, and the most important power remained in the hands of a single committee — Appropriations — in each house.[2]

In the House, the major change in the jurisdiction of committees occurred around 1880, when the Appropriations Committee lost much of its power. In 1877 its jurisdiction over funds for river and harbor improvements was transferred to the Committee on Commerce. This move prompted a debate that continued until 1885, when jurisdiction over appropriations bills was given to eight different committees, including the weakened Appropriations Committee.[3] Those who sought to distribute the appropriations function among several committees argued that Congress was not "simply engaged in a division of spoils"; they maintained that specialization and division of labor were essential to proper governance of the nation and that it was "not possible . . . for any one committee to . . . investigate and understand everything necessary and proper to originate legislation, to raise the money for it, and to divide and appropriate that money." On the contrary, it was claimed that because "each committee" had "relations . . . with the different Departments" and therefore had "special knowledge and special information that the Committee on Appropriations . . . can not have," each committee ought to have jurisdiction over appropriations bills related to its substantive field of expertise. As one congressman explained by way of example, it was "in the very nature of things reasonable and just that fifteen men who have had the matter of the building of the Navy as the one theme for their investigation during the entire session of Congress" should have "in their hands the naval appropriation bill," for they would give it "the most intelligent consideration."[4]

Congressional reformers were not concerned only with improving the performance of committees; they also seem to have wanted to terminate the power of a single committee "to execute the wish of the caucus" and thereby "enforce . . . the policy of its party" — in short, to "simply obey . . . the will of the majority."[5] Opponents of reform countered that "it would be almost fatal in a party sense to the party having control if they were to disperse among eight or ten different committees the subject of appropriations," because "whatever party may be in the ascendant in this House . . . party discipline" required "having a single head to control." The opponents also argued that "to distribute the work" of the Appropriations Committee would "make it practically impossible to secure anything like harmony of action and unity of purpose" in the legislative activity of the House.[6] Despite such warnings, congressmen who supported the distribution of appropriations bills persisted in advancing their program of change. They argued that "this oneness of design, this 'harmony of action,' this 'unity of purpose' . . . [was] not consistent with the genius and spirit of our institutions"; it was "not the object for which the framers of this Government labored." On the contrary, the framers had "sought not to concentrate power in the hands of a few men to the end that 'harmony of action' and 'unity of purpose' might be secured, but their great aim was the general diffusion of power." Hence, the object of the reformers was to create independent committees, each "responsible [only] to itself" rather than to a party majority.[7]

In short, the existence of independent committees would ensure not only greater expertise in the enactment of legislation. It would also lead to a dispersion of power — an important object of the framers of the Constitution. Most important, reorganization of the committee system would transform the legislative process. Committees would no longer be subject to the will of party managers and the party caucus, but would instead place themselves at the head of groups regularly concerned with their particular field of competence and legislate in accordance with common values accepted by all of those groups. As reformers explained, each substantive committee would develop "relations" of "an intimate and friendly character" both with its counterpart in the executive department and with the other interests concerned with its area of jurisdiction; each committee would be composed of "men who are friendly to that Department" and would work "constantly in close alliance and sympathy with that Department." Congressman William Hatch of Missouri, in discussing some bills prepared by the House Agriculture Committee, described the way in which the reformers hoped the new system would operate. He observed that "these bills had been so carefully considered by the Committee on Agriculture, that committee having such close relations with the Department of Agriculture, its individual members investigating and acquainting themselves with the working of every single division and bureau of that Department, that when this bill . . . [was] perfected and presented here it command[ed] the approbation of the House and passe[d] without challenge."[8]

Thus, at least some congressmen publicly took a reform-minded position in supporting the 1885 decision of the House to distribute appropriations bills — and hence, the power to formulate legislation — to eight separate committees. These congressmen made clear their rejection of the system of majoritarian party democracy as they sought to weaken the hold of political parties over the processes whereby legislation was formulated. They wanted legislation formulated by men who represented and took into account the interests of various groups concerned with the legislation. Although these reform-minded legislators favored use of the most modern tools of late nineteenth-century empirical social science to investigate the facts, their ultimate object remained the same as that of the aristocratic leaders of pre-Jacksonian communities — to devise legislative programs that would reconcile divergent interests and thus merit adoption by general approbation rather than by a mere majority party vote. They favored a system in which each committee would identify the interest groups within its sphere and seek to generate an affinity among them in support of a legislative program acceptable to as many as possible.

While the House of Representatives was distributing apropriations bills among eight committees, reform-minded senators sought to do the same in the upper chamber. In the Senate it was urged that each committee should make appropriations in its area of legislative competence because it had "special knowledge and special information that the Committee on Appropriations . . . [did] not have," as well as "intimate relations" with its companion department in the executive branch and other concerned interest groups.[9] In particular, senators contended that it was wrong to attach to appropriations bills substantive riders concerning matters about which the Appropriations Committee itself had no expertise. The Senate, however, acted more slowly than the House, and it was not until 1899 that a resolution for distributing appropriations bills among eight committees was adopted without debate.[10]

The loss of control by a small group of party leaders over the day-to-day work of congressional committees was accompanied by a loss of control over the appointment and tenure of committee chairmen. This diminution of power stemmed from the gradual acceptance of the seniority system in both houses of Congress. Whereas party leaders in the mid-nineteenth century had power to appoint committee chairmen who would faithfully carry out party policies and — at least in the Senate — to remove chairmen who failed to do so, by the early twentieth century the almost invariable practice in both houses was to name as chairman the member of the majority party who had served longest on a committee, even if he was merely a nominal member of the party with little loyalty to its programs.[11]

The seniority system like the dispersal of appropriations bills among numerous committees, worked to diminish the power of party and to render committees more responsive to the executive departments and other interest groups over whose affairs they had jurisdiction. Effective legislative power came to rest in committee chairmen and other senior committee members who, as a result of "long continuance of service on particular committees," had acquired "a knowledge of systems and of details," general expertise in particular substantive areas, and close ties to others interested in those areas. The seniority system made it possible to predict with substantial accuracy who future committee chairmen would be and thus enabled incumbent chairmen to devise arrangements with potential future chairmen, including ranking minority members of the committee; as a result, they were able to report legislation setting long-range priorities to which future leaders had already agreed. The capacity to predict was even more important to representatives of interest groups, for they could secure favorable committee action by influencing a few senior members of the relevant committee rather than a large portion of a party caucus. The result was a more consistent and "settled" line of "policy in any Department of the Government," for as long as the senior committee members of both parties coalesced around a particular policy, it was almost impossible to change that policy merely by placing the opposition party in control of Congress.[12]

Of course, political parties did not lose all their significance in the late nineteenth-century Congress. On the contrary, as the debates on rules changes indicate, many senators and congressmen clung to the conviction that political parties responsible to the majority of the people ought to dominate the proceedings of both houses. In fact, political parties may have had more influence in Congress late in the century than they had had in mid-century, for party regularity in floor votes seems to have increased.[13] The development of the seniority system and the increasing distribution of effective legislative power among a large number of committees, however, made effective party control of Congress more difficult. As a result, the mid-century tendency toward party government in Congress was slowed, and late nineteenth-century legislation became a product not merely of party forces, but both of party forces and of a more stable community of interest among various groups concerned with specific legislative policies.

Reform of the Executive Branch

Just as the influence of party did not disappear entirely in the workings of the late nineteenth-century Congress, so too party remained an important force in the functioning of the executive branch, if for no other reason than that the president remained a prominent creation and symbol of his party. Nevertheless, in the long run political chieftains suffered a significant loss of control over subordinate officials in the federal bureaucracy as a result of two major changes in the executive branch: the reformation of the civil service and the creation of the independent regulatory commission.

After the assassination of President Garfield in 1881 by a disappointed office seeker, public opinion shifted sharply in favor of elimination of the spoils system. In 1883 reform legislation was enacted. It created a Civil Service Commission and established fundamental rules for its operation, dividing the civil service into unclassified and classified segments and providing for the appointment of members of the classified service on the basis of merit, to be determined by competitive examinations open to all wishing to take them. Over the next several decades, increasing numbers of lower federal officials were added to the classified service, and civil service reform was extended to state and municipal governments. Thus the battle for reform, begun in the middle and late 1860s by political moralists turning their attention from antislavery and Reconstruction,[14] was ultimately triumphant.

In part, the reform movement was merely an attempt to eliminate corruption and improve performance within the lower bureaucracy.

Since Jackson's administration, commentators had argued that rotation in office led to deterioration of performance levels in government service; as one had observed "frequent change of the incumbents of office . . . [was] a wilful sacrifice of all the tact, skill, and knowledge which . . . [could] be gained from experience."[15] The reformers had also observed a marked increase in official corruption. One place where corruption was rife was the customs service in New York: Samuel Swartwout, Jackson's collector for the port, embezzled $1,225,705.69 in customshouse funds, and Jesse Hoyt, whom Van Buren appointed as his successor, stole between $150,000 and $200,000. Two decades later, Isaac Fowler, Buchanan's collector, fled to Mexico owing over $150,000. Similarly, an 1839 report showed that seventy-five receivers of public money in land offices were in arrears in their payments to the government. Although in many cases the amounts in arrears were small and in some reflected bona fide accounting differences, in others real delinquencies had occurred. Graft and corruption eventually reached the highest levels of the federal government in the Grant administration, and of municipal government under Boss Tweed in New York.[16]

Incompetence and corruption were obvious targets for the reformers. As Congressman Thomas Jenckes, the leader of the civil service reform movement in its earliest stages, remarked in one speech, "[the] true interests of the Government . . . [could] best be served, its expenses lessened, the character of its officers improved, and its business more effectually done, by an entire reformation in the mode of making appointments in civil service." Civil service reform would bring "competency" and "efficiency" along with "integrity" to the public service. The National Manufacturers' Association, at its first annual meeting in 1868, resolved that it was "indispensable that public affairs be conducted on business principles, and that the dangerous custom of giving public posts to political paupers and partisan servants, regardless of their fitness, should be discontinued, as such custom absorbs a large share of the public revenue." Administrators of some of the few federal agencies that were reformed at an early date also agreed that reform improved agency efficiency. The head of the lifesaving service, Sumner I. Kimball, for example, observed that in that "expert service" it was "absolutely indispensable" in securing the "very best obtainable men" "to adopt such means as would exclude politics" from their appointments. Carl Schurz, secretary of the interior under President Hayes, likewise concluded that the appointment of clerks only after a competitive examination, the keeping of efficiency records, and the promotion of the most efficient "proved to be a powerful stimulus" to "almost everyone . . . do[ing] his utmost."[17]

Inefficiency and corruption, however, were often perceived as symptoms of a deeper immorality in American political life. The civil service reformers, who, according to Wendell P. Garrison, came "nearer to being lineal descendants of the abolitionists than any other existing manifestation of the national conscience," endeavored to reconstruct the moral foundations of American politics. They believed "that the abolition of the spoils system . . . [was] second . . . in importance [only] to the abolition of slavery." They saw the link between the evil nature of politics and the wicked character of the men who became politicians and sought to reform the former by changing the latter. Thus, as Carl Schurz, an antislavery advocate who became an early leader of the reform movement, told the Senate: "The question whether the Departments at Washington are managed well or badly, is, in proportion to the whole problem, an insignificant question after all. Neither does the question whether our civil service is as efficient as it ought to be, cover the whole ground. The most important point to my mind is, how we can remove that element of demoralization which the now prevailing mode of distributing office has introduced into the body-politic."[18]

One aspect of that demoralization was the diversion of political parties from their proper function. That function, wrote George William Curtis, was "to divide upon questions of national policy . . . by appeal[ing] by public speech and in the public press to the judgment of the people" and to "strive . . . to elect to the various legislatures representatives who will put its policy into law." Civil service reform sought "not merely the observance of certain rules of examination" but "the restoration of political parties to their true function, which is the maintenance and enforcement of national policies." Reformers did "not, of course, contemplate the dissolution of parties," but proposed merely to "promote the legitimate power of party by making it a representative of opinion to a degree which, under the spoils system, is impossible."[19]

Ultimately the reformers carried their analysis of the evils of the spoils system even further. George William Curtis, their moral and intellectual leader, summarized the evils thus:

> What we affirm is that the theory which regards places in the public services as prizes to be distributed after an election, like plunder after a battle, the theory which perverts public trusts into party spoils, making public employment dependent upon personal favor and not on proved merit, necessarily ruins the self-respect of public employees, destroys the function of party in a republic, prostitutes elections into a desperate strife for personal profit, and degrades the national character by lowering the moral tone and standard of the country.[20]

Essentially, the reformers were seeking to transform the process of governmental decisionmaking from one in which those in power simply allocated the spoils of office among the party faithful into one that compelled administrators to act in accordance with autonomous, abstract standards. This concern with compelling officeholders to act objectively necessarily led not only to reform in the means of obtaining office but also to reform of abuses, as legislation relating to the postal service, the customs administration, and the land office demonstrates.

As discussed earlier, part of the political importance of the post office in mid-century had rested on the contracts it awarded for carriage of the mails. In the last third of the century, Congress enacted a complex series of reforms in the awarding of postal contracts. In theory the contracts had always gone to the lowest qualified bidder, but a number of techniques had been developed to circumvent the ideal. Among these techniques were inadequate advertising of the contracts to be let, the awarding of additional compensation to favored low bidders, and the awarding of contracts to a favored high bidder subsequent to nominal acceptance of straw bids.[21]

Congress outlawed these and some similar practices by a major piece of reform legislation in 1872, which required the post office to comply with detailed requirements for advertising before receiving bids for contracts, prohibited the award of additional compensation except in narrowly specified circumstances, compelled bidders to give security for the performance of their contracts before their bids would be opened, and even made failure to perform a bid accepted by the government a misdemeanor. The new requirements explicitly excluded contracts made with railroads, which by the 1870s had become the principal carriers of domestic mail; although the legislation set the rates of compensation for railroads, it gave the postmaster general discretion to make contracts with whichever roads he chose.[22]

For several reasons this discretion did not result in contracts being awarded on a political basis. First, until the 1860s the post office almost never had a choice among railroads to transport the mail: the rail network was so undeveloped that usually only one route was available between any two points. Second, just when the network developed sufficiently to permit interline competition, a small group of men with reform ideas and an extraordinary concern for postal efficiency created the railway mail service and established procedures for allocating the mail — and hence, payments for its carriage — among potential competitors on nonpolitical grounds. The procedures were based on a set of detailed schedules of interconnecting mail trains; clerks both at central post offices and in railway mail cars were directed to ship mail so that it would arrive at its destination most efficiently — that is, on the earliest possible train. The apolitical nature of this process was reinforced prior to 1889 by the fact that although railway mail clerks received probationary appointments on the recommendation of senators, permanent appointments and promotions were available only to those passing periodic efficiency tests; no one who passed these tests was removed from office. The apolitical character of the service was further reinforced after 1889 by the inclusion of railway mail clerks in the classified civil service.[23]

The administration of customs was also depoliticized. As discussed earlier, the political power of the customs service had rested largely on the ability of agents to practice favoritism in classifying and appraising the goods of friendly merchants. In the last two decades of the century, new efforts were made "to levy and collect duties [that were] uniform . . . for all persons throughout the United States." Those efforts culminated in the Customs Administration Act of 1890, which established a Board of General Appraisers, consisting of nine men who were appointed by the president with Senate confirmation for unspecified terms but could be removed from office only for cause. This board, one of the earliest of the federal administrative agencies, rapidly built up expertise and precedent that gave agents standards to follow in individual cases; although the new standards did not eliminate all possibilities of favoritism, they did provide a gauge by which specific decisions could be measured if favoritism was suspected.[24]

Reforms were also instituted in the General Land Office during the decades following the Civil War. An important element of the land office's business, it will be recalled, was the adjudication of competing land claims. Before the Civil War, records of those adjudications were disorganized and were available, if at all, only to clerks in the land office. Postwar reformers, however, in an effort to "systematize" land office practice, instituted a program of publishing past adjudications to be used as precedents. During the 1860s and 1870s three volumes of adjudications were published privately, and in 1881 the government began publishing a regular series of reports.[25] Cases in the first volume of the government series illustrate how apolitical and similar to the increasingly formalistic judicial process the adjudicatory process of the land office had become. One case mentioned "rules and well-established principles"; another declared that a particular "doctrine" should be treated not only "as having all the force of *stare decisis*, but of law." On another occasion, the secretary of the interior cited ten prior "decisions." A fourth case concerned whether a new rule, generated by overruling earlier authorities, should be applied retroactively or only prospectively.[26]

With the introduction of standards into the land office, one of its high officials observed that the "business transacted here is really a profession in itself." Such an office needed to be staffed not by political partisans but by "able men of legal education and mature judgment." Professional lawyers were in fact brought into the land office with the creation in 1881 of the Board of Law Review, consisting of the commissioner of the land office and two law assistants, to adjudicate land cases; a third law clerk was appointed in 1882.[27]

Meanwhile, standards were gradually being introduced elsewhere in the federal administrative system. As in the land office, the introduction of standards was often marked by the publication of agency decisions. Before the Civil War, the opinions of the attorney general and the decisions of the second comptroller constituted the only publications of federal administrative bodies. Then, in 1868, the Department of the Treasury began publishing its decisions under the customs laws, followed in 1869 by the Patent Office; in 1873 by the solicitor of the post office; in 1880 by the first comptroller; in 1881 by the land office; in 1887 by the Interstate Commerce Commission and the Pension Office; and in 1898 by the Internal Revenue Service. Throughout the federal government many jobs were also beginning to require special abilities, skills, and expertise. In the Department of Agriculture, for example, some newly developing jobs required scientific expertise, and others, statistical skills that could only be measured objectively. Throughout the bureaucracy, the introduction of office machinery such as typewriters and telephones created job opportunities for people with the technical skills needed to operate and repair them.[28]

Thus, by the end of the nineteenth century the administrative process was coming to be understood, in accordance with the scientific ideal of reformers, as one that required trained experts who made decisions and otherwise performed their tasks in accordance with autonomous, abstract standards. This transformation was not complete by the end of the century, especially at the state and local level; but the direction of change had become clear despite the failure of some reform efforts.

One early post–Civil War effort that ultimately failed, but that nevertheless reveals much about the character of the reform movement, arose in connection with the Bureau of Indian Affairs. Throughout the antebellum period strong links had existed between antislavery leaders and a smaller band of reformers seeking justice for the American Indian. In 1865 a number of reformers, most of whom had previously been involved in the antislavery movement, obtained the appointment of a joint congressional committee to inquire into corruption in the Indian bureau. During the next several years, a number of investigations occurred and various legislation was proposed, but real reform occurred only in 1869 with the beginning of the Grant administration. Grant organized an unpaid Board of Indian Commissioners consisting of eminent religious and philanthropic leaders. The board gave members of an informal community held together by shared attitudes and concerns toward Indians a voice in Indian affairs—a voice enhanced by the Grant administration's practice of appointing men recommended by religious leaders to many Indian agencies in lieu of making political appointments. Nonetheless, corruption and charges of corruption continued in the bureau, and Carl Schurz, the reform-minded secretary of the interior in the Hayes administration, concluded that Indian affairs could be more competently and honestly managed if religious influence was eliminated and full control over Indian matters restored to paid government servants. Thus ended the unique attempt to reform administration of a government program through the participation of a community of religious and philanthropic leaders. In the long run, the Bureau of Indian Affairs reverted to the spoils system until well into the twentieth century when it became part of the civil service system.[29]

Another reform failure occurred in 1888, when Congress defeated a bill to establish a Bureau of Harbors and Waterways that would have been a prototype for the independent regulatory commission. The bureau would have been staffed by a corps of "skilled and experienced" personnel having "tenure . . . for life," with promotion determined "partially by seniority and partly by merit." Such an arrangement would enable bureau members to exercise "independence of judgment free from dictation of superiors or pressure of influence." Charged with deciding what public works should be undertaken with federal funds, the bureau would have looked upon various proposed projects "as part of a system" and selected projects on the basis of some "well-defined, consistent, and rational" scheme. Instead, Congress continued well into the twentieth century to select projects for improving rivers and harbors on a purely political basis that maximized opportunities for legislative logrolling.[30] A more important example of failure occurred at the local governmental level, particularly in large cities containing massive immigrant populations. Although the reformers proposed to replace the spoils system in those cities with new commission and city-manager forms of government, the mid-nineteenth-century system of joining office and party together for purposes of enforcing law and maintaining order endured into the twentieth century, perhaps because it was the only means of governing the cities and slowly integrating their immigrant residents into the mainstream of American life.

The reformers met with a mixture of failure and success in their efforts to deal with perhaps the most difficult and important problem confronting late nineteenth-century government—the problem of railroad rate regulation. Numerous ills stemmed from railroad rate-setting practices in the late nineteenth century. In the words of the Senate committee that framed the Interstate Commerce Act of 1887, "no general question of governmental policy occupie[d] . . . so prominent a place in the thoughts of the people as that of controlling . . . corporate power," especially the power of railroads, the corporations that were most "conspicuously before the public eye" because their "operations so directly affect[ed] every citizen in the daily pursuits of his business."[31]

Before passage of the Interstate Commerce Act in 1887, two main constraints affected the setting of railroad freight rates. The first was competition from water transport: if railroads wanted to divert traffic from the Great Lakes and the Erie Canal or from the Mississippi River and its tributaries, their rates could not exceed the rates available from water carriers. As a result, cities such as Chicago, Cleveland, and St. Louis that had adequate transportation by water could also rely on railroad freight rates that did not exceed the cost of water transport. The other constraint on freight rates could drive them even lower: a city or even a single major industry that had access to two or more rail lines and generated enough traffic to induce the railroads to compete for it could obtain additional rate reductions, down to a rate that covered only a railroad's costs in handling a particular shipment exclusive of any allowance for sunk capital and fixed operating costs. The difficulty was that a municipality or business firm having access to only a single rail line could obtain no discount; even if the railroad charged that municipality or business only a rate calculated to compensate the railroad for its handling costs and a fair share of its capital and fixed operating costs, such a municipality or business would usually suffer discrimination in comparison with a competitor having access to two rail lines or to water transportation.[32]

Discriminatory rates, usually in the form of rebates, in favor of a municipality or business firm had troublesome consequences. One railroad executive, A. B. Stickney, labeled discrimination "the death of that fair competition as between individuals . . . which so long and justly has been styled 'the life of trade.'" Martin A. Knapp, a member of the Interstate Commerce Commission, found discrimination "in respect of a common necessity . . . repugnant to every notion of equality" and offensive to "the rudest conception of justice." Collis P. Huntington, the president of the Southern Pacific, observed that discrimination did "great harm to the small shippers, who are crowded out of the market" or otherwise "injured in their business to a very considerable extent." Commissioner Knapp developed the point in greater detail. In his view, discriminatory rates furnished "the large shipper . . . with a weapon against which skill, energy and experience are alike unavailing." "Favored shippers" obtained "an advantage by which they secured a monopoly of the markets through the ruin or withdrawal of their competitors." These "practices . . . aided the formation and fortified the power of those vast combinations of capital which have excited such widespread apprehension." Of the firms that had so procured monopolies through discriminatory rates, Standard Oil was the most obvious. Another "conspicuous illustration," in Stickney's view, was the four great Chicago meatpacking firms, whose "present business" had been "built up by rebates" and who thereafter "care[d] but little what rates they pay, provided they are less than are granted to other shippers, so that they may continue to maintain their present practical monopoly."[33]

An even more disturbing result of rate discrimination among localities was the concentration of population in major rail centers. As A. B. Stickney observed, "the city in whose favor discrimination is practiced . . . at once begins the process of 'swallowing' the trade and population of its unfortunate neighboring cities" as the "brightest business men" and "few manufacturing establishments that had started in a small way" in the smaller municipalities, recognizing that there was "no hope" in view of the rate discriminations against them, moved into the larger cities. Stickney's observation was not a new one; two decades earlier Charles Francis Adams, Jr. noted that smaller interior cities like Syracuse and Rochester could not compete with Atlantic coast cities like Boston or major midwestern centers like Chicago as a result of rate discrimination and that "a consciousness of this fact . . . ha[d] caused the breaking up of many manufacturing establishments at interior points." Martin A. Knapp of the Interstate Commerce Commission was also aware that "the relative rates" of rail lines "applied to competing towns determine[d] to a great extent the volume of their business and the measure of their growth." He added that railroads "can decree that one town shall be enriched by the impoverishment of its rival; that one community shall languish while another flourishes." Railroads had "enormous" power to "build up or destroy a commercial center," to "raise or reduce the prices of agricultural products," and even to "enhance or depress the salable value of wide areas of land." The ultimate danger was that railroad competition would injure the commerce of smaller towns and cities, thereby driving business to major commercial and industrial centers that were already too large to function as effective communities, and lead to the concentration of

> all the business of the country . . . [in] the hands of the few. Later on discrimination, as between these few, will reduce their numbers, and so on, till finally the prospect would seem to be that in addition to the Standard Oil Company, which we already have, there might be one Standard Mercantile Company, one Standard Manufacturing Company, one Standard Railway Company, four Presidents, four General Managers, a score of Directors, and the rest of the then probable population of 100,000,000 of people will be poor grangers, clerks and employees, all mere "strikers" and impotent "kickers," living, packed like sardines, in enormous tenement houses at "competitive points."[34]

A number of railroad executives were of the opinion that rate discrimination hurt railroads as much as it did the shippers and localities that were its victims. Collis P. Huntington of the Southern Pacific, for example, noted that discrimination "takes money from the railroad[s]," leaving many of them barely short of bankruptcy. A. B. Stickney similarly warned the railroads to "remember that by discrimination they have built up some manufacturing and mercantile concerns so big that they are now more powerful . . . inasmuch as they are able to dictate the rates that they will pay"; he gave as an example the Chicago meatpacking firms that had "become dictators of rates to all the great railway corporations." As president of the Union Pacific, Charles Francis Adams, Jr. also was of the view that discriminatory rates had "brought the railroad system to its present low condition," threatened "to carry it still lower," and would "inevitably lead to financial disaster of the most serious kind."[35] Although William H. Vanderbilt of the New York Central thought there was "an absolute hostility between the interests of the railroads and the public," the ill effects of discrimination led a committee appointed in 1879 by the New York legislature to conclude that such hostility did "not or, at least, should not exist" and that "public and railway interests will be identical and their efforts must be united."[36]

Many common late nineteenth-century reform ideas can be found in discussions of the railroad rate problem. The rhetoric about the need for railroads to behave morally and to set equal rates was reminiscent of the rhetoric of antislavery advocates. The historicist orientation was expressed in concern about the railroads' destruction of small, cohesive geographic communities and in the recognition of the possibility of creating new communities on the basis of common interest and affinity. Finally, other proposals for reform approximated the scheme that materialized in the Interstate Commerce Commission in the twentieth century, that of having rates set by experts on the basis of neutral and objective standards.

The modern scheme of having an independent regulatory commission to supervise railroads and set their maximum rates was advocated by Thomas M. Cooley, the first chairman of the Interstate Commerce Commission, and by Charles Francis Adams, Jr., the first chairman of a state regulatory commission.[37] But this plan was opposed in the 1890s because of "the impossibility of its being done directly by Congress or by any commission," the danger of "political *animus* . . . for partisan reasons," and "the repugnancy of the plan to the spirit of our institutions, and the American idea that a citizen should have at least a part in the management of his own business affairs." A second proposal — that the federal government assume ownership and operation of the lines — failed on two similar grounds: first, "the incapacity of Government for so huge and intricate a task", and second, the danger "in a country like the United States, where everything involving patronage is more or less partisan" of permitting government to employ nearly one million railroad workers.[38] A third proposal was to consolidate existing railroads into as few firms as possible so that those few firms could control rates. A fourth proposal was to enact legislation permitting railroads to turn to the courts to enforce agreements between them dividing traffic and fixing rates; at common law, agreements of this sort were deemed to be in restraint of trade and hence were illegal and unenforceable.[39] These last two proposals were rejected, however, out of a "popular fear" that they would "result in extortion" by the railroads.[40]

A more fruitful approach sought to induce railroads to behave consistently with moral and communitarian ideals. Some reformers hoped the railroads would respond voluntarily. For example, Charles Francis Adams, Jr., who found the source of the railroad problem to be "the covetousness, want of good faith, and low moral tone" of railroad managers — "the absence among them of any high standard of commercial honor" — contended that "the railroad system must heal itself." Similarly, A. B. Stickney maintained that railroad leaders had to learn "that no business can be permanently prosperous which is not founded on principles of justice." Other reformers, however, sought to bring morality to railroading by legislation, and the main piece of late nineteenth-century railroad legislation—the Interstate Commerce Act of 1887—can be read as little more than an injunction requiring railroads to behave morally in setting their rates.[41]

The Interstate Commerce Act was, of course, a product of conflicting pressures brought to bear upon the congressmen who framed and enacted it. Nonetheless, discussions before and after passage of the act, as well as the act itself, reveal a consistent approach to the railroad problem. This approach was based on the assumption that if specific abuses in rate setting could be controlled, the common interest of the railroads and the public would lead to rates that were reasonable and just from the point of view of that common interest. The principal substantive provisions of the act prohibited railroads from charging a higher rate "for a shorter than for a longer distance over the same line, in the same direction," under similar circumstances; defined and prohibited "unjust discrimination"; and prohibited the granting of "any undue or unreasonable preference or advantage to any person, company . . . or locality," or the subjecting of "any person, company . . . or locality . . . to any undue or unreasonable prejudice or disadvantage." Although the act also contained a general provision requiring all rates to be "reasonable and just,"[42] it is by no means clear that Congress intended this provision to give the Interstate Commerce Commission power to set maximum rates for the benefit of shipping interests; on the contrary, the provision could be and was read by the courts as merely barring practices detailed in the more specific sections.[43] In so reading the act the courts did not do violence to the legislative history. Two years before passage of the act, Thomas M. Cooley, who would be the first chairman of the Interstate Commerce Commission, had suggested that "the final solution for the 'railroad problem' " might be to treat "the railroad interest as constituting in a certain sense a section by itself of the political community"; this section could be combined with representatives of other sections into an agency possessing "the necessary authority to protect the public against unfair practices." Then government could "well leave the roads to quarrel over the infinite variety of detail in the adjustment of rates," apparently with confidence that the power of large shippers and the common interest of railroads and shippers in increasing the total amount of rail freight would keep rates in general from becoming excessive. In the same year, John H. Reagan, chairman of the House Committee on Commerce, told the full House that the bill that would become the House version of the Interstate Commerce Act should "not undertake to prescribe rates for the transportation of freight"; instead, it should require only that railroads "not discriminate in freight rates, but . . . be just and equal in their charges to the public." Similarly, Shelby M. Cullom, chairman of the Senate Committee on Interstate Commerce and author of the Senate version of the Interstate Commerce Act, wrote in 1892 that the act did "not seek to change property rights, but simply to enforce common law principles" and "common rules of fair dealing" prohibiting "extortion" and other "unjust discriminations." In retrospect, Cullom found that the act's "wise system of regulation" was of benefit "both to the public and to the railways"; it "protect[ed] the roads against each other," offered "men engaged in business on a limited scale . . . an even opportunity to do business with larger and richer competitors," and enabled "small towns . . . [to] have busy factories among them, and prosperity . . . [for] their people."[44]

In sum, there existed an approach to the problem of railroad rates that did not seek to lower or otherwise regulate rates in general — that is, to redistribute income from railroads to shippers — but sought only to eliminate "special privileges" and ensure "equality of rights." This approach, according to Augustus Schoonmaker, "assign[ed] to government its true function in the business pursuits of its citizens, as the great reserve force to secure justice and impartiality." The approach, wrote Thomas M. Cooley, was "neither . . . unphilosophical nor out of accord with the general spirit of our institutions," for it authorized government to protect what might be termed common moral values and thus, indirectly, the communitarian order out of which those values had sprung. It was successful at least in the short run, in that it received "serious consideration by law makers" and was put into practice by the commission in its earliest years. Ultimately, however, the conflicting interests of shippers and railroads overwhelmed their common interests; as a result, efforts to induce railroads to set just and reasonable rates failed, and in the twentieth century the Interstate Commerce Commission was given general ratemaking power.[45]

Thus, the progress of reform in the independent regulatory commissions, in the federal civil service, and in local government was beset with tension and ambiguity. On the one hand, reform was often slow, especially in local politics, where the Jacksonian system had greatest importance; in the absence of direct evidence, one can speculate that the Jacksonian system endured because there was no effective alternative to it. On the other hand, the more important development, especially for the future, was the emergence in the federal government of the professional bureaucracy, appointed on the basis of merit and at least sometimes governed by standards that could be passed off as objective to the groups most immediately concerned with the substantive activities of a particular bureaucratic agency.

The Judicial Branch: The Formal Style of Reasoning

It was in the judicial branch of government, at both state and federal levels, that decisionmaking in accordance with either moral or apolitical, professionally administered standards attained its fullest development. In the late nineteenth century, judges under the influence of reform-minded intellectuals conjoined antislavery jurisprudence with newer scientific ideas into an amalgam that subsequent scholars have loosely labeled legal formalism. It was also in the judicial branch that the greatest efforts were made to require officers of the courts, from Supreme Court justice down to attorney at law, to give evidence satisfactory to the legal community of their training and competence in manipulating the tools of their profession.

One important element in the late nineteenth-century style of formal legal reasoning was the higher-law jurisprudence of antislavery. Antislavery moral principles initially seemed capable of playing a special role in late nineteenth-century adjudication, in part because many judges of the time had begun their careers as antislavery leaders. As these men began to fill both state and federal judicial posts, ideas associated with antislavery jurisprudence began to surface in innumerable judicial opinions. In some states as early as the late 1840s, a few judges began again to speak about "natural right and justice" and about "protection to life, liberty, and property" as the great duty of all governments. Courts of law, according to these judges, were "no place for the doctrine of EXPEDIENCY" and ought not shape "their decisions with reference to predicted consequences"; the duty of courts was merely "to follow the . . . law as it is written, regardless of consequences."[46] Particularly in constitutional litigation, when property rights allegedly were being infringed by a legislative enactment, some judges in the 1850s argued that courts ought not to give effect to their own "speculative opinions in regard to the wisdom of the act, or the beneficial results likely to flow from it"; decisions in such cases should give effect to those "rights fully recognized as inherent and indefeasible in man . . . which human government can neither grant nor abolish, alter nor abridge." Even in litigation between private parties, some judges at mid-century referred to "elementary principle[s] in reference to private rights."[47]

The phenomenon of antislavery advocates ascending the bench and then giving effect to moralistic antislavery ideas finds ample illustration in the careers of Justices Bradley and Field. Bradley since his college days had believed that people could "NEVER consent to relinquish those rights which NATURE ha[d] given" them and had long believed that all individuals were entitled to "the enjoyment of all the natural liberty compatible with mutual security."[48] Moreover, before the outbreak of the Civil War Bradley had been a staunch Republican in New Jersey, the strongest Democratic state in the North.[49] Justice Field, the other prominent exponent of antislavery jurisprudence on the Supreme Court after the war, though a Democrat had also been a strong exponent of antislavery and its jurisprudence before the war. In an 1858 opinion delivered when he was a judge in California, Field had referred to Christianity as "the basis of our civilization" and had considered its infusion into the nation's law "as natural as that the national sentiment of liberty should find expression in the legislation of the country."[50] Field had also written that the nation would not be free until the infamous *Scott* decision was set aside and had been one of the first men in California to side with the Union once the Civil War began. Finally, he had always remained close to his brother, David Dudley Field, a longtime abolitionist and an organizer of the Republican party. Nor were Bradley and Field unique. Other judicial advocates of antislavery jurisprudence in the post–Civil War era, such as Justice Brewer of the Supreme Court, Chief Justice Doe of New Hampshire, and Judge Cooley of Michigan, had also been politically active opponents of slavery before the war and had been infuriated by the decision in *Scott*.[51]

It was natural for such judges to revert to notions of higher law and human rights once they ascended the bench. It was especially natural for antislavery ideas to proliferate in opinions dealing with enforcement of the Civil War amendments and the federal legislation enacted pursuant thereto. In one case, involving defendants who had been indicted for attempting to prevent some freedmen from exercising their right peaceably to assemble, a federal circuit court held that freedom of speech and the right peaceably to assemble were among the privileges and immunities of citizens protected by section 1 of the Fourteenth Amendment. The court reasoned that the amendment protected all rights "which may be denominated fundamental; which belong of right to the citizens of all free states." The court also alluded to the higher-law origin of those rights when it reported that "it is not claimed by counsel . . . that freedom of speech and the right peaceably to assemble are rights granted by the constitution, but . . . [only] that they are rights recognized and secured."[52]

Similarly, Justice Field, riding on circuit, invoked a combination of Christian ideals, and the inalienable rights of man regarding criminal procedure — both of which had been important elements of antislavery thought — in holding unconstitutional California legislation requiring that the hair of all persons imprisoned upon failure to pay fines be cut to a length of one inch. Field emphasized that the purpose of the ordinance was to authorize the state to cut the queues of Chinese convicts who did not pay their fines. The state had argued that only the prospect of the loss of his queue, which for a Chinese entailed disgrace among his countrymen and a constant dread of misfortune and suffering after death, would induce a Chinese defendant to pay his fine. But Field responded that "probably the bastinado, or the knout, or the thumbscrew, or the rack, would accomplish the same end," and concluded that it would "always be the duty of the judiciary to declare and enforce the paramount law of the nation" against such legislation, which was "unworthy of a brave and manly people." It was simply "not creditable to the humanity and civilization of our people, much less to their Christianity, that an ordinance of this character was possible," and he accordingly ruled that the Fourteenth Amendment, codifying the nation's humanity, civilization, and Christianity, made it impossible.[53]

Ideas about civil rights associated with the antislavery movement appeared in other cases as well. In *Leeper* v. *Texas* Chief Justice Fuller confirmed that states could deal freely with criminals within their borders, provided they did not subject "the individual to the arbitrary exercise of the powers of government unrestrained by the established principles of private right and distributive justice." Similarly, Justice Field spoke in *Ex parte Jackson* of "the great principle embodied in the fourth amendment of the Constitution." Most explicit of all was Justice Brewer, who in a state court opinion written before his appointment to the Supreme Court referred to bills of rights as "those essential truths, those axioms of civil and political liberty upon which all free governments are founded." In similar language, a Louisiana state judge viewed bills of rights as "declaratory of the general principles of republican government, and of the fundamental rights of the citizen, rights usually of so fundamental a character, that, while such express declarations may serve to guard and protect them, they are not essential to the creation of such rights, which exist independent of constitutional provisions."[54]

The antislavery ideal of equality was also commonplace in judicial opinions after the Civil War. Thus when a railroad argued before the Supreme Court in the 1870s that a common carrier had a right to make a contract disclaiming its common law liability on the principle that all people were "permitted to make their own agreements," Justice Bradley responded for the Court that "the carrier and his customer [did] not stand on a footing of equality." Bradley thus refused to protect the railroad's liberty of contact with the same rigor he would have applied to protect similar individual freedom, because protection of the railroad's contract rights would not secure liberty and equality for all men. Likewise, the Supreme Court of Mississippi refused to recognize an alleged property right of a railroad to be exempt from taxation, for the claim was thought to be inconsistent with that "equality in bearing a common burden, which is natural [and] right [and was] secured alike to the corporation and to the citizen."[55]

Finally, the antislavery concern with according special protection to property and contract rights was an important element in many postbellum cases, most notably the *Slaughter-House Cases*. Plaintiffs had challenged the constitutionality of state legislation conferring upon a corporation of seventeen persons the right to build the only plant for slaughter of animals in the city of New Orleans and requiring all butchers to use that plant. On circuit, Justice Bradley upheld the challenge, holding that the right to follow a lawful industrial pursuit, the right to hold property, and the right to equal protection of the laws were among the privileges and immunities of citizens of the United States. Bradley declared:

> Any government which deprives its citizens of the right to engage in any lawful pursuit, subject only to reasonable restrictions, or at least subject only to such restrictions as are reasonably within the power of government to impose, — is tyrannical and unrepublican. And if to enforce arbitrary restrictions made for the benefit of a favored few, it takes away and destroys the citizen's property without trial or condemnation, it is guilty of violating . . . one of the fundamental principles of free government.[56]

The Supreme Court disagreed with him by a vote of five to four, but Bradley adhered to his views. In a dissenting opinion, he wrote that citizenship in a free nation carried with it "certain incidental rights, privileges and immunities of the greatest importance" and "a sure and undoubted title to equal rights in any and every State in this Union." Thus, certain rights inhered in the very nature of republican government. Justice Field, even more explicitly, wrote that the Fourteenth Amendment "was intended to give practical effect to the declaration of 1776 of inalienable rights, rights which are the gift of the Creator; which the law does not confer, but only recognizes," including the rights to pursue an occupation and to acquire and hold property.[57]

Other opinions and arguments continuing the antislavery moralistic traditions with respect to property and contract rights reasoned, in the words of Justice Field, that regulatory laws could "not conflict with any . . . natural right," or, as one attorney argued, that "one of the fundamental objects of all civilized government was the preservation of the rights of private property," because those rights were "the very keystone in the arch upon which all civilized government rest[ed]." Mr. Justice Harlan similarly wrote in an opinion for the Court that private property was "founded in natural equity, and . . . laid down by jurists as a principle of universal law. Indeed, in a free government, almost all other rights would become worthless if the government possessed an uncontrollable power over the private fortune of every citizen." "The demands of absolute and eternal justice" thus prohibited "private property, legally acquired or legally held," from being "spoliated or destroyed in the interests of public health, morals or welfare without compensation."[58]

As before the Civil War, the right to use and dispose of property was viewed as a necessary consequence of the right to acquire and hold it. Every individual, that is, had a "natural right to sell or keep his commodities as best suit[ed] his own purpose." This concept of freedom of contract, according to the Illinois Supreme Court, embraced not only the right to use and dispose of property, but also "the right of every man to be free in the use of his powers and faculties, and to adopt and pursue such avocation or calling as he may choose." Judges spoke often of "the natural right to gain a livelihood by intelligence, honesty, and industry in the arts, the sciences, the professions, or other vocations"; Justice Field observed that "among [the] inalienable rights" proclaimed in the Declaration of Independence was "the right to pursue any lawful business or vocation."[59]

During the mid-1890s, judges used these antislavery notions of freedom of contract in a series of cases enjoining strikes and other activities by labor unions. Although a few judges and commentators maintained that enjoining a strike was "tantamount to decreeing a specific performance of a contract of service, which [would result] in a state of *slavery*" and "an invasion of one's natural liberty," others feared that many union activities would lead to "the obliteration of legal and natural rights." One such right, in the words of William Howard Taft, the future president and chief justice, was the worker's "inalienable right to bestow his labor where he will." Another, according to a federal court in Idaho, was the right of "every owner of property" to "work it as he will, by whom he pleases, at such wages, and upon such terms as he can make." These rights, particularly the right of the individual to bestow his labor as he pleased, were, it will be recalled, among those for which the Civil War had been fought. Hence, even in granting injunctions against unions that had not called strikes, but merely sought to "coerce" or "vex" workmen, judges who had received their education or begun their professional careers during the Civil War era were reasoning in a manner consistent with the values that had emerged triumphantly after the war. It was, they observed, "preposterous" that unions should take the place of former slavedrivers and "attempt to issue orders that free men are bound to obey."[60]

Antislavery ideas appeared in the legal scholarship as well as in the judicial opinions of the late nineteenth century. Some writers stressed the higher-law basis that had characterized much antislavery thought. Joel P. Bishop, a leading scholar of the criminal law, wrote that "the rules of right, and of rightful association, given by God to man, are . . . portions of the 'authority' which binds our tribunals." All legal institutions, he claimed, performed their labors "in subjection to one great, immutable, pre-existent law." For Bishop, law was thus not the product of human will, but of eternal standards of justice and morality. John F. Dillon agreed that it was neither "possible, or, if it were, . . . desirable, to separate dogmatically the domain of law from that of ethics." Dillon thought that judges, when formulating law, were "rightfully, because necessarily, within the domain of ethics"; that although "lawyers must discriminate law from morality, and . . . keep separate and distinct their respective provinces . . . these provinces always adjoin each other"; and that "ethical considerations can no more be excluded from the administration of justice, which is the end and purpose of all civil laws, than one can exclude the vital air from his room and live."[61]

Other writers placed primary emphasis on fundamental principles of republican government as a source of American law. Ferris Rihani, for example, thought that "law should be the sanctuary of liberty " and that if it did not remain so, "this glorious and grand country will be converted into a monarchy clothed in the garb of a republic." Another scholar held that "the distinctive and characteristic feature of the American system is equality before the law"—that the foundation of American law was "a government of equality of rights, equality of duties and equality of burdens." Most explicit of all was Thomas M. Cooley, who wrote of rights that "may well be regarded as 'absolutely necessary to preserve the advantages of liberty, and to maintain a free government' "; in particular, "the right of the people peaceably to assemble, and to petition the government for a redress of grievances, is one which 'would seem unnecessary to be expressly provided for in a republican government, since it results from the very nature and structure of its institutions.' "[62]

Although higher-law and human rights concepts associated with the antislavery movement attained influence as the movement's partisans ascended to the bench during the second half of the nineteenth century, acceptance of antislavery jurisprudence during the era of the Civil War was far from universal even in northern courts. In one of the leading cases discussed earlier, *Wynehamer* v. *People*, Judge Comstock, though agreeing that the statute at issue was unconstitutional and void, took special note of "the danger . . . when theories, alleged to be founded in natural reason or inalienable rights, but subversive of the just and necessary powers of government, attract the belief of considerable classes of men." Moreover, several judges disavowed the theory that a legislative act could be voided even if the act violated no express constitutional provision. The Supreme Court of Pennsylvania likewise rejected higher-law arguments in two pre–Civil War cases, with one judge observing that "there can be no organized authority superior to government itself . . . In civil matters there can be no moral principle of higher importance than . . . the principle of social order."[63]

Perhaps the most important influence on the jurisprudence of the period was the growing preoccupation with the scientific method, discussed in chapter 4. The scientific ideal became a central aspiration of the legal profession and reshaped the reasoning processes of many lawyers and courts. The concept of law as a science led much of the bar, as it had social scientists, to pay greater attention to the past in the form of using old cases as precedents and to emphasize processes of classification and categorization.

The concept of law as science had important practical effects, leading to a very different analysis of precedents from that used in the first half of the century. When presented with an alleged precedent, early nineteenth-century lawyers and judges typically asked first whether the precedent furthered a policy, such as economic development, that the law ought to further. If it did, they followed the precedent, often with little discussion of the policy itself or of other arguably relevant but conflicting lines of authority. If the precedent did not further the desired policy, the courts usually rejected it, arguing that they did not have to follow English cases, because American constitutions adopted the common law only when it furthered American needs, or that their own precedents could be jettisoned when the needs of society had changed and the consent of the people to a new rule of law could be presumed.[64] For most antebellum courts, precedents were convenient justifications because they had the sanction of the reception acts, but no precedent was conclusive if it did not further society's current needs.

For the legal scientists of the closing decades of the century, precedents had a very different significance. "Adjudged cases [were] to juridical science what ascertained facts and experiments [were] to the natural sciences"; the law library was to lawyers "all that the laboratories of the university [were] to the chemists and physicists, all that the museum of natural history [was] to the zoologists, all that the botanical garden [was] to the botanists." Just as the task of the natural scientist was "the classification of facts" and the formulation of conclusions on the basis of those facts, so too the task of the legal scientist, in the famous language of Dean Langdell, was "to select, classify, and arrange all the cases which . . . contributed . . . [to the] establishment of any of its essential doctrines." Normally the legal scientists of the late nineteenth century expected all precedents to be consistent, but if they were not, then the scientist had to reconcile the seeming contradictions. "To believe two contradictory propositions at the same time" was, according to John Chipman Gray, "no part of the duty of a legal writer." His task was to "search for a principle which shall reconcile all the authorities, or, if this is out of the question, a principle which shall reconcile as large a part of them as possible."

If the cases could not be reconciled, the final task of the scientist was to "determine which represent[ed] the main principle, and which the anomaly, the exception, and to do this he should look at the past."[65] Looking to the past meant, as a practical matter, looking to England, as did most casebook authors like Langdell; over 90 percent of the cases in his 1871 edition were British.[66] Cases that could be shown to "have no foundation in English jurisprudence" and "to be at variance with an unbroken line of precedents in the English books" were simply viewed as "depart[ing] from the rule of the common law."[67] While it may be that the legal scientists refused to follow precedents as often as earlier judges had, they did so on different grounds — on grounds of intellectual consistency rather than on grounds of policy.

Whereas a typical antebellum case like *M'Culloch* v. *Eagle Insurance Co.* had held that no contract arose when an acceptance of an offer crossed a revocation of the offer in the mails, on the ground that such a rule would be "reasonable in mercantile contracts," Langdell's "Summary" of the law of contracts, published in 1879, took a very different approach. Taking note of an argument "that the purposes of substantial justice and the interests of contracting parties as understood by themselves . . . [would] be best served by holding that the contract . . . [was] complete the moment the letter of acceptance . . . [was] mailed," Langdell responded that "the true answer to this argument is, that it is irrelevant." Later Langdell warned courts against adopting any rule "liable to the serious objection of involving judicial legislation" or "to the much greater objection, at least in a scientific point of view, that it could succeed only 'by involving' doctrine in infinite confusion." The same shift in legal reasoning was evident in cases dealing with the ancient law of waste. *Pynchon* v. *Stearns* had rejected the English rule that construction of a house and an entryway on a life estate would constitute waste, because such a rule, if "universally adopted in this country, would greatly impede the progress of improvement." *Gaines* v. *Green Pond Iron Mining Co.*, an 1881 New Jersey case, reached an analogous decision, holding that a life tenant could continue to extract ore from existing veins of a mine without committing waste;[68] but it arrived at that result on very different grounds. It carefully analyzed twenty-one cases, the majority of them English, and concluded that the English rule permitted the extraction of ore from existing veins and that the American rule was at least as broad.*

*The legal scientists' predilection for reconciling inconsistent cases was also apparent in the efforts of late nineteenth-century courts and commentators to harmonize a line of Massachusetts cases dealing with duties between neighbors. By the early 1870s Massachusetts had been left with a body of case law holding that a landowner could undermine his neighbor's cellar, see *Thurston* v. *Hancock*, 12 Mass. 220 (1815), but that a municipality could not flood it, see *Wilson* v. *City of New Bedford*, 102 Mass. 262 (1871); that one neighbor could deprive another of well water, see *Greenleaf* v. *Francis*, 35 Mass. (18 Pick.) 117 (1836) but could not pollute it, see *Ball* v. *Nye*, 99 Mass. 582 (1868); and that one man could injure his neighbor with a cane, as long as he struck him without fault, see *Brown* v. *Kendall*, 60 Mass. (6 Cush.) 292 (1850), but that he could not injure him with snow falling from his roof, even though he had taken every possible precaution to keep the snow from falling. See *Shipley* v. *Fifty Associates*, 106 Mass. 194 (1870). Thomas M. Cooley, the Michigan law professor and judge, made a number of attempts at harmonization. Focusing on *Ball* and *Greenleaf*, he reasoned in *Upjohn* v. *Board of Health*, 46 Mich. 542, 9 N.W. 845 (1881), that the law required a landowner to take whatever precautions were "practicable" not to injure his neighbor; he implied that whereas it might be practicable to keep filth within a vault, it might not be practicable to drill a well without interfering with the water supply of a neighboring well, because the course of underground streams was often unknown, 46 Mich. at 549, 9 N.W. at 848. As Cooley himself realized, however, this distinction was not a persuasive one. 46 Mich. at 549–550, 9 N.W. at 848. He had made a far more comprehensive attempt at harmonization in

The systematization demanded by the new legal science also led to reinterpretation of the 1842 English case of *Davies* v. *Mann* and thereby to the creation of the doctrine of last clear chance. *Davies* was a case in which a plaintiff had negligently left a donkey tied in a public highway, where it was struck by the defendant's wagon. The plaintiff nonetheless recovered damages for the defendant's negligence. The case was troublesome for late nineteenth-century systematizers who held that a plaintiff's contributory negligence was an absolute bar to recovery for a defendant's negligence, and much ink was spilled analyzing the case, with some writers explaining it on causation grounds and others calling for it to be overruled. The puzzle was not solved until 1886, when an anonymous writer in the *Law Quarterly Review* formulated the *Davies* case as follows: "the party *who last has a clear opportunity of avoiding the accident, notwithstanding the negligence of his opponent*, is considered solely responsible for it." Gradually this reading of the *Davies* case was accepted by other writers and by the courts, and by 1900 the doctrine of last clear chance was well established. During the same period a similar process led to the working out of the doctrine of assumption of risk.[69]

The notion of science thus contributed importantly to the jurisprudence of the postbellum era, mainly because it enabled judges to avoid discussing questions of policy and expediency, questions that were viewed as essentially legislative. In most cases, either the concept of law as a science or antislavery moralistic principles provided judges with a point of reference unalterable by any act of judicial will, from which the legal reasoning process could proceed by accepted

---

in this 1879 *A Treatise on the Law of Torts*. In part, he achieved apparent harmonization through his method of classifying the cases: *Brown* v. *Kendall* was discussed under "Accidental Injuries," ibid., p. 80, n. 2, *Thurston* v. *Hancock* under "Removing Lateral Support," ibid., p. 549, n. 6, and the other four cases in sections dealing with nuisances caused by water. See ibid., pp. 567–575. Even *Greenleaf* was discussed some ten pages away from the principal discussion of the three post– Civil War cases, under the heading "Subterranean Waters," ibid., p. 581, n. 1, thus making direct comparison of the cases unnecessary. Should a wary reader make the comparison, however, Cooley provided a principle of harmonization, for he discussed *Ball, Shipley,* and *Wilson* together with *Rylands* v. *Fletcher*, on which all three had relied, in sections of the book devoted to the liability of property owners who gathered objects such as filth, water, or snow on their premises. See ibid., pp. 567–575. *Brown, Thurston,* and *Greenleaf* were, of course, all distinguishable because they involved no such gathering.

modes of analysis. Some judges, like Rufus Peckham, turned to antislavery precepts for guidance; others, like Henry Brown, turned to the concept of law as a science. Still others, like Thomas Cooley and John Dillon, drew upon both sources.[70]

What the judges whom subsequent scholars have called formalists had in common was not any single well-developed style or method, but an aversion to explicit analysis of policy. It is, of course, impossible to know whether any particular judge totally ignored issues of policy in reaching a decision in any given case. But even if they did take policy considerations into account, most late nineteenth-century judges did "not like to discuss questions of policy," for "views of policy [were] taught by experience of the interests of life," and "those interests [were] fields of battle." Americans had just come from those fields and had no desire to return. Thus, most American judges sought to clothe their decisions in the language of formal "logical deduction" and to reason either from "general propositions" about the essential meaning of republicanism or from the immutable records of the English common law. They sought to make "legal reasoning seem like mathematics" and to convince themselves that, if men differed over a question of law, "it meant simply that one side or the other were not doing their sums right, and, if they would take more trouble, agreement inevitably would come."[71]

To avoid questions of policy, judges sometimes adopted as their initial point of reference some principle of human rights that was fundamental to a republican form of government; the existence of such a referent would justify a judge in refusing to promulgate a rule that would endanger such rights. But if, as was frequently true, concepts of human rights only limited and did not entirely eliminate the range of judicial choice, judges could then turn to another reference point — past judicial decisions — from which they could extract principles whereby to decide cases. Although the courts could "extend the application of the principles of common law" by applying old principles to new cases[72] and, as new cases accumulated, thereby transform the principles, no act of judicial will, not even overruling, could erase earlier decisions from the historical record. Moreover, the extraction of principles from the decisions was thought to be not an act of will, but an intellectual exercise; it required lawyers to reconcile and harmonize as many past decisions as possible and to reject only those that did not fit into the mainstream of case development. The process was one of sustained research and close analysis of the judicial record bequeathed by the past rather than one of determining desirable social policies for the future.

To ensure that judges avoided passing upon issues of policy, it became necessary for reform-minded intellectuals not only to elaborate the moralistic and scientific styles of reasoning and proclaim their merits, but also to train the profession as a whole in the two styles and to organize at least its leaders into groups that would impose those styles as the norms for legal reasoning. There were two reasons for this. The first was that, by the late nineteenth century, judges had come to be chosen from the ranks of the legal profession, and hence one way to train the bench of the future was to train the bar of the present. The second reason was that the bar had considerable creative and critical influence on the judicial process; under either style, which proclaimed that deciding cases was analogous to doing one's sums correctly, practicing lawyers had an important role to play in casting cases in formal rather than policy terms, in identifying the ways in which the doing of sums might be approached, and in identifying those judges who did their sums well and those who did them poorly. It therefore is not surprising that late nineteenth-century legal reformers organized lawyers both to raise standards for admission to the bar and to police their fellow attorneys.

The most important step in the raising of admissions standards was the emergence of law school training as the characteristic route for entry into the profession. In 1860 there were approximately 1,200 students attending 21 law schools in the United States; by 1900 there were 12,516 students in 102 law schools. The pattern of change is even more dramatic if one compares the year 1850, when there were only 400 law students, with the year 1910, when there were 19,567. The bar itself grew far less rapidly: there were 24,000 lawyers in 1850, 35,000 in 1860, 114,000 in 1900, and 122,000 in 1910.[73] These figures strongly suggest that law schools trained relatively few of the new lawyers entering the bar between 1850 and 1860, whereas they probably trained nearly all new lawyers during the decade 1900–1910.

It seems unlikely that the impetus for formal law school training grew out of any belief that such schools could provide a better practical education than apprenticeship did. Indeed, the leading law schools, notably Columbia and Harvard, consciously sought to provide a theoretical rather than a practical education. For Theodore Dwight, an antislavery advocate from upstate New York who was appointed to the Columbia faculty in 1858 and remained the dominant force there for some three decades, "principles before practice . . . [was] the true watchword." Similarly, Christopher Columbus Langdell, the scientific-minded dean of Harvard from 1870 to 1895, was an advocate of legal decisionmaking on grounds of principle rather than practical policy and sought so to train his students. In short, the "object" of the leading law schools, according to James B. Ames, was to train students "to know what legal reasoning is"—to teach students not to memorize specific legal rules, but to reason deductively from the moral and scientific foundations of the law to the solution of specific legal problems.[74]

Pioneers in the organization of bar associations expressed similar objectives. The new movement began in 1870 with the formation of the Association of the Bar of the City of New York.[75] The organizers of the association expressed all the common concerns of the period. Speaking at its first meeting, Samuel J. Tilden, the already powerful Democratic party leader who would oust Boss Tweed from office and run for the presidency in 1876, expressed his dissatisfaction with the "serious decline" that had occurred "in the character, in the training, in the education, and in the morality of our Bar." Tilden and others, according to the *Albany Law Journal*, were especially disturbed at recent manifestations of corruption in judges, corruption that resulted ineluctably from "expos[ure] . . . to partisan influences."[76] Tilden accordingly pressed his fellow attorneys "to organize yourselves into a body," which could through "the creation of more intimate relations" among lawyers and what the *Albany Law Journal* labeled "consultation and social intercourse . . . undertake . . . the work of purification, . . . revive a past renown," and "give new life to traditions which we believe to be only dormant, not extinct."[77] The organizers of the association knew that judges, for example, would be "compelled to pay that regard to their collective power which they fain would deny to that of the individual members." They hoped the association could use its power as a community to raise the moral tone of bench and bar—"to elevate its own standards . . . [and] for the common and public good."[78]

The founders and early supporters of the American Bar Association said similar things. They sought through the "encouragement of cordial intercourse" among lawyers from different parts of the nation "to advance," in the words of civil service reformer Dorman B. Eaton, "professional learning and character, and to raise the lawyer's sense of the duty and dignity of his profession." They also hoped to promote "more perfect harmony and concord" and bring "members together on a common ground now altogether wanting." The stated, if not the real, objective of the late nineteenth-century bar association movement, according to Alfred Reed, was thus to organize the legal profession into communities that would revive and enforce moral traditions on the basis of which lawyers could then "discharge professional responsibilities in the spirit of *noblesse oblige*."[79]

In their effort to avoid questions of policy, legal reformers of the late nineteenth century thus elaborated what later scholars have labeled a formal style of judicial reasoning, institutionalized legal education in its modern form, and organized elite members of the bar into communities to police the moral standards of the legal profession and, indeed, of government as a whole. The new jurisprudence of "logical method and form flatter[ed] that longing for certainty and for repose" that arose out of the fratricidal strife of the middle and the seeming social chaos of the end of the century, while the new institutions of learning and the new associations of lawyers responded to concerns about scientific expertise and the preservation of shared moral traditions. But as Oliver Wendell Holmes correctly foresaw at the end of the century, "certainty . . . and repose" would not be "the destiny" of American law in the years to come. Courts in the twentieth century would have to take "sides upon debatable and often burning questions" of "social advantage" and pass "judgment as to the relative worth and importance of competing legislative grounds."[80] For litigants would present twentieth-century courts with novel claims about the injustice of the existing distribution of wealth and power in American society, and those courts would find the late nineteenth century's formal style, grounded in eighteenth-century morality and propped up by nineteenth-century science, increasingly inapposite as a means for approaching those fundamental distributional issues. Nevertheless the formal style would remain a potent intellectual force well into the twentieth century; indeed, some of the institutions that arose in connection with it, notably the law schools and the bar associations, remain powerful and significant today.

In their dealings with the judicial branch, as in their dealings with the legislative and executive branches, the late nineteenth-century reformers achieved only partial long-term success. Their greatest success was the establishment of new institutions. For a while, they also succeeded in tying both their new institutions and the older, existing ones to new moralistic and scientific styles of thought. Indeed, they came close to excluding politics from the law. But they did not succeed entirely. Politics continued to intrude into law with the election of judges, and the instrumental style of reasoning, which recognized the political character of judicial decisionmaking, also persisted,* ready to be resurrected to new heights by the legal realists of the 1930s. In law, as in politics and administration, the main accomplishment of the late nineteenth-century reformers was the creation of institutions that have long outlived their original intellectual premises.

Substantive Due Process: The Constitutional Glue

One of the most striking developments in late nineteenth-century America was the maturation of the judicial practice of passing upon the constitutionality of acts of the legislative branch of government. This doctrine of judicial review developed in the late eighteenth and early nineteenth centuries and survived the democratic challenge of mid-century. Before the Civil War, however, courts invalidated leg-

---

*One postwar judge, for example, adhered to precedents permitting a suit for anticipatory breach of a contract for the delivery of goods, because those cases "rest[ed] on strong grounds of convenience, however difficult it may be to reconcile them with the strictest logic."; *Dingley* v. *Oler*, 11 Fed. 372, 374 (C.C.D. Me. 1881). Likewise, a New York judge refused to adopt the rule of strict liability adopted in *Rylands* v. *Fletcher*, L.R. 3 H.L. 330 (1868), aff'g L.R. 1 Ex. 265 (1866), on the ground that the natural right to exclusive possession of property must be modified to conform to the exigencies of "factories, machinery, dams, canals and railroads," which are "demanded by the manifold wants of mankind" and lie "at the basis of all our civilization." *Losee* v. *Buchanan*, (51 N.Y. 476, 484 (1875). An equally clear statement of the old instrumentalism came from another New York judge: "Society has an interest in the cultivation and improvement of lands, and in the reclamation of waste lands. It is also for the public interest that improvements shall be made, and that towns and cities shall be built. To adopt the principle that the law of nature must be observed in respect to surface drainage, would, we think, place undue restriction upon industry, and enterprise . . . The question should, we think, be determined largely upon considerations of public policy, and general utility." *Barkley* v. *Wilcox*, 86 N.Y. 140, 148 (1881).

islative acts infrequently. After it, instances of judicial review increased markedly.

The Supreme Court, for example, held only two acts of Congress invalid in reported opinions before the Civil War, in *Marbury* v. *Madison* and *Scott* v. *Sandford*.[81] From 1865 to 1898, on the other hand, the Court held twenty-one congressional statutes or resolutions unconstitutional. State courts followed a corresponding pattern. In Indiana, for example, the highest court held two legislative acts unconstitutional before 1850, thirty-three from 1850 to 1869, and sixty-one from 1870 to 1899. In Massachusetts, the Supreme Judicial Court struck down ten acts before 1860 and thirty-one between 1860 and 1893. In Minnesota, thirty-two state laws were invalidated between the state's admission to the Union and 1884 and approximately seventy between 1885 and 1899. The largest number of judicial review cases occurred in New York; figures on the number of statutes held void are listed below.

1777–1840	10
1841–1850	18
1851–1860	34
1861–1870	39
1871–1880	45
1881–1890	49
1891–1900	99

The Ohio Supreme Court also was very active in the 1880s and 1890s, invalidating fifty-seven acts. In Virginia only four laws were invalidated prior to 1860 but more than forty between 1861 and 1902. Even in Utah, admitted to the Union only in 1896, eleven acts were declared unconstitutional between then and the end of the century.[82]

Why did instances of judicial review increase so markedly in the last third of the century? Part of the explanation may lie in the trend, already noted, away from an instrumental toward a more formal style of judicial reasoning. Instrumentalist judges, who view questions of law as issues of policy to be decided in accordance with the will of a majority, are likely to hesitate before challenging an act adopted by a majoritarian legislature. On the other hand, judges who believe that cases should be decided in accordance with fixed principles derived either from moral norms or through scientific analysis will have less difficulty invalidating a statute inconsistent with those principles. Both the practice of judicial review and the formal style of judicial reasoning are effective instruments whereby minorities can obstruct the will of a majority and, as such, reflect what I understand to be the main thrust of the late nineteenth-century movement for governmental reform.

Another common explanation has been that substantive due process, the single most formidable doctrine in the judicial arsenal of antilegislative weapons, developed into an effective instrument by which the wealthy classes and their allies on the bench invalidated legislation that either redistributed the wealth of the rich to the poor or gave the poorer classes means of obtaining a greater share of that wealth.[83] Substantive due process can indeed be seen as an antiredistribution doctrine; that aspect of its character was made explicit by Chief Justice Chase as early as 1871 in his dissenting opinion in the *Legal Tender Cases*, where he declared that Congressional legislation making paper money legal tender "violate[d] that fundamental principle of all just legislation that the legislature shall not take the property of A. and give it to B." and hence amounted to "a manifest violation of this clause [the Fifth Amendment due process clause] of the Constitution." Two years later Justice Field, dissenting in the *Slaughter-House Cases*, similarly found that Louisiana legislation that created a corporation to centralize all butchering in New Orleans violated the due process clause of the Fourteenth Amendment, in that it took away "a right to pursue a lawful and necessary calling, previously enjoyed by every citizen" and vested the right "exclusively . . . in a single corporation." Two decades later Justice Field, this time concurring in the Court's invalidation of the federal income tax in *Pollock* v. *Farmers' Loan & Trust Co.*, again concluded that the Constitution prohibited "class legislation," which occurred "whenever a distinction is made in the burdens a law imposes or in the benefits it confers on any citizens by reason of their birth, or wealth, or religion."[84]

Thus, the doctrine of substantive due process can be understood as a species of class legislation favoring the rich at the expense of the poor. Indeed, if one believes that the primary activity of all branches of government is the distribution of the nation's wealth among competing interest groups, then it is hard to perceive the doctrine of substantive due process as anything but an excuse for class legislation by the courts. Such an analysis, however, loses sight of the doctrine's immense scope and breadth. In concentrating upon twentieth-century cases like *Lochner* v. *New York*,[85] in which the Court struck down a legislative effort to provide assistance to the poor, historians have failed to recognize the larger role played by the doctrine in cases before 1900, both in the Supreme Court and in the highest courts of the states.

In the *Slaughter-House Cases*, the dissenting opinions of Justices Field and Bradley, from which the due process doctrine is understood to have sprung, were not written in the service of special privilege. As Field wrote in two later opinions in which Bradley concurred, the two justices did not oppose legislation "to promote the health, peace, morals, education, and good order of the people" or "to increase the industries of the State, develop its resources, and add to its wealth and prosperity." Indeed, they did not even oppose laws "to protect all persons from the physical and moral debasement which comes from uninterrupted labor," for they found those laws "beneficent and merciful laws, especially to the poor and dependent, [and] to the laborers in our factories and workshops and in the heated rooms of our cities."[86] On the contrary, Field and Bradley dissented in the *Slaughter-House Cases* because they understood that Louisiana had conferred a special privilege upon the small group of butchers who had been formed into a corporation and given the exclusive right to operate a slaughterhouse in the New Orleans metropolitan area. As Field wrote, the "act of Louisiana present[ed] the naked case . . . where a right to pursue a lawful and necessary calling . . . in connection with which a thousand persons were daily employed, is taken away and vested exclusively . . . in a single corporation." Field and Bradley opposed the use of legislative power to redistribute wealth in such a manner from the masses to the few. As Bradley noted in a companion case that came before the Court several years later, the Louisiana legislation had created "a mere monopoly, and nothing else" — "a monopoly of an ordinary employment and business, which no legislature has power to farm out by contract." Indeed, Bradley considered "monopolies" to be "the bane of our body politic at the present day," for "in the eager pursuit of gain they . . . [were] sought in every direction . . . [and] exhibit[ed] themselves in corners in the stock market and produce market, and in many other ways."[87]

The majority in the *Slaughter-House Cases* did not overtly reject the substantive due process doctrines proclaimed by Justices Field and Bradley in dissent. A more important source of disagreement was how to interpret the facts. In writing the opinion of the Court, Justice Miller found that the Louisiana act did not "creat[e] a monopoly" or "confer . . . odious and exclusive privileges upon a small number of persons at the expense of the great body of the community of New Orleans." If Miller had understood the act to benefit the few at the expense of the multitude, he might have joined Field and Bradley in holding it unconstitutional. In fact two years later, in *Loan Association* v. *Topeka*, Miller wrote an opinion for the Court invalidating a state law that had pledged the tax power to support the repayment of bonds donated to a private bridge manufacturing company in order to induce it to construct a factory in Topeka. In language that could have been written by the most ardent proponents of substantive due process, Miller observed: "The merchant, the mechanic, the innkeeper, the banker, the builder, the steamboat owner are equally promoters of the public good, and equally deserving the aid of the citizens by forced contributions. No line can be drawn in favor of the manufacturer which would not open the coffers of the public treasury to the importunities of two-thirds of the business men of the city or town."[88]

Like the *Slaughter-House Cases* and *Loan Association* v. *Topeka*, *Allgeyer* v. *Louisiana*,[89] in which a majority of the Supreme Court first joined in an opinion deciding a matter on substantive due process grounds, did not involve legislation benefiting the masses at the expense of the few. At issue in *Allgeyer* was a Louisiana statute that prohibited a resident of the state who had previously made a contract in New York with a New York firm from mailing a notification pursuant to the contract. The real issue in *Allgeyer* was whether the Court would tolerate state impediments to the transaction of interstate business; following its practice throughout the nineteenth century, the Court declined to do so. If the legislation that the Court invalidated in *Allgeyer* had any distributional effect it was to benefit special interests in Louisiana at the expense of most of its people, by prohibiting the people from doing business with a New York firm that was a more effective competitor than its local Louisiana counterpart. Thus, if the Court's opinion had any distributional effect, it was not to protect the rich from the poor, but rather to protect the poor from the rich.

Similarly in the states, substantive due process was not a device used by the courts solely to protect the rich from the redistributive onslaughts of the poor. For example, in *Wynehamer* v. *People*, a famous case decided by the New York Court of Appeals before the Civil War, the issue was whether state legislation prohibiting the sale of alcoholic beverages could be applied to liquors owned by individuals before passage of the act; it is difficult to imagine how either the legislation itself or the court's invalidation of it brought about any significant redistribution of wealth. Likewise, in *People* v. *Gillson*, in which the New York Court of Appeals invalidated an act that prohibited the Atlantic and Pacific Tea Company from giving a teacup and saucer to consumers who purchased its coffee, what was at stake was not any redistribution of wealth but the right of "citizen traders" to sell and consumers to buy a cup, a saucer, and coffee, rather than coffee alone, for the price of the coffee.[90]

In other states the doctrine of substantive due process was used to challenge a wide variety of special interest legislation. Thus, the Maryland courts questioned the constitutionality of an act providing that "no Black Republican . . . shall be appointed to any office" within the jurisdiction of the Baltimore Board of Police;[91] and the Iowa courts struck down Iowa legislation that permitted the use of oil for lighting purposes only in lamps made by a particular manufacturer, but not in other lamps. In another case involving state legislation, the Supreme Court struck down an Illinois statute exempting from its operation only producers of agricultural products and raisers of livestock. Although the due process clause was used at times to invalidate redistributive legislation, that was neither its sole nor its principal function.[92]

The main function of substantive due process was to prevent conflict within the political process between groups that were competing for wealth and power in late nineteenth-century America. In the words of one state governor, the late nineteenth century witnessed "the birth and growth of new schools of political thought, each clamoring to have its policy engrafted into fundamental law" and "the development and clash of powerful class influences struggling for control of the body politic." Those forces had to be restrained unless all the nation's energies were to be absorbed in "general unrest and disturbance in society." Indeed, Justice Field argued in *Pollock* v. *Farmers' Loan & Trust Co.* that if those forces were not constrained, "our political contests will become a war of the poor against the rich; a war constantly growing in intensity and bitterness." If the rich were concerned, however, by the prospect of depredations by the poor, it was also the case that the poor were concerned with "the exactions of . . . monopolists . . . unfair taxes and . . . all varieties of 'class laws' " whereby the rich appropriated the fruits of their labor. In the language of onetime antislavery and reform politician Carl Schurz, average Americans had watched as "the great corporations . . . by hook or crook accumulate[d] enormous fortunes in single hands," grew "more greedy and unscrupulous," and ultimately sought "to control" for their own "purposes governments and legislatures." And they agreed with Schurz that "unless this dangerous tendency be checked . . . our social life will be disastrously demoralized" and "our political contests will become mere wrangles between different bands of public robbers, legislation only a matter of purchase and sale and the whole government a festering mass of corruption."[93]

Substantive due process was a weapon for invalidating any legislative act in which private interests, rich or poor, put the power of government to use for their own ends at the expense of others. Thus, Justice Field found the due process clause offended by any law that imposed a burden or conferred a benefit "on any citizens by reason of their birth, or wealth, or religion," characterizing such laws as "the same in essential character as . . . the English income statute of 1691, which taxed Protestants at a certain rate, Catholics, as a class, at double the rate of Protestants, and Jews at another and separate rate." Unlike legislation enacted "solely for the general good of the community," such unequal laws "attract[ed] . . . that prejudice or jealousy . . . which naturally would arise . . . from the consideration that the latter were obtained with a view to the benefit of particular individuals, and the apprehension that their interests might be promoted at the sacrifice, or to the injury, of those others whose interests should be equally regarded." As the Civil War had demonstrated, such prejudice and jealousy set men against each other and destroyed the internal harmony of groups and communities as well as the peace between them. And, as the corruption of the Tweed

Ring in New York showed at the very time substantive due process was receiving early impetus from the dissents of Justices Field and Bradley in the *Slaughter-House Cases*, government could not even be conceived in moral terms once its power to distribute wealth and property among citizens was recognized. The creation of a political order either on the basis of antislavery moral precepts or on the basis of newer forms of scientific morality simply required denying to legislatures the power to "take the property of A. and give it to B."[94]

Conclusion:
The Unresolved Tensions

For two centuries a tension has existed in American political thought between the ideal of popular self-government and the concern for protecting individual and minority rights. On the one hand, American political thinkers have always assumed that those who occupy office with a mandate from the majority of the people should have power to make the political program of the majority effective. Simultaneously there has existed a pluralistic vision of America as a nation of distinctive individuals and innumerable minorities who possess rights that majorities may not infringe. Americans, that is, have long believed in "the republican principle of the supremacy of the will of the majority" while simultaneously "acknowledg[ing], in general, a strong sympathy with minorities." The "demanding and delicate" task has been to "fix . . . the definition and content of the . . . personal rights held against popular will" and thereby to determine when an individual or a minority can obstruct that will.[1] Many ideas have been advanced as to how this task should be performed, but none has obtained widespread, lasting acceptance.

Underlying the tension in American political thought is an analogous tension in American social reality. In the past two centuries Americans have created political, economic, and social institutions that have made the United States a true nation. But, during those two centuries, the United States has always been a nation of great heterogeneity as well. In the eighteenth century, Americans were highly conscious of their local heritage and of sectarian differences even though most were Protestants of British ancestry. Today American society is riven by racial, religious, and ethnic differences.

156

Throughout its history the United States has been paradoxically a single nation of many peoples, no one of which has attained permanet ascendency over the others. Government has possessed powers required to ensure the well-being of the nation as a whole, yet it has simultaneously been subjected to restraints designed to protect the nation's different groups from one another.

The tension between the ideal of majority rule and the pluralistic concern for protecting individual and minority rights is thus rooted deeply in the unities and divisions of American society. Given these deep roots, the failure of Americans to resolve the tension during the past two centuries is not surprising. Indeed, there is every reason to expect that the tension will endure until the United States becomes a far more homogenized nation than it has ever been. The conclusion of this book is not that the United States over time has or should become more or less solicitous of individual and minority rights. Americans have been, are now, and probably will remain convinced that majorities should govern and that individuals and minorities should enjoy their rights. What have changed are the institutional forms in which the tension between the two convictions has worked itself out.

The Civil War was the great watershed in the nineteenth century. Until 1860, the tension between majority rule and minority right was focused around issues of federalism as those who lacked power in one sovereign political forum frequently called upon allies in another for help. After losing the presidential election of 1860, for example, southerners turned to state governments to protect themselves against national power. A few years earlier, in cases like *Ableman* v. *Booth*, antislavery stalwarts had similarly sought to interpose state power to prevent enforcement of legislation enacted by a congressional majority. At the same time, individuals who believed they had been deprived of their rights by majorities in the states could turn to federal institutions for protection. Throughout the first half of the century, victims of such deprivations turned, in particular, to the federal courts, which frequently provided them with protection in a series of cases stretching back to *Fletcher* v. *Peck*.[2]

People in the first half of the nineteenth century who felt they had been deprived of their rights could also make arguments derived from theories of natural law or natural right, and in an age when moral principles were taken seriously, arguments based on morality sometimes had the capacity to sway a majority from its predetermined course. Moral arguments had even greater success when, as was typically the case, they were presented to a forum other than the one in which the majority had initially settled upon its policy.

For several decades before the Civil War, the indeterminate character of the federal system and the weight accorded by society to diverse moral arguments preserved the pluralist quality of American society. When a group gained even temporary control of the national government, its awareness that the minority held deeply rooted moral views often led it to compromise rather than insist on rigid adherence to its own point of view; the period 1820–1850, in particular, was one of frequent compromises between sectional groups with divergent policies and viewpoints. And when compromise did not occur, as in the case of treatment of fugitive slaves, losers in the national political forum could present their moral arguments to state forums, which often agreed with the arguments and which possessed significant though indeterminate power to interfere with enforcement of national legislative policy.

In the 1860s two changes occurred in this pattern. Antislavery moralists gained great, if not dominant, power in the national government only to discover that moral principles provided little guidance or impediment to a majority's exercise of its authority. More important, the Civil War and Reconstruction established the military and political supremacy of the federal government over states. Although states continued to possess vast powers in the last third of the century, they could no longer threaten, as they had until the Civil War, to stop a determined majority in Congress from imposing its will on a dissident minority.[3] Accordingly, during Reconstruction the pluralistic quality of America appeared to be threatened as it never had been before and never has been since. New institutional structures seemed necessary if American pluralism was to be preserved.

Over the next three decades those new institutions came into being. Civil service reform and the creation of independent regulatory commissions gave subordinate officials in the executive branch independence from both the president and Congress and gradually created bonds of loyalty between groups of officials and the particularistic interest groups they were charged with aiding or regulating. Meanwhile, as the judiciary moved from what has been labeled an instrumental to a formal style of reasoning, it too became less responsive to the political process as a whole and more closely allied to a single, small segment of American society — the legal profession. Even in Congress, substantial power was transferred from party caucuses and from one or two dominant committees in each house staffed by party leaders to a number of quasi-autonomous committees under the control of senior members of Congress. In all branches of government, training and expertise came substantially under control of the universities, themselves quite independent of the national political process and allied to several different segments of American society, ranging from state political establishments through the business community to intellectual elites. With the development of these new institutions, power within the federal government became fragmented. This fragmentation of power institutionalized pluralism.

In tracing the transformation of nineteenth-century government from a party-centered to a bureaucratic system of authority, I have not attempted to provide answers to two fundamental theoretical questions that American political thinkers must ask as they analyze how the nation's government should be organized. First, do Americans continue to want, as they have in the past, a governmental structure that reflects the pluralism of American society and gives diverse groups in that society access to the levers of power? If so, should pluralism be institutionalized through a genuine federalism of the sort existing prior to the Civil War? Or should bureaucratic communities with discrete loyalties to different groups in society serve as the bulwarks of pluralism? In short, should American pluralism be structured along lines of geographic propinquity or lines of social affinity? Second, do Americans believe that significant social reform should occur in the United States in the coming years? If so, do they understand social reform to consist in the imposition of some determinate conception of the good society on the populace as a whole — a kind of reform that would undermine a pluralist social structure? Or do they understand reform to consist in giving access to the levers of power to groups that have not previously enjoyed such access?

I have no doubt about the society in which and the governmental structure under which we live. American society today is a pluralist one organized along lines of social affinity, not geographic propinquity, and most existing communities of affinity have access to mechanisms of power. Government in the United States is presently structured to thwart social reform of the first sort noted above — that is, the imposition on the populace as a whole of some determinate conception of the good society. Most political changes in the United States in the twentieth century have not brought the nation closer to any utopian vision of the good society, but have simply given access to power to groups that have previously lacked it.

The late nineteenth-century reformers whose political thought and activity gave birth to the modern bureaucratic state and thereby institutionalized pluralism were not reformers in either of the senses outlined above. They did not possess and did not seek to impose on others any determinate conception of the good society. Nor were they seeking to grant access to political power to groups who did not yet enjoy that access. Their goal was more limited; they strove only to reshape the structure of American government in a way that would protect them from the imposition of other people's utopian schemes and enable them to continue to "enjoy an untroubled night's sleep"⁴ in the America they had always known.

The fact that the mugwumps or genteel reformers were not true reformers in either of the modern-day senses noted above does not, however, make them the quintessential men of self-interest that some historians have painted them to be. The genteel reformers of the late nineteenth century should be understood in the contexts of their own time and of the earlier milieu from which they emerged. For the mugwumps, comfortable nativeborn scions of the upper and middle classes, the demise of the moral and communitarian values they had been taught to revere as youths threatened to result in a lawless society in which neither they nor anyone else would know either their social place or the rules of daily life. They therefore sought to protect their traditional place in society and to restore rules with which they were familiar. Although some reformers may have been aware intellectually of growing injustice in the distribution of wealth and property, that injustice had little effect on their daily lives and hence could not prevent them from focusing on the problem that did affect their lives — the problem of preserving their place and restoring the familiar rules. On the other hand, for members of the lower class, who often had had no indoctrination in eighteenth- and early nineteenth-century moral and communitarian or pluralist values, the injustice of the existing distribution of wealth was the central issue that controlled their lives and prompted political effort. Those lower classes did not care whether they had to sacrifice traditional American values that they hardly understood in order to give government the power to redistribute wealth in their favor. The perspective of the upper class was no more self-interested than that of the lower class; in both cases, what might be called self-interest probably arose more from bitter confrontations with the problems of daily life than from any truly selfish lack of concern about the problems of other people.

Indeed, neither the genteel reformers nor their lower-class contemporaries were either more or less afflicted with self-interest than those who read this book. Viewed in the abstract, late nineteenth century society, like late twentieth-century society, had many problems. But people who lived then, like those who live today, could appreciate only the problems that affected either their lives or the lives of those with whom they could empathize. Most important, perhaps, people of the late nineteenth century, like people today, developed solutions only for what they perceived as problems.

Ultimately, then, I suspect that each reader's attitude toward the late nineteenth-century builders of the modern bureaucratic state will depend on what he perceives to be the problems facing American society today. If he believes that American society is fundamentally unjust and that its injustices can be corrected only if he and other people utilize governmental power to impose their vision of justice on others, then he will have no sympathy either with the late nineteenth-century reformers or with the bureaucratic governmental institutions they created. Such a reader will want a government capable of being harnessed toward utopian ends and will be critical of people and pluralist institutions that impede attainment of those ends. If, on the other hand, a reader fears both what he may do to others and what others may do to him if either he or they are given untrammeled power, he will empathize with the late nineteenth-century reformers, will recognize them as his intellectual forefathers, and will value his inheritance from them. And, when he fails to translate some specific policy objective into law, he will attribute his failure not to the malice or pigheadedness of his opponents but to a pluralistic structure of authority that protects his opponents from his political whims just as it protects him from theirs.

Notes

Introduction: Origins of Authority

1. Benjamin F. Wright, ed., *The Federalist*, no. 39 (Madison) (Cambridge, Mass.: Harvard University Press, 1961), pp. 280-281; John H. Ely, *Democracy and Distrust: A Theory of Judicial Review* (Cambridge, Mass.: Harvard University Press, 1980), p. 7.

2. Charles F. Adams, ed., *Works of John Adams*, vol. 6 (Boston, 1851), p. 63; Wright, *The Federalist*, no. 78 (Hamilton), p. 494; Jesse H. Choper, *Judicial Review and the National Political Process: A Functional Reconsideration of the Role of the Supreme Court* (Chicago: University of Chicago Press, 1980), p. 64. See also Ely, *Democracy and Distrust*, pp. 73–87.

3. I am attempting to define bureaucracy in a manner consistent with the definition of Max Weber. For Weber's criteria for defining bureacracy, see Alexander M. Henderson and Talcott Parsons, trans., *Max Weber: The Theory of Social and Economic Organization* (New York: Oxford University Press, 1947), pp. 333–334.

4. See generally Burton J. Bledstein, *The Culture of Professionalism: The Middle Class and the Development of Higher Education in America* (New York: Norton, 1976); Alexandra Oleson and John Voss, eds., *The Organization of Knowledge in Modern America* (Baltimore: Johns Hopkins University Press, 1979).

5. The best recent work includes George B. Galloway, *History of the House of Representatives* (New York: Crowell, 1961); Ari A. Hoogenboom, *Outlawing the Spoils: A History of the Civil Service Reform Movement, 1865–1883* (Urbana: University of Illinois Press, 1961); David J. Rothman, *Politics and Power: The United States Senate, 1869–1901* (Cambridge, Mass.: Harvard University Press, 1966); Leonard D. White, *The Republican Era: A Study in Administrative History, 1869–1901* (New York: Macmillan, 1958).

6. See Max Weber, "The Presuppositions and Causes of Bureaucracy," in *Reader in Bureaucracy*, ed. Robert K. Merton et al. (Glencoe, Ill.: Free Press, 1952), pp. 60–68; Henderson and Parsons, *Max Weber*, pp. 73–340.

7. See Douglas T. Miller, *Jacksonian Aristocracy: Class and Democracy in New York, 1830–1860* (New York: Oxford University Press, 1967), pp. 3–25; Edward Pessen, *Riches, Class, and Power before the Civil War* (Lexington, Mass.: D. C. Heath, 1973), pp. 2–3, 304–305; William E. Nelson, "The Eighteenth-Century Background of John Marshall's Constitutional Jurisprudence," *Michigan Law Review*, 76 (1978), 893, 932–956; John L. O'Sullivan, "The Democratic Principle," in *Notions of the Americans, 1820–1860*, ed. David Grimsted (New York: G. Braziller, 1970), p. 86.

8. For general discussion of the reformers and their work see Hoogenboom, *Outlawing the Spoils*; Morton Keller, *Affairs of State: Public Life in Late Nineteenth Century America* (Cambridge, Mass.: Harvard University Press, 1977); John G. Sproat, *"The Best Men": Liberal Reformers in the Gilded Age* (New York: Oxford University Press, 1968).

9. David Beetham, *Max Weber and the Theory of Modern Politics* (London: Allen & Unwin, 1974), p. 70.

10. I thus disagree with what I understand to be the thrust of Robert H. Wiebe, *The Search for Order. 1877–1920* (New York: Hill and Wang, 1967).

11. Hoogenboom, *Outlawing the Spoils*; Matthew Josephson, *The Politicos, 1865–1896* (New York: Harcourt, Brace, 1938); Arnold M. Paul, *Conservative Crisis and the Rule of Law: Attitudes of Bar and Bench, 1887–1895* (Ithaca, N.Y.: Cornell University Press, 1960); and Sproat, *"The Best Men,"* exemplify this point of view.

12. See Hoogenboom, *Outlawing the Spoils,* pp. 21, 34–36, 186–197; Paul, *Conservative Crisis,* pp. 76–81, 128–132, 159–160; Sproat, *"The Best Men,"* pp. 55–60.

13. Quoted in Choper, *Judicial Review*, p. 67.

1. The Emergence of the Majoritarian Authority Structure

1. See William W. Freehling, *Prelude to Civil War: The Nullification Controversy in South Carolina, 1816–1836* (New York: Harper & Row, 1966), pp. 106–108, 136–138, 292–293; Glyndon G. Van Deusen, *The Jacksonian Era, 1828–1848* (New York: Harper, 1959), pp. 39, 60, 76–79, 164–166, 201–204; Morton J. Horwitz, *The Transformation of American Law, 1780–1860* (Cambridge, Mass.: Harvard University Press, 1977), pp. 34–53; Harry N. Scheiber, *Ohio Canal Era: A Case Study of Government and the Economy, 1820–1861* (Athens: Ohio University Press, 1969).

2. See Sanford H. Cobb, *The Rise of Religious Liberty in America: A History* (New York: Macmillan, 1902), pp. 67–398; Edwin S. Gaustad, *A Religious History of America* (New York: Harper & Row, 1966), pp. 41–42, 54–55, 74–79, 84, 107.

3. See Sidney E. Ahlstrom, *A Religious History of the American People* (New Haven: Yale University Press, 1972), pp. 415–490, 501–509, 635–669.

4. On population see generally J. Potter, "The Growth of Population in America, 1700–1860," in *Population in History: Essays in Historical Demography*, ed. D. V. Glass and D. E. C. Eversley (Chicago: Aldine, 1965),

p. 631; Yasukichi Yasuba, *Birth Rates of the White Population of the United States, 1800–1860: An Economic Study* (Baltimore: Johns Hopkins University Press, 1962). On wealth see generally Paul W. Gates, *The Farmer's Age: Agriculture, 1815–1860* (New York: Holt, Rinehart and Winston, 1960); Curtis P. Nettels, *The Emergence of a National Economy, 1775–1815* (New York: Holt, Rinehart and Winston, 1962); George R. Taylor, *The Transportation Revolution: Industry, 1815–1860* (New York: Rinehart, 1951). On the concept of aristocrat see James Fenimore Cooper, *The American Democrat*, 3d ed. (1838; New York: Funk & Wagnalls, 1969), pp. 70–87. In Cooper's words, "Social station, in the main . . . [was] a consequence of property." (p. 71).

5. See William E. Nelson, *Dispute and Conflict Resolution in Plymouth County, Massachusetts, 1725–1825* (Chapel Hill: University of North Carolina Press, 1981), pp. 133–134, 150–152; William E. Nelson, "The Eighteenth-Century Background of John Marshall's Constitutional Jurisprudence," *Michigan Law Review*, 76 (1978), 893, 902–924.

6. See Gordon S. Wood, *The Creation of the American Republic, 1776–1787* (Chapel Hill: University of North Carolina Press, 1969), pp. 181–188, 319–389, 532–536, 593–615.

7. See Nelson, *Dispute and Conflict Resolution*, pp. 133–134, 150–152; idem, "Eighteenth-Century Background," pp. 902–924.

8. On disestablishment and the important issues that it raised see Richard R. Beeman, *The Old Dominion and the New Nation, 1788–1801* (Lexington, Ky.: University Press of Kentucky, 1972), pp. 93–95, 198–199; Hamilton J. Eckenrode, *Separation of Church and State in Virginia: A Study in the Development of the Revolution* (Richmond: D. Bottom, 1910); Paul Goodman, *The Democratic-Republicans of Massachusetts* (Cambridge, Mass.: Harvard University Press, 1964), pp. 86–96, 162–166; William E. Nelson, *Americanization of the Common Law: The Impact of Legal Change on Massachusetts Society, 1760–1830* (Cambridge, Mass.: Harvard University Press, 1975), pp. 104–109. See also the materials cited in notes 2 and 3 above. On decriminalization of sexual standards see David H. Flaherty, "Law and the Enforcement of Morals in Early America," *Perspectives in American History*, 5 (1971), 201, 245–253; William E. Nelson, "Emerging Notions of Modern Criminal Law in the Revolutionary Era: An Historical Perspective," *New York University Law Review*, 42 (1967), 450–462.

9. See Nelson, *Americanization of the Common Law*, pp. 36–63.

10. Of course we must not underestimate the difficulty even of these tasks, particularly in the vast wilderness that constituted early nineteenth-century America. That revenue collection was not always simple is demonstrated by such events as the Whisky Rebellion of 1794 and South Carolina's attempt at tariff nullification in 1833; on both occasions the government's normal enforcement mechanisms required strengthening. See Leonard D. White, *The Federalists: A Study in Administrative History* (New York: Macmillan, 1948), pp. 419–420, and *The Jacksonians: A Study in Administrative History, 1829–1861* (New York: Macmillan, 1954), pp. 512–516. Nor was enforcement of the judgments of the federal courts always an easy

task. It must be remembered that the diversity jurisdiction was created for the purpose of removing from the state courts difficult cases that might result in unpopular judgments that would be more difficult than usual to enforce. See Henry J. Friendly, "The Historical Basis of the Diversity Jurisdiction," *Harvard Law Review,* 41 (1928), 483. Throughout the first seventy years of the federal government's existence there was in fact a series of cases in which state officials sought to interpose their power to prevent execution of federal judgments, and federal officials were required to take special steps to have the judgments enforced. See Edward S. Corwin, "National Power and State Interposition," in *Select Essays on Constitutional Law,* ed. Association of American Law Schools, vol. 3 (Chicago: Foundation Press, 1937), p. 1176; Charles Warren, "Federal and State Court Interference," in ibid., p. 1096; idem, "Legislative and Judicial Attacks on the Supreme Court," *American Law Review,* 47 (1913), 1.

11. See generally Walter W. Jennings, *The American Embargo, 1807–1809* (Iowa City: University of Iowa Press, 1921); Louis M. Sears, *Jefferson and the Embargo* (Durham, N.C.: Duke University Press, 1927).

12. For evidence that these tasks were not always easy ones, see David M. Ellis, *Landlords and Farmers in the Hudson–Mohawk Region, 1790–1850* (Ithaca, N.Y.: Cornell University Press, 1946), pp. 34–35, 154–155, 232; Oscar Handlin and Mary F. Handlin, *Commonwealth: A Study of the Role of Government in the American Economy, Massachusetts, 1774–1861,* rev. ed. (Cambridge, Mass.: Harvard University Press, 1969), pp. 32–33, 43–47.

13. See Handlin and Handlin, *Commonwealth,* pp. 128–129, 215–224; Edward C. Kirkland, *Men, Cities, and Transportation: A Study in New England History, 1820–1900,* 2 vols. (Cambridge, Mass.: Harvard University Press, 1948), 2: 230–267. On the inefficacy of regulation see J. Willard Hurst, *Law and Economic Growth: The Legal History of the Lumber Industry in Wisconsin, 1836–1915* (Cambridge, Mass.: Harvard University Press, 1964), pp. 453, 559–560.

14. See generally Robert S. Hunt, *Law and Locomotives: The Impact of the Railroads on Wisconsin Law in the Nineteenth Century* (Madison: State Historical Society of Wisconsin, 1958), pp. 98–131, 140–143.

15. Pennsylvania Archives, 4th ser., 7, p. 392 (report by Governor Johnston, 1850); ibid., 6, p. 130 (statement by Governor Wolf, 1836); ibid., 6, p. 620 (statement by Governor Porter, 1842); *Pennsylvania House of Representatives Journal,* 33d Assembly, p. 622 (1822).

16. See Louis Hartz, *Economic Policy and Democratic Thought: Pennsylvania, 1776–1860* (Cambridge, Mass.: Harvard University Press, 1948), pp. 262, 265–266; James C. Mohr, *The Radical Republicans and Reform in New York During Reconstruction* (Ithaca, N.Y.: Cornell University Press, 1973), pp. 25–53, 86–114, 149–152; Michael Les Benedict, "Contagion and the Constitution: Quarantine Agitation from 1859 to 1866," *Journal of the History of Medicine,* 25 (1970), 177.

17. See Paul W. Gates, *History of Public Land Law Development* (Washington, D.C.: Government Printing Office, 1968), pp. 121–247,

387-434, 531-562; Hurst, *Law and Economic Growth*, pp. 62-142, 341-386; Malcolm J. Rohrbough, *The Land Office Business: The Settlement and Adminis- tration of American Public Lands, 1789-1837* (New York: Oxford University Press, 1968), pp. 89-249.

18. See Carter Goodrich, *Government Promotion of American Canals and Railroads, 1800-1890* (New York: Columbia University Press, 1960), pp. 51-168; Hartz, *Economic Policy and Democratic Thought*, pp. 37-180; Kirk- land, *Men, Cities, and Transportation*, 1: 32-59 and 2: 237-240, 248, 250; Nelson, *Americanization of the Common Law*, pp. 146-147; Harry N. Scheiber, *Ohio Canal Era: A Case Study of Government and the Economy, 1820-1861* (Athens: Ohio University Press, 1969).

19. See Hartz, *Economic Policy and Democratic Thought*, pp. 55, 96-100; Handlin and Handlin, *Commonwealth*, pp. 71-73, 76-77, 87, 103-105.

20. See Marvin Meyers, *The Jacksonian Persuasion: Politics and Belief* (Stanford: Stanford University Press, 1957), pp. 158-162, 176-177; Arthur M. Schlesinger, Jr., *The Age of Jackson* (Boston: Little, Brown, 1945), pp. 90-92, 144-209, 306-321, 334-349.

21. See Lee Benson, *The Concept of Jacksonian Democracy: New York as a Test Case* (Princeton: Princeton University Press, 1961), pp. 97-109; E. Merrick Dodd, *American Business Corporations until 1860* (Cambridge, Mass.: Harvard University Press, 1954), pp. 311-321; W. Stull Holt, *The Office of the Chief of Engineers of the Army: Its Non-Military History, Activities, and Organi- zation* (Baltimore: Johns Hopkins University Press, 1923), p. 33; Scheiber, *Ohio Canal Era*, pp. 88-113.

22. See Dixon R. Fox, *The Decline of Aristocracy in the Politics of New York* (New York: Columbia University Press, 1919), pp. 229-269; Schlesinger, *Age of Jackson*, pp. 30, 343-344. The principle of majority rule was not, of course, a new one. It had been defended during the American Revolution, for example, on the ground that "mankind being in a state of nature equal, the larger Number (Caeteris paribus) is of more worth than the lesser." Statement of Berkshire County Representatives, November 17, 1778, in *The Popular Sources of Political Authority: Documents on the Massachusetts Constitu- tion of 1780*, ed. Oscar Handlin and Mary F. Handlin (Cambridge, Mass.: Harvard University Press, 1966), pp. 374, 375; and John Locke had earlier defended it on the ground that "if the consent of the majority shall not in reason be received as the act of the whole and conclude every individual," then a society could "not act as one body, and consequently . . . [would] be immediately dissolved." *Two Treatises of Government: Book II, Of Civil Govern- ment* (London, 1690), §98. But although the idea of majority rule was not new, the emphasis the Jacksonians placed on it was: the will of the majority of the people became the ultimate foundation of government that gave sanction to all law — even to law that failed to give maximum freedom to in- dividuals or that treated unequally individuals who were equal.

23. See Herbert McCloskey, "The Fallacy of Absolute Majority Rule,"*Journal of Politics*, 11 (1949), 637, 638-639.

24. See Freehling, *Prelude to Civil War*, pp. 260-297; Thomas D. Morris,

Free Men All: The Personal Liberty Laws of the North, 1780–1861 (Baltimore: Johns Hopkins University Press, 1974); Jon C. Teaford, *The Municipal Revolution in America: Origins of Modern Urban Government, 1650–1825* (Chicago: University of Chicago Press, 1975), pp. 79–115; Van Deusen, *Jacksonian Era*, pp. 52, 65–67; Gerald E. Frug, "The City as a Legal Concept," *Harvard Law Review*, 93 (1980), 1057, 1105–09, 1113–17.

25. U.S., Congress, House, *Congressional Globe*, 26th Cong., 2d sess., 1840, p. 239, quoted in DeAlva S. Alexander, *History and Procedure of the House of Representatives* (Boston: Houghton Mifflin, 1916), p. 67. Accord, *Congressional Globe*, 35th Cong., 1st sess., 1857, p. 40 (remarks of Senator Bayard). See generally Alexander, *House of Representatives*, pp. 66–70.

26. See Noble E. Cunningham, Jr., *The Jeffersonian Republicans: The Formation of Party Organization, 1789–1801* (Chapel Hill: University of North Carolina Press, 1957), pp. 71, 82–91, 162–166; Manning J. Dauer, *The Adams Federalists* (Baltimore: Johns Hopkins University Press, 1953), pp. 225–245; David H. Fischer, *The Revolution of American Conservatism: The Federalist Party in the Era of Jeffersonian Democracy* (New York: Harper & Row, 1965), pp. 1, 5–10, 17–20.

27. Daniel Webster to Charles March, June 19, 1813, in *The Letters of Daniel Webster*, ed. Claude H. Van Tyne (New York: McClure, Phillips, 1902), pp. 42, 43; *Annals of Congress*, 13th Cong., 1st sess., 1813, p. 461n.

28. See Noble E. Cunningham, *The Jeffersonian Republicans in Power: Party Operations, 1801–1809* (Chapel Hill: University of North Carolina Press, 1963), pp. 78–82; Richard E. Ellis, *The Jeffersonian Crisis: Courts and Politics in the Young Republic* (New York: Oxford University Press, 1971), pp. 83–107.

29. A. Lawrence Lowell, "The Influence of Party upon Legislation in England and America," *Annual Report of the American Historical Association for the Year of 1901*, vol. 1 (Washington, D.C.: Government Printing Office, 1902), pp. 319, 336. For the percentages see the table in ibid., p. 538. The figures in the second column of that table are for the occasions on which both parties voted along party lines; those in the fourth, for occasions on which one party so voted.

30. Ibid., pp. 336–337.

31. See Joseph Cooper, "The Origins of the Standing Committees and the Development of the Modern House," *Rice University Studies*, 56, no. 3 (1970), 84–85, 104.

32. See George L. Robinson, "The Development of the Senate Committee System" (Ph.D. diss., New York University, 1955), pp. 171–178, 268–269, 280.

33. U.S., Congress, House, *Congressional Debates*, 27th Cong., 1st sess., 1841, p. 153, quoted in Alexander, *House of Representatives*, p. 191. See generally Alexander, *House of Representatives*, pp. 191, 234–235; George B. Galloway, *History of the House of Representatives* (New York: Crowell, 1961), p. 131. See also Harold M. Hyman, *A More Perfect Union: The Impact of the Civil War and Reconstruction on the Constitution* (New York: Alfred A. Knopf, 1973), pp. 182–183, who notes that the power of the Speaker and the evolu-

tion of committees nourished each other during the 1860s.

34. Charles F. Adams, *Memoirs of John Quincy Adams*, vol. 7 (Philadelphia, 1875), p. 373; Asher C. Hinds, *Precedents of the House of Representatives* (Washington, D.C.: Government Printing Office, 1908), §4477, n. 2; *Congressional Globe*, 35th Cong., 1st sess., 1857, p. 40 (remarks of Senator Bayard).

35. See Alexander, *House of Representatives*, p. 240; David J. Rothman, *Politics and Power: The United States Senate, 1869–1901* (Cambridge, Mass.: Harvard University Press, 1966), p. 17; Robinson, "Senate Committee System," pp. 69–72.

36. *Congressional Globe*, 29th Cong., 1st sess., 1846, p. 972 (remarks of Senator Allen); ibid., 34th Cong., 1st sess., 1856, p. 1396 (remarks of Senator Hamlin).

37. See Rothman, *Politics and Power*, pp. 14, 21–24.

38. *Congressional Globe*, 42nd Cong., 1st sess., 1871, pt. 1, p. 130 (quoted in remarks of Representative Garfield); ibid., 27th Cong., 2d sess., 1841, vol. 2, pp. 158–159 (remarks of the Speaker and of Representative Adams); ibid., 36th Cong., 2d sess., 1860, pt. 1, p. 22 (remarks of Representative Hawkins).

39. Robinson, "Senate Committee System," pp. 120–121; James D. Richardson, ed. and comp., *A Compilation of the Messages and Papers of the Presidents*, 11 vols. (New York: Bureau of National Literature, 1911), 7: 523, 531. Rothman, *Politics and Power*, seemingly takes a contrary view that mid-nineteenth-century party organization "could not maintain significant control over the legislative process" (p.13).

40. Richardson, *Messages and Papers*, 2: 448, 449.

41. Ibid., p. 449.

42. Jesse Hoyt to Martin Van Buren, March 21, 1829, quoted in William L. Mackenzie, *The Lives and Opinions of Benj'n Franklin Butler . . . and Jesse Hoyt . . .* (Boston, 1845), pp. 51–52; William T. Barry to Susan Taylor, June 11, 1829, quoted in *American Historical Review*, 16 (1911), 333; William T. Barry to Nathaniel Mitchell, October 3, 1834, in *Niles' Weekly Register*, 47 (November 22, 1834), 186.

43. William M. Gouge, *A Short History of Paper Money and Banking in the United States*, 2nd ed. (New York, 1835), pp. 30–33. On the collapse of traditional centers of social power see Matthew A. Crenson, *The Federal Machine: Beginnings of Bureaucracy in Jacksonian America* (Baltimore: Johns Hopkins University Press, 1975), pp. 143–145. On the theme of a need for restoration see Meyers, *Jacksonian Persuasion*, pp. 16–33.

44. Edward Everett to John McLean, August 1, 1828, in *Proceedings of the Massachusetts Historical Society*, 3d ser., 1 (1907), 361; William T. Barry to Andrew Jackson, April 1, 1835, quoted in Dorothy G. Fowler, *The Cabinet Politician: The Postmasters General, 1829–1909* (New York: Columbia University Press, 1943), p. 17; Barry to S. L. Gouverneur, July 14, 1829, quoted in Fowler, *Cabinet Politician*, p. 16; Barry to Susan Taylor, May 16, 1829, *American Historical Review*, 16 (1911), 332.

45. See U.S., Congress, *House Reports*, no. 103, 23d Cong., 2d sess., 1835, pp. 28–29, 212. There were 10,693 postmasters in 1834, and they received $896,063; in the same year contractors received $1,922,431. See also U.S., Congress, *Senate Reports*, no. 422, 23d Cong., 1st sess., 1834, pp. 11–13.

46. See Amos Kendall to B. F. Butler, June 30, 1835, quoted in Crenson, *Federal Machine*, p. 95; Leonard D. White, *The Jeffersonians: A Study in Administrative History, 1801–1829* (New York: Macmillan, 1951), p. 329.

47. William Stickney, ed., *Autobiography of Amos Kendall* (Boston, 1872), pp. 343–344. See also Crenson, *Federal Machine*, pp. 104–115; Francis P. Weisenburger, *The Life of John McLean: A Politician on the United States Supreme Court* (Columbus: Ohio State University Press, 1937), p. 44.

48. Speech of James Buchanan before the United States Senate, February 14, 1839, quoted in George T. Curtis, *The Life of James Buchanan*, vol. 1 (New York, 1883), p. 381; Richardson, *Messages and Papers*, 2: 460–461. On the suppression of abolitionist tracts see Gilbert H. Barnes, *The Antislavery Impulse,, 1830–1844* (New York: D. Appleton–Century, 1933), pp. 100–101, 247 nn. 1 and 2; Russel B. Nye, *Fettered Freedom: Civil Liberties and the Slavery Controversy, 1830–1860* (East Lansing: Michigan State University Press, 1949), pp. 54–69; Clement Eaton, "Censorship of the Southern Mails," *American Historical Review*, 48 (1942), 266. Local postmasters were deprived of the franking privilege by the Post Office Frauds Act, 5 Stat. 732 (1845).

49. *National Intelligencer*, April 18, 1839, p. 3; U.S., Congress, House, *Executive Documents*, no. 103, 23d Cong., 2d sess., 1835, p. 212.

50. See House, *Executive Documents*, no. 10, 34th Cong, 1st sess., 1853, p. 10; ibid., no. 3, 35th Cong., 2d sess., 1858, pp. 247–249; ibid., no. 2, pt. 2, 49th Cong., 1st sess., 1885, p. xxv; *Senate Reports*, no. 1990, 49th Cong., 2d sess., 1887, p. 73. More than three-fourths of the federal government's total revenue came from customs receipts in the port of New York.

51. See *North American Review*, 91 (1860), 449–450, reporting a public protest by twenty-two sea captains against the delays and bribery required. See also William J. Hartman, "Politics and Patronage: The New York Customs House, 1852–1902" (Ph.D. diss., Columbia University, 1952), pp. 204–205.

52. See *House Reports*, no. 740, 24th Cong., 1st sess., 1836, p. 1.

53. On a merchant's judicial remedies see Nelson, *Americanization of the Common Law*, pp. 17–18, 31, 92–93. The Tariff of 1842, §17, 5 Stat. 564, granted review of original appraisals by two discreet and experienced merchants. If the two agreed, their decision was final; otherwise the collector decided.

54. See U.S., Congress, *House Executive Documents*, no. 2, pt. 2, 49th Cong., 1st sess., 1885, pp. xxiv–xxv. The Customs Administration Act of 1890, 26 Stat. 131, discussed in chapter 5, provided for the creation of a body of precedents against which future evaluations could be compared. The previous system of two merchants, in effect under the 1842 law, could not provide a similar body of precedent because judgments of different

pairs of merchants were too disparate and were inadequately published. For a discussion of an analogous set of problems see Nelson, *Americanization of the Common Law*, pp. 165–170.

55. *House Executive Documents*, no. 2, pt. 2, 49th Cong., 1st sess., 1885, p. xxv; Democratic leader, quoted in Fowler, *Cabinet Politician*, pp. 14–15.

56. *Senate Documents*, no. 460, 26th Cong., 1st sess., 1840, pp. 4–5. See Crenson, *Federal Machine*, pp. 84–87; Malcolm J. Rohrbough, *The Land Office Business: The Settlement and Administration of American Public Lands, 1789–1837* (New York: Oxford University Press, 1968), pp. 21, 32, 96–97, 113–114, 186–189, 197–199, 272, 291.

57. See Paul W. Gates, *History of Public Land Law Development* (Washington, D.C.: Government Printing Office, 1968), pp. 87–103.

58. Quoted in Rohrbough, *Land Office Business*, p. 277. See ibid., pp. 279–283.

59. See generally Alexander H. Meneely, *The War Department, 1861: A Study in Mobilization and Administration* (New York: Columbia University Press, 1928), pp. 100–139, 252–279; Edmund J. Danziger, Jr., *Indians and Bureaucrats: Administering the Reservation Policy during the Civil War* (Urbana.: University of Illinois Press, 1974), pp. 6–7, 11–12; Flora W. Seymour, *Indian Agents of the Old Frontier* (New York: D. Appleton-Century, 1941), pp. 2–3; Herman J. Viola, *Thomas L. McKenney: Architect of America's Early Indian Policy* (Chicago: Swallow Press, 1974), pp. 223–233; White, *Jacksonians*, pp. 187–205, 219–288.

60. Richardson, *Messages and Papers*, 2: 449; William M. Dickson, "The New Political Machine," *North American Review*, 134 (1882), 40, 50.

61. White, *Jacksonians*, pp. 558–560; *Congressional Globe*, 40th Cong., 3d sess., 1869, p. 263 (remarks of Congressman John A. Logan).

62. Theodore Sedgwick, *A Treatise on the Rules Which Govern the Interpretation and Application of Statutory and Constitutional Law* (New York, 1857), p. 141. See generally Horwitz, *Transformation of American Law*, pp. 1–30; Nelson, *Americanization of the Common Law*, pp. 170–174. Legislative awareness of the lawmaking capacity of courts was apparent in the requirement that courts publish their opinions so that the law they made could become known to the people. See Act of February 18, 1864, Iowa Laws of 1864, ch. 22; Willets v. Ridgeway, 9 Ind. 367 (1857); Baker v. Kerr, 13 Iowa 384 (1862).

63. See generally Albert Fishlow, *American Railroads and the Transformation of the Ante-Bellum Economy* (Cambridge, Mass.: Harvard University Press, 1965), pp. 205–261; Paul W. Gates, *The Farmer's Age: Agriculture, 1815–1860* (New York: Holt, Rinehart and Winston, 1960); Constance Green, *American Cities in the Growth of the Nation* (New York: J. DeGraff, 1957), pp. 9–14, 47–50, 62, 80–82; J. Willard Hurst, *Law and the Conditions of Freedom in the Nineteenth-Century United States* (Madison: University of Wisconsin Press, 1956), pp. 3–70; Marvin Meyers, *The Jacksonian Persuasion: Politics and Belief* (Stanford: Stanford University Press, 1957), pp. 121–141; Curtis P. Net-

tels, *The Emergence of a National Economy, 1775–1815* (New York: Holt, Rinehart and Winston, 1962); George R. Taylor, *The Transportation Revolution, 1815–1860* (New York: Rinehart, 1951), p. 207; Harvey H. Segal, "Canals and Economic Development," in *Canals and American Economic Development*, ed. Carter Goodrich (New York: Columbia University Press, 1961), pp. 216, 221–248.

64. Steele v. Curle, 34 Ky. (4 Dana) 381, 390 (1836); Allison v. McCune, 15 Ohio 726, 730 (1846); Pierce v. Proprietors of Swan Point Cemetry, 10 R.I. 227, 241 (1872). See also Joseph Story, "Value and Importance of Legal Studies: A Discourse Pronounced at the Inauguration of the Author as Dane Professor of Law in Harvard University, Aug. 25, 1829," in *The Miscellaneous Writings of Joseph Story*, ed. William W. Story (Boston, 1852), pp. 503, 526.

65. Potter v. Hall, 20 Mass. (3 Pick.) 368, 373 (1825); Silva v. Low, 1 Johns. Cas. 184, 190 (N.Y. Sup. Ct. 1799); McFarland v. Pico, 8 Cal. 626, 631 (1857). Accord, Thurston v. Koch, F. Cas. No. 14,016 (C.C.D. Pa. 1803); Winton v. Saidler, 3 Johns. Cas. 185, 196 (N.Y. Sup. Ct. 1802); Palmer v. Mulligan, 3 Cai. R. 307, 314 (N.Y. Sup. Ct. 1805); Liebert v. The Emperor, Bee's Admiralty Rep. 339, 343 (Pa. 1785); Watkins v. Crouch & Co., 32 Va. (5 Leigh) 522, 530 (1834). See generally Karl N. Llewellyn, *The Common Law Tradition: Deciding Appeals* (Boston: Little, Brown, 1960), pp. 64–72. Early nineteenth-century courts consistently searched for the policy reasons underlying rules; if a rule had a basis in policy, the courts would follow it, but if "the reason of the rule ha[d] ceased," the courts would cease to follow the rule. Campbell v. Johnson, 11 Mass. 184, 187 (1814).

66. Pynchon v. Stearns, 52 Mass. (11 Met.) 304, 312 (1846). The eighteenth-century precedent ignored by the *Pynchon* court was Nash v. Boltwood (Mass. Sup. Jud. Ct. 1783), in William Cushing, "Notes of Cases Decided in the Superior and Supreme Judicial Court of Massachusetts, 1772–1789" (Harvard Law School Library, Cambridge, Mass., 1789), fol. 35a. The court in *Nash* ruled that improvements on virgin land were not a bar to a writ of dower. *Nash* had been cited in a previous opinion of the Massachusetts court. See Webb v. Townsend, 18 Mass. (1 Pick.) 21, 22 (1822). For cases in accord with *Pynchon* v. *Stearns*, see Hastings v. Crunkleton, 3 Yeates 261, 262 (Pa. 1801); Findlay v. Smith, 20 Va. (6 Munf.) 134, 142 (1818). Cf. Van Ness v. Pacard, 27 U.S. (2 Pet.) 137 (1829). See generally Morton J. Horwitz, "The Transformation in the Conception of Property in American Law, 1780–1860," *University of Chicago Law Review*, 40 (1973), 248, 279–284.

67. M'Culloch v. Eagle Insurance Co., 18 Mass. (1 Pick.) 277, 281 (1822). *M'Culloch* was never the majority rule in this country. See Samuel Williston, *A Treatise on the Law of Contracts*, 3d ed., vol. 1 (Mt. Kisco, N.Y.: Baker, Voorhis, 1957), pp. 266–267, n. 4 and the cases cited therein.

68. Parker v. Foote, 19 Wend. 309, 318 (N.Y. Sup. Ct. 1838). Accord, Pierre v. Fernald, 26 Me. 436 (1847); Haverstick v. Sipe, 33 Pa. 368 (1859); Hubbard v. Town, 33 Vt. 295 (1860). See Horwitz, "Transformation in the Conception of Property," pp. 248, 264–265.

69. See Thurston v. Hancock, 12 Mass. 220 (1815); Lasala v. Holbrook, 4 Paige 169 (N.Y. Ch. 1833); Richardson v. Vermont Central R.R., 25 Vt. 465 (1853).

70. See Horwitz, *Transformation of American Law*, pp. 1–30.

71. Proprietors of the Charles River Bridge v. Proprietors of the Warren Bridge, 36 U.S. (11 Pet.) 420, 451–452 (1837) (argument of counsel); Proprietors of the Charles River Bridge v. Proprietors of the Warren Bridge, 24 Mass. (7 Pick.) 344, 508 (1829) (Parker, C. J., dissenting); Proprietors of the Charles River Bridge v. Proprietors of the Warren Bridge, 36 U.S. (11 Pet.) 420, 642 (1837) (Story, J., dissenting); ibid., 547 (opinion of the Court by Taney, C. J.). Like many other cases of the period, *Charles River Bridge* did not follow established American authority. Compare ibid., 567 (McLean, J., concurring), and ibid., 583 (Baldwin, J., concurring), with Chadwick v. Proprietors of the Haverhill Bridge, in Nathan Dane, *A General Abridgement and Digest of American Law*, vol. 2 (Boston, 1823), p. 686; and with L. Kinvin Wroth and Hiller B. Zobel, eds., *Legal Papers of John Adams*, vol. 1 (Cambridge, Mass.: Harvard University Press, 1965), pp. 11, 16. Phillips v. Earle, 25 Mass. (8 Pick.) 182, 184–185 (1829), rejected the same precedents.

72. Gibbons v. Ogden, 22 U.S. (9 Wheat.) 1, 190 (opinion of the Court), 167 (argument of counsel) (1824); Brown v. Maryland, 25 U.S. (12 Wheat.) 419, 434 (1827) (argument of counsel); Swift v. Tyson, 41 U.S. (16 Pet.) 1, 9 (argument of counsel), 20 (opinion of the Court) (1842); Cooley v. Board of Wardens, 53 U.S. (12 How.) 229, 317 (1851). See also United States v. Coombs, 37 U.S. (12 Pet.) 72 (1838); Willson v. Black Bird Creek Marsh Co., 27 U.S. (2 Pet.) 245 (1829). Of course, the idea of national unity to which the Supreme Court gave effect in these cases was more than a merely economic one; it also involved assumptions about America's spiritual and libertarian mission. See generally Frederick Merk, *Manifest Destiny and Mission in American History: A Reinterpretation* (New York: Alfred A. Knopf, 1963), pp. 24–60; Paul C. Nagel, *One Nation Indivisible: The Union in American Thought, 1776–1861* (New York: Oxford University Press, 1964), pp. 145–231. But, as many historians have recognized, the goals of national economic growth and national economic greatness were important elements in the broader concept of national unity. See James McClellan, *Joseph Story and the American Constitution* (Norman: University of Oklahoma Press, 1971), pp. 252–261; Nagel, *One Nation Indivisible*, pp. 19–22, 168–170.

73. On changes in insurance law see James v. Lycoming Insurance Co., F. Cas. No. 7182 (C.C.D. Mass. 1824); Jolly v. Baltimore Equitable Soc'y, 1 Harris & Gill 295 (Md. 1827); Stetson v. Massachusetts Mutual Fire Insurance Co., 4 Mass. 330 (1808). Cf. Thorndike v. Bordman, 21 Mass. (4 Pick.) 471 (1827) (deviation by merchant vessel from route prescribed in marine insurance contract). On the development of the doctrine of substantial performance see Hayward v. Leonard, 24 Mass. (7 Pick.) 181 (1828); Britton v. Turner, 6 N.H. 481 (1834); Fenton v. Clark, 11 Vt. 557 (1839).

74. See Horwitz, *Transformation of American Law*, pp. 160–210, 237–245; Nelson, *Americanization of the Common Law*, pp. 136–144, 154–158.

75. Commonwealth v. M'Closkey, 2 Rawle 369, 374 (Pa. 1803).
76. See State Bank v. Cooper, 10 Tenn. 599 (1831); Fisher's Negroes v. Dabbs, 14 Tenn. 119 (1834). On the divisive character of the issue of government aid to banks, see Hartz, *Economic Policy and Democratic Thought*, pp. 69–79; Schlesinger, *Age of Jackson*, pp. 90–97. On the imposition of stricter controls on blacks see John Hope Franklin, *The Free Negro in North Carolina, 1790–1860* (Chapel Hill: University of North Carolina Press, 1943), pp. 58–120; Charles S. Sydnor, *The Development of Southern Sectionalism, 1819–1848* (Baton Rouge: Louisiana State University Press, 1948), pp. 227–229; Alice F. Tyler, *Freedom's Ferment* (Minneapolis: University of Minnesota Press, 1944), pp. 513–519.
77. For eminent domain cases see Taylor v. Porter, 4 Hill 140, 145–146 (N.Y. 1843); Bloodgood v. Mohawk & H.R.R., 18 Wend. 9, 63 (N.Y. Ct. Err. 1837) (opinion of Senator Tracy). For cases involving the constitutionality of debtor relief legislation see Sturges v. Crowninshield, 17 U.S. (4 Wheat.) 122 (1819); Blair v. Williams, 14 Ky. (4 Littell) 34 (1823); Lapsley v. Brashears, 14 Ky. (4 Littell) 47 (1823). See also Grimball v. Ross, T. Char't 175 (Ga. 1808), where the court sustained debtor relief legislation. See generally Charles Warren, *The Supreme Court in United States History*, rev. ed., vol. 1 (Boston: Little, Brown, 1926), pp. 29–35; Harry N. Scheiber, "The Road to Munn: Eminent Domain and the Concept of Public Purpose in the State Courts," *Perspectives in American History*, 5 (1971), 327, 360–376.
78. See Hartz, *Economic Policy and Democratic Thought*, pp. 104–109, 204–219; Tyler, *Freedom's Ferment*, pp. 347–350, 459–460.
79. See Nougues v. Douglass, 7 Cal. 65 (1857) (erection of state capitol); Beebe v. State, 6 Ind. 501 (1855) (alcoholic beverages); Wynehamer v. People, 13 N.Y. 378 (1856) (alcoholic beverages); Westervelt v. Gregg, 12 N.Y. 202 (1854) (married women's rights); Newell v. People ex rel. Phelps, 7 N.Y. 9 (1852) (canals); White v. White, 5 Barb. 474 (N.Y. Sup. Ct. 1849) (married women's rights); Holmes v. Holmes, 4 Barb. 295 (N.Y. Sup. Ct. 1848) (married women's rights).
80. See Debow v. People, 1 Denio 9 (N.Y. 1845). On the divisiveness of issues relating to banking see Schlesinger, *Age of Jackson*, pp. 286–287, 336–339.
81. See Opinion of the Supreme Court, 3 R.I. 299 (1854). For a discussion of the Dorr War see George M. Dennison, *The Dorr War: Republicanism on Trial, 1831–1861* (Lexington, Ky.: University of Kentucky Press, 1976); Marvin E. Gettleman, *The Dorr Rebellion: A Study in American Radicalism: 1833–1849* (New York: Random House, 1973).
82. DeBow v. People, 1 Denio 9, 19 (N.Y. 1845); Ward v. Barnard, 1 Aikens 121, 126 (Vt. 1825); Regents of the University of Maryland v. Williams, 9 Gill & Johns. 365, 383 (Md. 1838); Goddin v. Crump, 35 Va. (8 Leigh) 120, 150 (1837).
83. Dorman v. State, 34 Ala. 216, 235 (1859); Fisher's Negroes v. Dabbs, 14 Tenn. 119, 166 (1834); Bloodgood v. Mohawk & H.R.R., 18 Wend. 9, 31 (N.Y. Ct. Err. 1837). Accord, Ex parte Martin, 13 Ark. 198,

206 (1853); Wynehamer v. People, 13 N.Y. 378, 411, 475 (1856).

84. Quoted in William T. Utter, "Judicial Review in Early Ohio," *Mississippi Valley Historical Review*, 14 (1927), 3, 17. See generally ibid., pp. 9-11, 16-18.

85. See Albert B. Saye, *A Constitutional History of Georgia, 1732-1968*, rev. ed. (Athens: University of Georgia Press, 1970), pp. 190-191.

86. Quoted in William D. Lewis, ed., *Great American Lawyers*, vol. 2 (Philadelphia: John C. Winston, 1907), p. 251. For a description of the two Kentucky decisions — Blair v. Williams, 14 Ky. (4 Littell) 34 (1823), and Lapsley v. Brashears, 14 Ky. (4 Littell) 47 (1823) — invalidating the 1819 stay law and the events surrounding them, see Lewis, *Great American Lawyers*, 2: 253-258.

87. Eakin v. Raub, 12 S. & R. 330, 344, 346-347, 349-351, 355 (emphasis in original). For a discussion of Gibson's views on judicial review see Stanley I. Kutler, "John Bannister Gibson, Judicial Restraint and the 'Positive State,' " *Journal of Public Law*, 14 (1865), 181.

88. Bennett v. Boggs, F. Cas. No. 1319 (C.C.D.N.J. 1830); Commonwealth v. M'Closkey, 2 Rawle 369, 374 (Pa. 1830); Cochran v. Van Surlay, 20 Wend. 365, 382 (N.Y. Ct. Err. 1838). Accord, Beekman v. Saratoga & S.R.R., 3 Paige 45, 49 (N.Y. 1831).

89. DeChastellux v. Fairchild, 15 Pa. 18, 20 (1850).

90. See Evan Haynes, *The Selection and Tenure of Judges* (Newark, N.J.: National Conference of Judicial Councils, 1944), pp. 101-135.

91. See Kermit L. Hall, *The Politics of Justice: Lower Federal Judicial Selection and the Second Party System, 1829-1861* (Lincoln: University of Nebraska Press, 1979), pp. 169-170.

92. See Haynes, *Selection and Tenure of Judges*, pp. 89-101.

93. See ibid., pp. 99-100, 117.

2. The Antislavery Movement and Moralistic Objections to Majoritarian Democracy

1. See Don E. Fehrenbacher, *The Dred Scott Case: Its Significance in American Law and Politics* (New York: Oxford University Press, 1978), pp. 135-147; David M. Potter, *The Impending Crisis, 1848-1861* (New York: Harper & Row, 1976), pp. 171-176.

2. See Fehrenbacher, *Dred Scott Case*, pp. 134-135, 139, 154-156, 367-384; Potter, *Impending Crisis*, p. 60.

3. "The Address of the People of South Carolina, Assembled in Convention, to the People of the Slaveholding States of the United States," in *South Carolina Secedes*, ed. John A. May and Joan R. Faunt (Columbia: University of South Carolina Press, 1960), p. 82. On the analogy between the American Revolution and the Civil War see Emory M. Thomas, *The Confederacy as a Revolutionary Experience* (Englewood Cliffs, N.J.: Prentice-Hall, 1971), pp. 1-2, 35, 44-51. On Calhoun and interposition see August O.

Spain, *The Political Theory of John C. Calhoun* (New York: Bookman Associates, 1951), pp. 105–157; Charles S. Sydnor, *The Development of Southern Sectionalism, 1819–1848* (Baton Rouge: Louisiana State University Press, 1948), pp. 211–214.

4. William E. Channing, "Likeness to God," in *The Transcendentalists: An Anthology*, ed. Perry Miller (Cambridge, Mass.: Harvard University Press, 1950), pp. 21, 24–25; Theodore Parker, *The Previous Question between Mr. Andrews Norton and His Alumni* (Boston, 1840), p. 23; idem, *A Discourse on the Transient and Permanent in Christianity*, 2d ed. (Boston, 1841), p. 28; idem, "The Administration of President Polk," in idem, *The Rights of Man in America*, ed. F. B. Sanborn (Boston: American Unitarian Association, 1911), pp. 48, 88; Charles G. Finney, *Sermons on Gospel Themes* (New York, 1876), p. 252; Lyman Beecher, *Letters of the Rev. Dr. Beecher and Rev. Mr. Nettleton, on the "New Measures" in Conducting Revivals of Religion* (New York, 1828), pp. 90, 93. See also *Baptist Register*, 14 (1837), 74, quoted in Whitney R. Cross, *The Burned-Over District* (Ithaca, N.Y.: Cornell University Press, 1950), p. 201. On the power of religion, especially evangelical religion, in nineteenth-century American life, see Perry Miller, *The Life of the Mind in America from the Revolution to the Civil War* (New York: Harcourt, Brace & World, 1965), pp. 3–95. One evangelical preacher, Theodore Weld, who also served as an antislavery activist throughout New York and the Western Reserve of Ohio, encapsulated the religious position against slavery: "The cause we are wedded to is the cause of *changeless eternal right*. God has decreed its ultimate triumph, and if the signs of the times are not mockers, the victory shout will ring around the world before the generation that now is, goes to the dead." Theodore Weld to Elizur Wright, Jr., January 10, 1833, in *Letters of Theodore Dwight Weld, Angelina Grimke Weld and Sara Grimke, 1822–1844*, ed. Gilbert H. Barnes and Dwight L. Dumond, vol. 1 (New York: D. Appleton–Century, 1934), p. 100. For a biography of Weld see Benjamin P. Thomas, *Theodore Weld: Crusader for Freedom* (New Brunswick, N.J.: Rutgers University Press, 1950).

5. Orestes A. Brownson, "New Views of Christianity, Society, and the Church," in Miller, *The Transcendentalists*, pp. 114, 118; George Ripley, "James Mackintosh," in ibid., pp. 65–66; James Marsh, "Preliminary Essay," in ibid., pp. 34, 37; Frederic H. Hedge, "Progress of Society," in ibid., pp. 72, 74; Ralph Waldo Emerson, "Self-Reliance," in *The Golden Age of American Literature*, ed. Perry Miller (New York: G. Braziller, 1959), pp. 101, 112.

6. See Miller, *The Transcendentalists*, pp. 124, 449; preface by F. B. Sanborn in Parker, *Rights of Man*, pp. iii–xxxviii; Thomas, *Theodore Weld*, pp. 68–87, 191–214.

7. Quoted in David Donald, *Charles Sumner and the Coming of the Civil War* (New York: Alfred A. Knopf, 1960), pp. 100, 133; John P. Hale to Mrs. Hale, April 18, 1843, quoted in Richard H. Sewell, *John P. Hale and the Politics of Abolition* (Cambridge, Mass.: Harvard University Press, 1965), pp. 33–34; Ralph V. Harlow, *Gerrit Smith, Philanthropist and Reformer* (New

York; H. Holt, 1939), p. 193; Octavius B. Frothingham, *Gerrit Smith* (New York, 1878), pp. 172–173.

8. See Cross, *Burned-Over District*, pp. 218–226; Thomas, *Theodore Weld*, p. 211.

9. See Bernard Bailyn, *The Ideological Origins of the American Revolution* (Cambridge, Mass.: Harvard University Press, 1967), pp. 175–198; Gordon S. Wood, *The Creation of the American Republic* (Chapel Hill: University of North Carolina Press, 1969), pp. 259–305. Some antislavery thinkers contended that rights were bestowed on man by God; others contended that they were inherent in the concept of man or were bestowed by nature. See Winthrop D. Jordan, *White over Black: American Attitudes toward the Negro, 1550-1812* (Chapel Hill: University of North Carolina Press, 1968), pp. 292–294. For the distinction between right-based political theories, like those of the eighteenth-century American revolutionaries, and duty-based theories, like those based upon the law of God, see Ronald Dworkin, "The Original Position," *University of Chicago Law Review*, 40 (1973), 500, 519–524. Dworkin distinguishes both from goal-based theories, like nineteenth-century instrumentalism.

10. Commonwealth v. White (Mass. Sup. Jud. Ct., Cumberland County 1787), in Robert T. Paine, "Criminal Trials: Minutes of the Attorney General, 1780–1789," Massachusetts Historical Society, Boston; Commonwealth v. Green, 17 Mass. 515, 517 (1822). The increasing concern over procedural rights of defendants in criminal trials was also reflected in the courts of other states. See State v. Ledford, 3 Mo. 75, 76–77 (1832) (holding based upon right of defendent not to be deprived of "life, liberty, and property, but by the law of the land"); In re Thorn, 4 City Hall Rec. 81, 86 (N.Y. Mayor's Ct. 1819) (holding confessions made under a promise of favor invalid and inadmissible as evidence at trial); State v. Hobbs, 2 Tyler 380 (Vt. 1803) (holding right against self-incrimination guaranteed in state criminal prosecutions).

11. Petition of Negro Slaves, 1777, quoted in Jordan, *White over Black*, p. 291 (emphasis deleted); Commonwealth v. Jennison (Mass. 1783), in William Cushing, "Notes of Cases Decided in the Superior and Supreme Judicial Court of Massachusetts, 1772–1789" (Harvard Law School Library, Cambridge, Mass., 1789), fols. 50, 51; St. George Tucker, ed., *Blackstone's Commentaries*, vol. 2 (Philadelphia, 1803), app., pp. 41–42. See generally Jordan, *White over Black*, pp. 287–304.

12. James Kent, *Commentaries on American Law*, 4 vols. (New York, 1826–1830), 2:1 and 1: 419; Gardner v. Village of Newburgh, 2 Johns. Ch. 162, 166 (N.Y. 1816); Terret v. Taylor, 13 U.S. (9 Cranch) 43, 50, 52 (1815).

13. See Ellis v. Marshall, 2 Mass. 269 (1807); Gardner v. Village of Newburgh, 2 Johns. Ch. 162 (N.Y. 1816); Ham v. M'Claws, 1 Bay 93, 98 (S.C. 1789).

14. Calder v. Bull, 3 U.S. (3 Dall.) 386, 388 (1798); Terret v. Taylor, 13 U.S. (9 Cranch) 43, 50–52 (1815); Wilkinson v. Leland, 27 U.S. (2 Pet.) 627, 657 (1829).

15. Taylor v. Porter, 4 Hill 140, 145 (N.Y. Sup. Ct. 1843); Regents of the University of Maryland v. Williams, 9 G. & J. 365, 408 (Md. 1838); Goshen v. Inhabitants of Stonington, 4 Conn. 209, 224–225 (1822); Langdon v. Strong, 2 Vt. 234, 256 (1829). For additional cases supporting, at least in dictum, the judiciary's inherent power, independent of constitutional provisions, to invalidate legislative enactments as contrary to fundamental principles of justice, see Varick v. Smith, 5 Paige 137 (N.Y. Ch. 1835); Rogers v. Bradshaw, 20 Johns. 735 (N.Y. Ct. Err. 1823); People v. Platt, 17 Johns. 195 (N.Y. Sup. Ct. 1819); Raleigh & G.R.R. v. Davis, 2 Dev. & Bat. 451 (N.C. 1837); Bradee v. Brownfield, 2 W. & S. 271, 278 (Pa. 1841); Hatch v. Vermont Central R.R., 25 Vt. 49 (1852); Lyman v. Mower, 2 Vt. 517, 519 (1830).

16. Bennett v. Boggs, F. Cas. No. 1319 (C.C.D.N.J. 1830). See also Theodore Sedgwick, *A Treatise on the Rules Which Govern the Interpretation and Application of Statutory and Constitutional Law* (New York, 1857), pp. 180–187.

17. See Wynehamer v. People, 13 N.Y. 378, 428–429 (1856) (Selden, J.); People v. Edmonds, 15 Barb. 529 (N.Y. Sup. Ct. 1853); Benson v. Mayor of New York, 10 Barb. 223 (N.Y. Sup. Ct. 1850); People ex rel. Fountain v. Board of Supervisors, 4 Barb. 64 (N.Y. Sup. Ct. 1848); Sharpless v. Mayor of Philadelphia, 21 Pa. 147, 164 (1853).

18. See Jordan, *White over Black*, pp. 349–356; Aileen S. Kraditor, *Means and Ends in American Abolitionism* (New York: Pantheon, 1969), pp. 185–189; Russel B. Nye, *Fettered Freedom: Civil Liberties and the Slavery Controversy, 1830–1860* (East Lansing: Michigan State University Press, 1963), pp. 235–244; William M. Wiecek, *The Sources of Antislavery Constitutionalism in America, 1760–1848* (Ithaca, N.Y.: Cornell University Press, 1977), pp. 228–248. Wiecek explores fully the ambiguities in antislavery thought.

19. The first gag rule, known as the Pickney gag rule, was enacted for the duration of the current House session on May 26, 1836. See U.S., Congress, House, *Congressional Globe*, 24th Cong., 1st sess., 1836, pp. 505–506. In each of the next three years, the House voted for a session-long gag rule on slavery-related petitions, and in January 1840 it enacted the toughest gag rule of all as Standing Rule 21. See *Congressional Globe,* 25th Cong., 2d sess., 1837, p. 45; ibid., 26th Cong., 1st sess., 1839, p. 89; ibid., 26th Cong., 1st sess., 1840, pp.150–151. This rule stood for five sessions of Congress, until the abolitionists, their friends, and other defenders of civil liberties gathered sufficient strength to repeal it. See *Congressional Globe*, 28 Cong., 2d sess., 1844, p. 7.

20. On the barring of the mails see Gilbert H. Barnes, *The Antislavery Impulse, 1830–1844* (New York: D. Appleton–Century, 1933), pp. 100–101; Nye, *Fettered Freedom*, pp. 67–70, 80–85. For typical accounts of the attacks on abolitionist editors, see Barnes, *Antislavery Impulse*, p. 39; Nye, *Fettered Freedom*, pp. 117–218. For the views of antislavery advocates on the Mexican War see Martin B. Duberman, *Charles Francis Adams, 1807–1886* (Boston: Houghton Mifflin, 1961), pp. 87–89, 110–112; Frederick Merk, *Manifest Destiny and Mission in American History: A Reinterpretation* (New York:

Alfred A. Knopf, 1963), pp. 21–22; Nye, *Fettered Freedom*, p. 296; Sewell, *John P. Hale*, pp. 47–48.

21. John Quincy Adams, quoted in Barnes, *Antislavery Impulse*, p. 110; William W. Slade, *Speech on the Right of Petition . . . Delivered in the House of Representatives, on the 18th and 20th January, 1840* (Washington, D.C. 1840), p. 4; John Quincy Adams, quoted in Nye, *Fettered Freedom*, p. 49. See also *Congressional Globe*, 24th Cong., 1st sess., 1836, p. 506; Cincinnati *Philanthropist*, January 1, 1836, p. 3; ibid., March 31, 1840, p. 1.

22. *Dayton Republican*, quoted in Nye, *Fettered Freedom*, pp.79–80; Cincinnati *Philanthropist*, July 8, 1836, p. 4.

23. *Cincinnati Daily Gazette*, August 4, 1836, p. 2; ibid., July 20, 1836, p. 2; *St. Louis Observer*, November 5, 1835; Massachusetts Anti-Slavery Society, *Annual Report of the Board of Managers*, vol. 5 (Boston, 1837), p. 6; *St. Louis Observer*, November 5, 1835. For further expressions of such sentiments see Massachusetts Anti-Slavery Society, *An Account of the Interviews Which Took Place on the Fourth and Eighth of March, between a Committee of the Massachusetts Anti-Slavery Society, and the Committee of the Legislature* (Boston, 1836), p. 11; Cincinnati *Philanthropist*, February 12, 1836. Similarly, William E. Channing, the New England divine, saw the abolitionists as "sufferers for liberty of thought, speech, and the press" and believed that for "maintaining this liberty amidst insult and violence, they deserve[d] a place among its most honored defenders " William E. Channing, *Works*, vol. 2 (Boston, 1843), p. 159.

24. Lysander Spooner, quoted in Jacobus TenBroek, *The Antislavery Origins of the Fourteenth Amendment* (Berkeley: University of California Press, 1951), p. 54, n. 17; William E. Channing, *Slavery*, 4th rev. ed. (Boston, 1836), p. 31; *Address by William Swain to the People of North Carolina on the Evils of Slavery*, quoted in Nye, *Fettered Freedom*, p. 224; statement by the American Anti-Slavery Society Convention, 1833, quoted in Nye, *Fettered Freedom*, p. 224; *Anti-Slavery Bugle*, March 3, 1856; John Quincy Adams, quoted in TenBroek, *Antislavery Origins*, pp. 62–63, n. 20; Joel Tiffany, quoted in ibid., p. 62, n. 20; John Quincy Adams, quoted in ibid., p. 62–63, n. 20. See also Channing, *Slavery*, p. 31. For some, however, "the Constitution . . . [was] a temple of liberty" because it incorporated the principles stated in the Declaration of Independence; Gerrit Smith to Salmon P. Chase, in *Albany Patriot*, November 10, 1847.

25. Argument by Salmon P. Chase in *Matilda's Case*, Court of Common Pleas of Hamilton County, Ohio, March 11, 1837, quoted in TenBroek, *Antislavery Origins*, p. 39; *Congressional Globe*, 33d Cong., 1st sess., 1854, app., p. 138 (remarks of Senator Chase); *National Anti-Slavery Standard*, February 21, 1857; Parker, *The Previous Question*, p. 363.

26. William Birney, *James G. Birney and His Times* (New York, 1890), p. 243 (emphasis deleted); New York *Evening Post*, November 18, 1837; *Emancipator*, July 22, 1834, p. 1; Henry B. Stanton, *Remarks in the Representatives Hall on the 23rd and 24th of February, 1837, before the Committee of the House of Representatives of Massachusetts*, 5th ed., (Boston, 1837), p. 34: Gerrit

Smith to Salmon P. Chase, in *Albany Patriot*, November 10, 1847. See also *Chicago Democrat*, November 5, 1860.

27. Stanton, *Remarks in the Representatives Hall*, p. 34; *Congressional Globe*, 35th Cong., 2d sess., 1859, p. 346 (remarks of Senator Giddings); Charles Olcott, quoted in TenBroek, *Antislavery Origins*, p. 26; Stanton, *Remarks in the Representatives Hall*, p. 34; William H. Seward, *Works*, ed. George E. Baker, rev. ed., vol. 4 (Boston, 1884), p. 302.

28. "Call for the Macedon Convention, 1847," quoted in TenBroek, *Antislavery Origins*, p. 117, n. 2; Schuyler Colfax, quoted in Ovando J. Hollister, *Life of Schuyler Colfax* (New York, 1886), p. 161; *North Star*, September 22, 1848.

29. Roy P. Basler, ed., *The Collected Works of Abraham Lincoln*, vol. 2 (New Brunswick, N.J.: Rutgers University Press, 1953), p. 405; "Call for the Macedon Convention, 1847," quoted in TenBroek, *Antislavery Origins*, pp. 117–118, n. 2; Laura E. Richards, ed., *Letters and Journals of Samuel Gridley Howe* (Boston: D. Estes, 1909), p. 385.

30. See Eric Foner, *Free Soil, Free Labor, Free Men: The Ideology of the Republican Party before the Civil War* (New York: Oxford University Press, 1970), pp. 11–39.

31. See Potter, *Impending Crisis*, pp. 154–162; Arthur M. Schlesinger, Jr., *The Age of Jackson* (Boston: Little, Brown, 1945), p. 463.

32. "Speech of Senator Douglas, on the Occasion of His Public Reception at Chicago, July 9, 1858," in *Political Debates between Abraham Lincoln and Stephen A. Douglas* (Cleveland, 1895), pp. 12, 13.

33. See Andrew W. Crandall, *The Early History of the Republican Party, 1854–1856* (Boston: R. G. Badger, 1930), pp. 17–26, 43–53.

34. "First Joint Debate, at Ottawa, Ill., August 21, 1858," in *Political Debates between Lincoln and Douglas*, pp.101, 126–127.

35. Prigg v. Pennsylvania, 41 U.S. (16 Pet.) 539, 611 (1842); Proprietors of the Charles River Bridge v. Proprietors of the Warren Bridge, 36 U.S. (11 Pet.) 420, 547 (1837). In upholding Prigg's contentions—first, that the fugitive-slave clause of the Constitution gave Congress exclusive power to legislate on the subject of fugitive slaves; second, that even if legislative power in the area were concurrent, congressional exercise of the power displaced all state legislation; and third, that even if state legislative power had not been displaced, the state statute was directly inconsistant with the Fugitive Slave Act of 1793 and hence was void—Justice Story was interested chiefly in gaining southern support for his long-held views on the issues of preemptation and the scope of federal legislative power. See Gerald Dunne, *Justice Joseph Story and the Rise of the Supreme Court* (New York: Simon and Schuster, 1970), pp. 398–402; James P. McClellan, *Joseph Story and the American Constitution: A Study in Political and Legal Thought with Selected Writings* (Norman: University of Oklahoma Press, 1971), pp. 261–263. For other examples of Story's instrumentalism and of his concern for national unity and economic growth, see Joseph Story, "Value and Importance of Legal Studies: A Discourse Pronounced at the Inauguration of the Author

as Dane Professor of Law in Harvard University, Aug. 25, 1829," in *The Miscellaneous Writings of Joseph Story*, ed. William W. Story (Boston, 1852), pp. 503, 526; Joseph Story, "Review of David Hoffman's Course of Legal Study," *North American Review*, 6 (1817), 45, 49. As his two recent biographers have noted, Story was "a firm advocate of growth and expansion" who "was keenly desirous of encouraging commerce and trade" (McClellan, *Joseph Story*, pp. 50, 252) by creating "a relevant and authentically American law of commerce" (Dunne, *Justice Joseph Story*, p. 387). See generally Dunne, *Justice Joseph Story*, pp. 101–102, 386–387; McClellan, *Joseph Story*, pp. 50–52, 252–261. At the same time, Story was a firm believer in natural law and in the inalienable rights of free men. See generally McClellan, *Joseph Story*, pp. 61–117, 194–237. Story's adherence to such seemingly inconsistent views of law raises a paradox that cannot be explored fully here. A possible explanation may be that he died a mere two years after the decision in *Prigg*, so that he was never forced to confront the inconsistency between instrumentalism and concepts of higher law and human rights except, perhaps, in *Prigg* itself. In his opinion in *Charles River Bridge*, for example, the various styles of reasoning all led to consistent results.

36. *Liberator*, November 4, 1842, p. 175. The case is also reported as Latimer Case, 5 Law Rep. 481 (Mass. 1843). On Shaw's instrumentalism see Leonard W. Levy, *The Law of the Commonwealth and Chief Justice Shaw* (Cambridge, Mass.: Harvard University Press, 1957), pp. 118–182. For the text of Massachusetts's Personal Liberty Law, see [1837] Laws of Mass., ch. 221. The act gauranteed to anyone "imprisoned, restrained of his liberty, or held in duress" a "writ of personal replevin," unless such detention was "in the custody of some public officer . . . by force of a lawful warrant or other process . . . issued by a court of competent jurisdiction."

37. Jones v. Van Zandt, 46 U.S. (5 How.) 215, 229 (1847).

38. *Liberator*, March 18, 1842, p. 41; ibid., March 11, 1842, p. 39; 5 Law Rep. 492 (1843); *Liberator*, November 4, 1842, p. 175; Jacob W. Schuckers, *The Life and Public Services of Salmon Portland Chase* (New York, 1874), p. 63, quoting Chase's argument in Van Zandt. For similar criticisms of these court decisions see Massachusetts Anti-Slavery Society, *Annual Report of the Board of Managers*, vols. 11 (Boston, 1843), pp. 70–71, 76; 12 (Boston, 1844), p. 4; and 16 (Boston, 1848), pp. 54–55; *Emancipator and Free American*, November 3, 1842.

39. Act of September 18, 1850, ch. 60, 9 Stat. 462; Massachusetts Anti-Slavery Society, *Annual Report of the Board of Managers*, vol. 19 (Boston, 1851), pp. 42, 45 (emphasis deleted); United States v. Hanway, F. Cas. No. 15,299, at 111 (C.C.E.D. Pa. 1851) (referring to denunciations of the Fugitive Slave Act by antislavery conventions); ibid., 123; Oliver v. Kauffman, F. Cas. No. 10,497 (C.C.E.D. Pa. 1850); Sim's Case, 61 Mass. (7 Cush.) 285, 319 (1851).

40. Ableman v. Booth, 62 U.S. (21 How.) 506 (1859), reversing In re Booth, 3 Wis. 1 (1854), and In re Booth, 3 Wis. 157 (1854).

41. In re Booth, 3 Wis. 1, 41–42, 91. See also ibid., 7–39.

42. Ableman v. Booth, 62 U.S. (21 How.) 506, 515, 517 (1859). For a leading example of Chief Justice Taney's instrumentalist bent, see his opinion for the Court in Proprietors of the Charles River Bridge v. Proprietors of the Warren Bridge, 36 U.S. (11 Pet.) 420 (1837).

43. For a summary of the views of such historians see Thomas J. Pressly, *Americans Interpret Their Civil War* (Princeton: Princeton University Press, 1954), pp. 204-214, 257-292.

44. 60 U.S. (19 How.) 393 (1857). Two recent books on the case are Walter Ehrlich, *They Have No Rights: Dred Scott's Struggle for Freedom* (Westport, Conn.: Greenwood Press, 1979), and Fehrenbacher, *Dred Scott Case*.

45. 51 U.S. (10 How.) 82 (1850). For a recent discussion of the *Strader* case see Paul Finkelman, *An Imperfect Union: Slavery, Federalism, and Comity* (Chapel Hill: University of North Carolina Press, 1981), pp. 271-274.

46. Scott v. Sandford, 60 U.S. (19 How.) 393, 455 (1857) (Wayne, J., concurring). For the text of the Missouri Compromise, see Act of March 6, 1820, ch. 22, §8, 3 Stat. 548. For the Northwest Ordinance, see An Ordinance for the Government of the Territory of the United States North-west of the River Ohio, July 13, 1787, art. 6, 1 Stat. 51n., reenacted as Act of August 7, 1789, ch. 8, 1 Stat. 50.

47. "Report to the New York Senate and Assembly, April 9th 1857," in *Case of Dred Scott* (New York, 1857), p. 102. For a survey of the reaction to Scott v. Sandford, see Fehrenbacher, *Dred Scott Case*, pp. 417-443.

48. Lemmon v. People, 20 N.Y. 562, 617, 628 (1860); ibid., 634 (Clerke, J., dissenting). The case is discussed in Finkelman, *Imperfect Union*, pp. 296-312.

49. *New York Tribune*, March 11, 1857, p. 4. See Fehrenbacher, *Dred Scott Case*, pp. 437-438, 444-445; Finkelman, *Imperfect Union*, pp. 313-336.

50. See Warren, *Supreme Court*, 2: 360-367.

51. Not only the radicals but also most moderate and conservative Republicans had strong antislavery convictions. See Foner, *Free Soil, Free Labor, Free Men*, pp. 186-225. The Republican party, of course, won every national election during the 1860s and majority of national elections during the remainder of the century.

3. The Triumph and Failure of Antislavery and the Transformation of Federalism

1. B.F. Morris, *Christian Life and Character of the Civil Institutions of the United States, Developed in the Official and Historical Annuals of the Republic* (Philadelphia, 1864), pp. 670, 682; Charles E. Norton, "American Political Ideas," *North American Review*, 101 (1865), 550, 559; Charles Sumner, quoted in Walter T. Mills, *The Science of Politics*, rev. ed. (New York, 1881), p. 186; Albert B. Hart, quoted in Paul Buck, ed., *The Social Sciences at Harvard, 1860-1920* (Cambridge, Mass.: Harvard University Press, 1965), p. 130. See also John G. Sproat, *"The Best Men": Liberal Reformers in the Gilded Age* (New York: Oxford University Press, 1968), pp. 52, 68.

2. " 'Politics' and Dirt," *Nation*, 32 (1881), 198, 199; Carl Schurz, "Address to the People," in *Speeches, Correspondence, and Political Papers of Carl Schurz*, ed. Frederic Bancroft, 6 vols. (New York: G.P. Putnam, 1913), 3: 240, 242; "The Republican Troubles," *Nation*, 5 (1867), 314; *Springfield Republican*, November 1, 1872, quoted in Sproat, "*The Best Men*," p. 52; "Civil Service Reform: An Address Delivered before the American Social Science Association at its Meeting in New York, in October 1869," in *Orations and Addresses of George William Curtis*, ed. Charles E. Norton, vol. 2 (New York, 1894), pp. 1, 28; "The Republican Troubles," *Nation*, 5 (1867), 314; Charles F. Adams, Jr., "Railroad Inflation," *North American Review*, 108 (1869), 130, 159.

3. Orestes A. Brownson, *The American Republic: Its Constitution, Tendencies, and Destiny* (New York, 1866), pp. 131, 272–273.

4. See, e.g., U.S., Congress, House, *Congressional Globe*, 39th Cong., 1st sess., 1866, app., pp. 133–135 (remarks of Congressman Rogers). Another Democrat who showed his disdain for the popular will was Grover Cleveland. Early in his term as governor of New York, he vetoed a popular rapid transit fare-reduction bill on the ground that the legislature was breaching its promise to the transit owners that the "State should not only be strictly just, but scrupulously fair, and in its relations to the citizen every legal and moral consideration should be recognized." Quoted in Allan Nevins, *Grover Cleveland: A Study in Courage* (New York: Dodd, Mead, 1932), p. 117.

5. "Roger Brooke Taney," *Atlantic Monthly*, 15 (1865), 151, 153–155; *Congressional Globe*, 38th Cong., 2d sess., 1865, p. 1013 (remarks of Senator Hale); William G. Sumner, *Andrew Jackson* (Boston: Houghton Mifflin, 1899), p. 427. See generally Harold M. Hyman, *A More Perfect Union: The Impact of the Civil War and Reconstruction on the Constitution* (New York: Alfred A. Knopf, 1973), pp. 504–505, 540–542; Stanley I. Kutler, *Judicial Power and Reconstruction Politics* (Chicago: University of Chicago Press, 1968); Phillip S. Paludan, *A Covenant with Death: The Constitution, Law, and Equality in the Civil War Era* (Urbana: University of Illinois Press, 1975), pp. 123, 227–233.

6. Samuel J. Barrows, *Municipal Reform* (New York, 1888), p. 17; speech by Carl Schurz, "Why James G. Blaine Should Not Be President," August 5, 1884, in Bancroft, *Speeches . . . of Carl Schurz*, 4: 224, 267; "What Mr. Cleveland Has Done," *Nation*, 44 (1887), 202. For Schurz's transformation from an advocate of antislavery into a civil service reformer, see Hans L. Trefousse, "Carl Schurz, the South, and the Politics of Virtue," in *Before Watergate: Problems of Corruption in American Society*, ed. Abraham S. Eisenstadt et al. (Brooklyn: Brooklyn College Press, 1978), p. 99. See generally Sproat, "*The Best Men*," pp. 266–267.

7. See David Donald, *Charles Sumner and the Rights of Man* (New York: Alfred A. Knopf, 1970), pp. 218–229, 231; William Gillette, *The Right to Vote: Politics and the Passage of the Fifteenth Amendment* (Baltimore; Johns Hopkins University Press, 1965), pp. 22–32; Joseph B. James, *The Framing of the Fourteenth Amendment* (Urbana: University of Illinois Press, 1956). pp. 3–20.

8. Bingham made the following seemingly incongruous statement on the House floor: "To be sure we all agree, and the great body of the people of this country agree, and the committee thus far in reporting measures of reconstruction agree, that the exercise of the elective franchise, though it be one of the privileges of a citizen of the Republic, is exclusively under the control of the States." *Congressional Globe*, 39th Cong., 1st sess., 1866, p. 2542. I understand Bingham to be stating that, although states have plenary control over the right to vote, all states have in fact granted the privilege of voting to citizens and have thereby transformed voting into a privilege guaranteed by the new Fourteenth Amendment, which privilege must be administered fairly and equally. I am currently working on an essay on what Bingham and others in the Thirty-ninth Congress understood section 1 of the Fourteenth Amendment to mean.

9. See Michael Les Benedict, *A Compromise of Principle: Congressional Republicans and Reconstruction, 1863–1869* (New York: Norton, 1974), pp. 125–126; Eric L. McKitrick, *Andrew Johnson and Reconstruction* (Chicago: University of Chicago Press, 1960), pp. 99–119; Paludan, *Covenant with Death*, p. 41.

10. See Michael Les Benedict, *The Impeachment and Trial of Andrew Johnson* (New York: Norton, 1973), pp. 173–180; Claude G. Bowers, *The Tragic Era: The Revolution after Lincoln* (Boston: Houghton Mifflin, 1929), pp. 196–197; Lloyd P. Stryker, *Andrew Johnson: A Study in Courage* (New York: Macmillan, 1929), pp. 732–733; Hans L. Trefousse, *Impeachment of a President: Andrew Johnson, the Blacks and Reconstruction* (Knoxville: University of Tennessee Press, 1975), pp. 169–181; Ralph J. Roske, "The Seven Martyrs?" *American Historical Review*, 64 (1959), 323.

11. Henry Adams, *The Education of Henry Adams* (Boston: Houghton Mifflin, 1918), pp. 260, 263, 280–281.

12. E. L. Godkin, "Commercial Immorality and Political Corruption," *North American Review*, 107 (1868), 248, 253; Adams, *Education*, pp. 328–329; Charles Eliot Norton to E. L. Godkin, July 26, 1872, quoted in Sproat, *"The Best Men,"* p. 51; James Russell Lowell, *Complete Works: Poems*, vol. 4 (Boston: Houghton Mifflin, 1910), p. 96; Adams, *Education*, pp. 259, 280–281.

13. "The Senate and the Chief Executive," *Nation*, 10 (1870), 188.

14. See Hepburn v. Griswold, 75 U.S. 603 (1870); Legal Tender Cases, 79 U.S. 457 (1871).

15. New York *World*, January 21, 1870, quoted in Charles Warren, *The Supreme Court in United States History*, rev. ed., vol. 2 (Boston: Little, Brown, 1922), p. 510; Adams, *Education*, p. 277; Legal Tender Cases, 79 U.S. 457, 529 (1871). On the impact of the cases on the business community, see Charles Fairman, *Reconstruction and Reunion, 1864–88, Part One* (New York: Macmillan, 1971), pp. 768–771.

16. New York *World*, January 21, 1870, quoted in Warren, *Supreme Court*, 2: 510; "The Senate and the Chief Executive," p. 188; Hepburn v. Griswold, 75 U.S. 603, 622, 624 (1870); Legal Tender Cases, 79 U.S. 457,

580, 582 (1871) (Chase, C. J., dissenting); ibid., 670 (Field, J., dissenting). For Field's antislavery credentials see Carl B. Swisher, *Stephen J. Field: Craftsman of the Law* (Washington, D.C.: Brookings Institution, 1930). pp. 116–118. See also chapter 5.

17. Legal Tender Cases, 79 U.S. 457, 561 (1871) (Bradley, J., concurring); ibid., 542 (Strong, J., concurring); ibid., 564 (Bradley, J. concurring). For a discussion of Bradley as an antislavery advocate on the bench, see chapter 5.

18. Civil Rights Cases, 109 U.S. 3, 34, 42 (1883) (Harlan, J., dissenting); ibid., 17; ibid., 42 (Harlan, J., dissenting). Justice Harlan agreed, of course, that purely private concerns could not be regulated under the Fourteenth Amendment.

19. See John Dewey, "The Influence of Darwin on Philosophy," in *The Influence of Darwin on Philosophy and Other Essays in Contemporary Thought* (New York: H. Holt, 1910), pp. 1, 10–13; Stow Persons, *American Minds: A History of Ideas* (New York: H. Holt. 1958), pp. 237–244; idem, "Evolution and Theology," in *Evolutionary Thought in America*, ed. Stow Persons (New Haven: Yale University Press, 1950), pp. 422–451; Francis P. Weisenburger, *Ordeal of Faith: The Crisis of Church-Going America, 1865–1900* (New York: Philosophical Library, 1959), pp. 61–79.

20. Benjamin F. Butler, "Minority Report," in *Official Proceedings of the National Democratic Convention, 1884* (New York, 1884), p. 205; *Congressional Globe*, 40th Cong,. 3d sess., 1869, p. 262 (remarks of Congressman Logan); ibid., 42d Cong., 2d sess., 1872, p. 1102 (remarks of Congressman Williams).

21. Benjamin F. Wright, ed., *The Federalist*, no. 28 (Hamilton) (Cambridge, Mass.: Harvard University Press, 1961), p. 225.

22. For a discussion of the standoff during nullification see William W. Freehling, *Prelude to Civil War: The Nullification Controversy in South Carolina* (New York: Harper & Row, 1966), pp. 260–297. For the legislation arising from the nullification controversy see Act of March 2, 1833, §7, 4 Stat. 634 (1833). For cases prior to that act in which state courts heard suits against federal officials, see, e.g., Slocum v. Mayberry, 15 U.S. (2 Wheat.) 1 (1817); Harris v. Dennie, 28 U.S. (3 Pet.) 292 (1830).

23. See, e.g., Commonwealth v. Cushing, 11 Mass. 67 (1814); State v. Dimick, 12 N.H. 197 (1841); In re Stacy, 10 Johns. 327 (N.Y. 1813); Commonwealth v. Murphy, 4 Binney 487 (Pa. 1812). See generally William F. Duker, *A Constitutional History of Habeas Corpus* (Westport, Conn.: Greenwood Press, 1980), p. 178, n. 192. Duker concludes that the federal Constitution meant to leave state courts with power to issue the writ in behalf of prisoners in federal custody. See ibid., pp. 126–135. He finds support for this position both in state court practice and in an opinion by Attorney General Caleb Cushing as late as 1853. See ibid., pp. 149–150. The power of state courts was terminated in Ableman v. Booth, 62 U.S. (21 How.) 506 (1859).

24. The principal acts were Civil Rights Act of 1866, 14 Stat. 27 (1866); Enforcement Act of May 31, 1870, 16 Stat. 140 (1870); Ku Klux Klan Act

of 1871, 17 Stat. 13 (1871); Civil Rights Act of 1875, 18 Stat. 336 (1875). Cases in which legislation was declared unconstitutional were United States v. Cruikshank, 92 U.S. 542 (1876); and Civil Rights Cases, 109 U.S. 3 (1883).

25. Freedmen's Bureau Act, 14 Stat. 113 (1866). For the bureau's interpretation of the act see Donald G. Nieman, *To Set the Law in Motion: The Freedmen's Bureau and the Legal Rights of Blacks, 1865–1868* (Millwood, N.Y.: KTO Press, 1979), p. 144.

26. See Nieman, *Freedmen's Bureau*, pp. xiii–xvii, 3–8, 11–15, 18–20, 49–53, 64–65, 133, 144–147, 221–222; George Bentley, *A History of the Freedmen's Bureau* (Philadelphia: University of Pennsylvania Press, 1944), p. 152. Bentley, who examined the dispositions of fifteen bureau courts, found that more than two-thirds of the cases were decided in favor of blacks. See ibid., p. 159.

27. See Benedict, *Compromise of Principle*, pp. 124–126, 210–243, 315–324.

28. See Paul M. Bator, Paul J. Mishkin, David L. Shapiro, and Herbert Wechsler, eds., *Hart and Wechsler's The Federal Courts and the Federal System* (Mineola, N.Y.: Foundation Press, 1973), pp. 844–847.

29. See Murray v. Patrie, F. Cas. No. 9,967 (C.C.S.D.N.Y. 1866); In re Martin, F. Cas. No. 9,151 (C.C.S.D.N.Y. 1866).

30. See In re Turner, F. Cas. No. 14,247 (C.C.D.Md. 1866) (enslavement case); United States v. Quinn, F. Cas. No. 16,110 (C.C.S.D.N.Y. 1870) (voting fraud); United States v. Foote, F. Cas. No. 15,128 (C.C.S.D.N.Y. 1876) (mailing obsene material); United States v. Bott, F. Cas. No. 14,626 (C.C.S.D.N.Y. 1873) (mailing contraceptive drug); United States v. Anthony, F. Cas. No. 14,459 (C.C.N.D.N.Y. 1873) (voting fraud).

31. For the cases against businessmen see Counselman v. Hitchcock, 142 U.S. 547 (1892); Boyd v. United States, 116 U.S. 616 (1886); United States v. Hughes, F. Cas. No. 15,417 (C.C.S.D.N.Y. 1875). The habeas corpus cases were Ableman v. Booth, 62 U.S. (21 How.) 506 (1859), and Tarble's Case, 80 U.S. 397 (1872).

32. A number of opinions arising out of the case are reported. See In re Sykes, F. Cas. No. 13,707 (D.C.S.D.N.Y. 1878); United States v. Tilden, F. Cas. No. 16,519 (D.C.S.D.N.Y. 1878); United States v. Tilden, F. Cas. No. 16,520 (D.C.S.D.N.Y. 1878): United States v. Tilden, F. Cas. No. 16,521 (D.C.S.D.N.Y. 1879); United States v. Tilden, F. Cas. No. 16,522 (D.C.S.D.N.Y. 1879). The case never came to trial but was finally discontinued in 1882 by virtue of an agreement between Tilden and the government. See Alexander C. Flick, *Samuel Jones Tilden: A Study in Political Sagacity* (New York: Dodd, Mead, 1939), p. 441.

33. In re Sykes, F. Cas. No. 13,707 (D.C.S.D.N.Y. 1878) (contempt proceeding against vice-president of Chicago & Northwestern R.R.); United States v. Tilden, F. Cas. No. 16,522 (D.C.S.D.N.Y. 1879) (subpoena of stockbroker); United States v. Tilden, F. Cas. No. 16,521 (D.C.S.D.N.Y. 1879) (argument of counsel); United States v. Tilden, F. Cas. No. 16,520

(D.C.S.D.N.Y. 1878) (government motion to unseal evidence).

34. Tenure of Office Act, 14 Stat. 430 (1867); Army Appropriations Act, 14 Stat. 485 (1867). See Hyman, *More Perfect Union,* pp. 510–511; Leonard D. White, *The Republican Era; A Study in Administrative History, 1869–1901* (New York: Macmillan, 1958), p. 23.

35. *New York Tribune,* August 5, 1864; *Diary of Gideon Welles,* vol. 2 (Boston: Houghton Mifflin, 1911), p. 426; Henry Adams, "The Session," *North American Review,* 111 (1870), 29, 34.

36. Adams, "The Session," p. 41; John R. Young, *Around the World with General Grant,* vol. 2 (New York, 1879), pp. 265–266; George F. Hoar, *Autobiography of Seventy Years,* vol. 2 (New York: C. Scribner's Sons, 1903), p. 46; *Congressional Globe,* 41st Cong., 3d sess., 1871, p. 293 (remarks of Senator Sherman); Young, *Around the World with Grant,* 2: 265–266.

37. See White, *Republican Era,* pp. 54–57.

38. Blyew v. United States, 80 U.S. 581, 585 (1872). For the 1866 act see 14 Stat. 27 (1866).

39. Blyew v. United States, 80 U.S. 581, 598 (1872); United States v. Ortega, 24 U.S. (11 Wheat.) 467 (1826).

40. John N. Pomeroy, *An Introduction to the Constitutional Law of the United States,* 5th ed. (Boston, 1880), p. 61; James Schouler, *Constitutional Studies, State and Federal* (New York, 1897), pp. 209–210.

4. The Quest for a Scientific Morality

1. Henry Adams, *The Education of Henry Adams: An Autobiography* (Boston: Houghton Mifflin, 1918), pp. 280–281.

2. E. L. Godkin, "Commercial Immorality and Political Corruption," *North American Review,* 107 (1868), 248, 253; idem, "The Prospects of the Political Art," *North American Review,* 110 (1870), 398, 417; Robert L. Church, "The Economists Study Society: Sociology at Harvard, 1891–1902," in *Social Science at Harvard, 1860–1920,* ed. Paul Buck (Cambridge, Mass.: Harvard University Press, 1965), pp. 18, 19; quoted in Richard T. Ely, *Ground under Our Feet* (New York: Macmillan, 1938), p. 140.

3. A. Lawrence Lowell, "The Influence of Party upon Legislation in England and America," *Annual Report of the American Historical Association for the Year 1901,* vol. 1 (Washington, D.C.: Government Printing Office, 1902), pp. 319, 350; "Annual Report of the American Historical Association for 1891," quoted in William R. Shepherd, "John William Burgess," in *American Masters of Social Science,* ed. Howard W. Odum (New York: H. Holt, 1927), pp. 23, 49; R. Jackson Wilson, *In Quest of Community: Social Philosophy in the United States, 1860–1920* (New York: Wiley, 1968), p. 65.

4. Herbert L. Osgood, "Review of John Fiske's American Revolution (1891)," quoted in Dixon R. Fox, *Herbert Levi Osgood: An American Scholar* (New York: Columbia University Press, 1924), pp. 48, 51; John W. Burgess, *Reminiscences of an American Scholar* (New York: Columbia Univer-

sity Press, 1934), p. 290; Herbert B. Adams, "New Methods of Study in History," *Johns Hopkins University Studies in Historical and Political Science*, 2 (1884), 24, 64; idem, "Seminary Libraries and University Extension," *Johns Hopkins University Studies in Historical and Political Science*, 5 (1887), 455; Ephraim Emerton, "The Practical Method of Higher Historical Instruction," in *Methods of Teaching History*, ed. G. Stanley Hall (Boston, 1884), pp. 31, 59–60; Albert B. Hart, "Imagination in History," *American Historical Review*, 15 (1910), 227, 232.

5. Edward J. Phelps, quoted in "Methods of Legal Education," *Yale Law Journal*, 1 (1892), 139, 142; Christopher C. Langdell, ed., *A Selection of Cases on the Law of Contracts*, 2nd ed. (Boston, 1879), p. viii; William Keener, quoted in "Methods of Legal Education," *Yale Law Journal*, 1 (1892), 139, 144; Ephraim W. Gurney to Charles W. Eliot, spring 1883, in Arthur E. Sutherland, *The Law at Harvard: A History of Ideas and Men, 1817–1967* (Cambridge, Mass.: Harvard University Press, 1967), pp. 187, 188.

6. See Thomas Bender, "Science and the Culture of American Communities: The Nineteenth Century," *History of Education Quarterly*, 16 (1976), 63, 70–73. Precisely what late nineteenth-century scientists meant by theory and the extent to which the scientific community perceived a need for it are questions beyond the scope of this book. Although scientists today increasingly view their discipline as involving dynamic and ultimately personal processes of theory formulation, followed by experiments seeking empirical verification of theory, followed in turn by a reformulation of theory, a leading historian of science maintains that until recently science was almost uniformly viewed as a series of techniques for gathering data and as the logical operations employed in classifying and organizing those data into coherent, nonidiosyncratic scientific laws. See Thomas S. Kuhn, *The Structure of Scientific Revolutions*, 2nd ed. (Chicago: University of Chicago Press, 1970), pp. 1–5. Techniques for gathering data and logical operations for organizing them are, of course, not without theoretical content, and Professor Kuhn probably would not understand late nineteenth-century American science to have been totally lacking in theory. But it does seem likely that nineteenth-century conceptions of theory differed from today's; in particular, it appears that scientists then regarded theory formulation as a more impersonal task than they do today. This topic of the meaning of theory to American scientists is, however, one requiring a book in itself.

7. Karl Pearson, *The Grammar of Science* (New York, 1895), p. 7. This concept of science, which Pearson believed to be applicable to the social as well as the physical sciences (see ibid., pp. 6–7), was adopted by William Graham Sumner, perhaps the leading sociologist of the day. See William G. Sumner, "The Scientific Attitude of Mind," in *Sumner Today: Selected Essays of William Graham Sumner with Comments by American Leaders*, ed. Maurice R. Davie (New Haven: Yale University Press, 1940), p. 127.

8. *Atlantic Monthly*, 14 (1864), 775–776, quoted in Richard Hofstadter, *Social Darwinism in American Thought, 1860–1915* (Philadelphia: University of Pennsylvania Press, 1945), p. 33.

9. *American Railroad Journal,* 27 (1854), 549. See generally Alfred D. Chandler, Jr., *The Visible Hand: The Managerial Revolution in American Business* (Cambridge, Mass.: Harvard University Press, 1977), pp. 103, 110–111.

10. See Robert H. Bremner, *From the Depths: The Discovery of Poverty in the United States* (New York: New York University Press, 1956), p. 72.

11. See note 6 above.

12. Nicholas P. Gilman, *Socialism and the American Spirit* (Boston, 1893), p. 14.

13. E. L. Godkin, quoted in John G. Sproat, *"The Best Men:" Liberal Reformers in the Gilded Age* (New York: Oxford University Press, 1968), p. 144; Lord Bryce, discussed in ibid., pp. 50–51; speech by Abram S. Hewitt in the House of Representatives, May 25, 1876, quoted in Allan Nevins, *Abram S. Hewitt with Some Account of Peter Cooper* (New York: Harper & Brothers, 1935), p. 304.

14. Adams, *Education,* pp. 47, 50, 343.

15. Rutherford B. Hayes, *Letters and Messages Together with Letter of Acceptance and Inaugural Address* (Washington, D.C., 1879), p.6; Samuel J. Tilden to the Democratic State Committee of New York, August 1873, Tilden Papers, quoted in Sproat, *"The Best Men,"* p. 144.

16. Henry Adams, *History of the United States of America During the Administrations of Jefferson & Madison,* vols. 1 (New York, 1889), pp. 195–196, 235; 7 (1891), p. 401; and 2 (1889), p. 223.

17. G. Stanley Hall, "Boy Life in a Massachusetts Country Town Thirty Years Ago," *Proceedings of the American Antiquarian Society,* n.s. 7 (1890–1891), 107, 120; G. Stanley Hall, *Life and Confessions of a Psychologist* (New York: D. Appleton, 1923), p. 144; Hall, "Boy Life," p. 108; "Humanitarianism," *Nation,* 6 (1868), 68, 69.

18. Diary of Henry Cabot Lodge, entry for September 23, 1874, Henry Cabot Lodge Papers, quoted in Sproat, *"The Best Men,"* p. 53; quoted in ibid., p. 272; Carl Schurz, "Memorial Address," in *Report of the George William Curtis Memorial Committee* (Orange, N.J.: Chronicle Press, 1905), pp. 12, 26–27; Woodrow Wilson, "Character of Democracy in the United States," *Atlantic Monthly,* 64 (1889), 577, 586.

19. *Springfield Republican,* July 21, 1884, p. 4; Adams, *History of the United States,* 1: 76, 227; "Standards of Manners," *Nation,* 37 (1883), 7.

20. Carl Schurz, "Address to the People," in *Speeches, Correspondence, and Political Papers of Carl Schurz,* ed. Frederic Bancroft, vol. 3 (New York: G.P. Putnam, 1913), p. 245; John W. Burgess to Frederic A. P. Barnard, February 20, 1880, in *A History of the Faculty of Political Science, Columbia University,* ed. R. Gordon Hoxie (New York: Columbia University Press, 1955), p. 11; Richard T. Ely, "Fundamental Beliefs in My Social Philosophy," *Forum,* 18 (1894), 173; Henry Adams to Charles F. Adams, November 21, 1864, in *A Cycle of Adams Letters, 1861–1865,* ed. Worthington C. Ford, vol. 1 (Boston: Houghton Mifflin, 1920), pp. 195–197; Ely, "Fundamental Beliefs," p. 183.

21. U.S., Congress, *Senate Executive Documents,* no. 53, 43d Cong., 1st

sess., 1874, app. G, p. 148; John W. Burgess to Frederick A. P. Barnard, February 20, 1880, in Hoxie, *A History of the Faculty*, p. 11; Woodrow Wilson, "The Study of Administration," *Political Science Quarterly*, 2 (1887), 197, 216; Albert B. Hart, "The Future of the Mississippi Valley," *Harper's New Monthly Magazine*, 100 (1900), 422; Herbert Croly, *Progressive Democracy* (New York: Macmillan, 1914), p. 377.

22. Wendell Phillips, *Speeches, Lectures, and Letters*, 2d ser. (Boston, 1891), p. 163; "Religion and Politics," *Nation*, 3 (1866), 188, 189; Jurgen Herbst, *The German Historical School in American Scholarship* (Ithaca, N.Y.: Cornell University Press, 1965), p. 116; Adams, *History of the United States*, 1: 5, 136; Hall, "Boy Life," pp. 107–108; Edward A. Ross, *Social Control: A Survey of the Foundations of Order* (New York: Macmillan, 1901), pp. 434, 436; Josiah Royce, *Race Questions, Provincialism, and Other American Problems* (New York: Macmillan, 1908), pp. 62–67, 185.

23. G. Stanley Hall, *Adolescence: Its Psychology and Its Relations to Physiology, Anthropology, Sociology, Sex, Crime, Religion, and Education* (New York: D. Appleton, 1904), quoted in Wilson, *In Quest of Community*, p. 116; Hall, "Boy Life," p. 108; James M. Baldwin, *The Individual and Society, or Psychology and Sociology* (Boston: R. G. Badger, 1911), p. 127; Wilson, *In Quest of Community*, pp. 75, 89; "Humanitarianism," *Nation*, 6 (1868), 68, 69.

24. Simon Sterne, "The Administration of American Cities," *International Review*, 4 (1877), 631, 642; Royce, *Race Questions*, p. 87; Ross, *Social Control*, p. 434.

25. Godkin, "Prospects of the Political Art," pp. 413, 416–418; Francis E. Abbot, quoted in Thomas L. Haskell, *The Emergence of Professional Social Science: the American Social Science Association and the Nineteenth-Century Crisis of Authority* (Urbana: University of Illinois Press, 1977), p. 66; Herbert B. Adams to Daniel C. Gilman, July 3, 1882, in *Historical Scholarship in the United States, 1876–1901: As Revealed in the Correspondence of Herbert B. Adams*, ed. W. Stull Holt (Baltimore: Johns Hopkins University Press, 1938), p. 55.

26. Adams, *Education*, pp. 382, 450–451, 454, 495.

27. Charles S. Peirce, "Some Consequences of Four Incapacities," in *Collected Papers of Charles Sanders Peirce*, ed. Charles Hartshorne and Paul Weiss, vol. 5 (Cambridge, Mass.: Harvard University Press, 1960), pp. 156, 157, 186, 189; idem, "How to Make Our Ideas Clear," in ibid., pp. 248, 268. For backround information on Peirce, see Wilson, *In Quest of Community*, pp. 32–59.

28. See generally Wilson, *In Quest of Community*.

29. American Social Science Association, *Constitution, Address, and List of Members of the American Association for the Promotion of Social Science* (Boston, 1866), pp. 3, 15. For a discussion of the founding of the association, see Haskell, *Emergence of Professional Social Science*, pp. 97–106. For the founding of the historical and economic associations, see ibid., pp. 168–189. For a discussion of the founding of the American Bar Association, see chapter 5.

30. Thomas M. Cooley, "The Interstate Commerce Act — Pooling and Combinations Which Affect Its Operation," in *Compendium of Transportation*

Theories, ed. C.C. McCain (Washington, D.C., 1893), pp. 242, 248.

31. "The Labor Crisis," *North American Review*, 105 (1867), 177, 178.

32. F. H. Giddings, "Co-Operation," in *The Labor Movement: The Problem of To-day*, ed. George E. McNeil (Boston, 1887), pp. 508, 511, 530–531. On Wright's support of profit sharing see James Leiby, *Carroll Wright and Labor Reform: The Origin of Labor Statistics* (Cambridge, Mass.: Harvard University Press, 1960), p. 143.

33. Leiby, *Carroll Wright*, p. 153. See generally ibid., pp. 152–153.

34. *Hour Week Journal of New York*, August 5, 1882, quoted in Stanley Buder, *Pullman: An Experiment in Industrial Order and Community Planning, 1880–1930* (New York: Oxford University Press, 1967), p. 45; Richard T. Ely, "Pullman: A Social Study," *Harper's New Monthly Magazine*, 70 (1885), 452, 459; quoted in Buder, *Pullman*, pp. 95–96; Ely, "Pullman," p. 465. See also Buder, *Pullman*, p. 61.

35. Quoted in Buder, *Pullman*, pp. 44, 61, 63; "United States Strike Commission's Report on the Chicago Strike of June-July, 1894," *Senate Executive Documents*, no. 7, 53d Cong., 3d sess., 1895, p. 529.

36. Quoted in Buder, *Pullman*, pp. 83, 95, 99. See also ibid., pp. 95, 126.

37. Ibid., p. 228. On Wright's support for the model town, see ibid., p. 188.

38. Carroll D. Wright, *Outline of Practical Sociology* (New York, 1899), p. 297; Charles F. Adams, Jr., *Investigation and Publicity as Opposed to "Compulsory Arbitration"* (Boston, 1902), pp. 2, 4, 6.

39. See Buder, *Pullman*, pp. 155, 229; Leiby, *Carroll Wright*, pp. 160–161.

40. "Annual Report of the New York and Erie Railroad Company for 1855," in Alfred D. Chandler, Jr., *The Railroads: The Nation's First Big Business: Sources and Readings* (New York: Harcourt, Brace & World, 1965), pp. 101, 102.

41. See William E. Nelson, *Dispute and Conflict Resolution in Plymouth County, Massachusetts, 1725–1825* (Chapel Hill: University of North Carolina Press, 1981), pp. 13–44.

42. See Stanley N. Katz, "The Politics of Law in Colonial America: Controversies over Chancery Courts and Equity Law in the Eighteenth Century," *Perspectives in American History*, 5 (1971), 257, 262–265.

43. I understand this definition of boundary to have been the main object of Oliver Wendell Holmes, Jr., *The Common Law* (Boston, 1881).

44. *Twenty-first Annual Report of the President and Directors to the Stockholders of the Baltimore & Ohio Rail-Road Company* (Baltimore, 1847), p. 13; "Annual Report," in Chandler, *Railroads*, p. 102.

45. See Chandler, *Railroads*, pp. 102–103; idem, *Visible Hand*, pp. 99–100.

46. "Annual Report," in Chandler, *Railroads*, p. 101.

47. See Chandler, *Visible Hand*, pp. 125–126.

48. See *Annual Report of the Louisville & Nashville Railroad Company for the Year Ending June 30, 1874*, in Chandler, *Railroads*, pp. 108–117; Chandler, *Visible Hand*, pp. 111–117.

49. See Chandler, *Visible Hand*, pp. 227, 304–305, 403–407.

50. See generally John S. Whitehead, *The Separation of College and State: Columbia, Dartmouth, Harvard, and Yale, 1776–1876* (New Haven: Yale University Press, 1973), pp. 9–190.

51. Charles W. Eliot, *A National University: Report Made by Charles W. Eliot, President of Harvard University, to the National Education Association, August 5, 1873* (Cambridge, Mass., 1874), pp. 9–10, 21; John W. Burgess, *The American University: When Shall It Be? Where Shall It Be? What Shall It Be?* (Boston, 1884), in *American Higher Education: A Documentary History*, ed. Richard Hofstadter and Wilson Smith, vol. 2 (Chicago: University of Chicago Press, 1961), pp. 652, 661.

52. See *Catalogue of the Officers and Students of Yale College, November, 1822* (n.p.), p. 24; *Catalogue of the Officers and Students in Yale College, 1829–1830* (n.p.), p. 25; Richard Hofstadter and Walter P. Metzger, *The Development of Academic Freedom in the United States* (New York: Columbia University Press, 1955), pp. 303–306; Whitehead, *Separation of College and State*, p. 94.

53. See John W. Burgess, *The American University*, in Hofstadter and Smith, *American Higher Education*, 2: 654, 661; Samuel Eliot Morison, *Three Centuries of Harvard, 1636–1936* (Cambridge, Mass.: Harvard University Press, 1936), pp. 372–373; Andrew D. White, *Autobiography*, vol. 1 (New York: Century, 1905), pp. 435–436; Charles W. Eliot, "Congratulatory Address," in *Addresses at the Inauguration of Daniel C. Gilman as President of the Johns Hopkins University, Baltimore, February 22, 1876* (Baltimore, 1876), p. 7.

54. See Walter P. Rodgers, *Andrew D. White and the Modern University* (Ithaca, N.Y.: Cornell University Press, 1942), pp. 150–153; Walter Quincy Scott to Herbert B. Adams, June 13, 1894, in Holt, *Historical Scholarship in the United States*, pp. 230, 233.

55. W. C. Russel to Gentlemen of the Executive Committee, March 31, 1881, in Rodgers, *White and the Modern University*, p. 152; Herbert B. Adams to W. I. Chamberlain, June 4, 1894, in Holt, *Historical Scholarship in the United States*, pp. 225, 226; Noah Porter to William G. Sumner, December 6, 1879, in Harris E. Starr, *William Graham Sumner* (New York: H. Holt, 1925), p. 346; William G. Sumner to the Corporation and Permanent Officers of Yale College, June, 1881, in Starr, *Sumner*, pp. 357, 358, 360.

56. See Starr, *Sumner*, p. 369.

57. Charles W. Eliot, "The Unity of Educational Reform," in *Educational Reform: Essays and Addresses* (New York, 1898), pp. 313, 326, 330; W. T. Harris, "The Necessity for Five Co-Ordinate Groups of Studies in the Schools," *Education Review*, 11 (1896), 323, 324. On patterns of teaching in early nineteenth-century American colleges, see Hofstadter and Metzger, *Development of Academic Freedom*, p. 289.

58. Eliot, "Unity of Educational Reform," p. 331; *Biblical Repertory and Princeton Review*, 17, pp. 505–557, quoted in Thomas J. Wertenbacher, *Princeton, 1746–1896* (Princeton: Princeton University Press, 1946), p. 233; Charles W. Eliot, "Inaugural Address as President of Harvard College," in

Educational Reform, pp. 1, 11. See generally John Hingham, "The Matrix of Specialization," in *The Organization of Knowledge in Modern America, 1860–1920,* ed. Alexandra Oleson and John Voss (Baltimore: Johns Hopkins University Press, 1979), p. 3; Hofstadter and Metzger, *Development of Academic Freedom,* p. 288; Dewey, "Influence of Darwin on Philosophy," pp. 1, 10.

59. Eliot, "Inaugural Address," pp. 11–12.

60. See Ernst Mayr, *Principles of Systematic Zoology* (New York: McGraw-Hill, 1969), pp. 56–62.

61. William G. Sumner, "Sociology," in *Social Darwinism: Selected Essays of William Graham Sumner,* ed. William E. Leuchtenburg and Bernard Wishy (Englewood Cliffs, N.J.: Prentice-Hall, 1963), pp. 9, 12; idem, "Speech," in *Herbert Spencer on the Americans and the Americans on Herbert Spencer,* ed. E. L. Youmans (New York, 1883), pp. 35, 39; idem, "The Scientific Attitude of Mind," in Davie, *Sumner Today,* p. 127; idem, *Folkways: A Study of the Sociological Importance of Usages, Manners, Customs, Mores, and Morals* (Boston: Ginn, 1906), p. 40.

62. G. Stanley Hall to Charles Eliot Norton, June 8, 1879, quoted in Nathan G. Hale, Jr., *Freud and the Americans: The Beginnings of Psychoanalysis in the United States, 1876–1917* (New York: Oxford University Press, 1971), p. 54; E. A. Freeman, *Comparative Politics* (New York, 1874), p. 23; U.S., Congress, Senate, *Congressional Record,* 55th Cong., 3d sess., 1899, p. 1424 (remarks of Senator Daniel). On the development of categories in the fields of sociology and psychology see Hale, *Freud and the Americans,* pp. 84–86; Albert Deutsch, *The Mentally Ill in America: A History of Their Care and Treatment from Colonial Times,* 2nd ed. (New York: Columbia University Press, 1949), pp. 354–355.

5. Building Bureaucratic Authority Structures

1. George B. Galloway, *History of the House of Representatives* (New York: Crowell, 1961), p. 96; Woodrow Wilson, *Congressional Government: A Study in American Politics* (Boston, 1885), p. 61.

2. See DeAlva S. Alexander, *History and Procedure of the House of Representatives* (Boston: Houghton Mifflin, 1916), pp. 235–236; Lauros G. Mc-Conachie, *Congressional Committees: A Study of the Origins and Development of our National and Local Legislative Methods* (New York, 1898), pp. 171–181; George L. Robinson, "The Development of the Senate Committee System" (Ph.D. diss., New York University, 1955), pp. 269–270.

3. See Alexander, *House of Representatives,* pp. 236–250.

4. U.S., Congress, House, *Congressional Record,* 49th Cong., 1st sess., 1885, pp. 172, 173, 202, 285.

5. Ibid., pp. 291, 316.

6. Ibid., 46th Cong., 2d sess., 1880, p. 711; ibid., 49th Cong., 1st sess., 1885, pp. 171, 283. Accord, ibid., pp. 172, 235.

7. House, *Congressional Record,* 49th Cong., 1st sess., 1885, pp. 235, 237. Accord, ibid., 46th Cong., 2d sess., 1880, p. 711.

8. House, *Congressional Record*, 49th Cong., 1st sess., 1885,   pp. 173, 279, 287–288. Accord, ibid., p. 171.

9. Senate, *Congressional Record*, 48th Cong., 1st sess., 1883, p. 209.

10. See Robinson, "Senate Committee System," pp. 281–297.

11. See David J. Rothman, *Politics and Power: The United States Senate, 1869–1901* (Cambridge, Mass.: Harvard University Press, 1966), pp. 51–52; Nelson W. Polsby, Miriam Gallaher, and Barry S. Rundquist, "The Growth of the Seniority System in the U.S. House of Representatives," *American Political Science Review*, 63 (1969),   787.

12. House, *Congressional Record*, 49th Cong., 1st sess., 1885, p. 172.

13. See A. Lawrence Lowell, "The Influence of Party upon Legislation in England and America," *Annual Report of the American Historical Association for the Year 1901*, vol. 1 (Washington, D.C.: Government Printing Office, 1902), pp. 319, 336–337.

14. See Ari A. Hoogenboom, *Outlawing the Spoils: A History of the Civil Service Reform Movement, 1865–1883* (Urbana: University of Illinois Press, 1961), pp. 212–214, 239–248; Paul P. Van Riper, *History of the United States Civil Service* (Evanston, Ill.: Row, Peterson, 1958), pp. 96–532; Leonard D. White, *The Republican Era: A Study in Administrative History, 1869–1901* (New York: Macmillan, 1958), pp. 300–301; idem, *Trends in Public Administration* (New York: McGraw-Hill, 1933), pp. 239–258. For the Civil Serice Act, see 22 Stat. 403 (1883). For the antislavery backgrounds of prominent civil service reformers such as Charles Sumner, G. W. Curtis, and Horace Greeley, see David H. Donald, *Charles Sumner and the Coming of the Civil War* (New York: Alfred A. Knopf, 1960); David H. Donald, *Charles Sumner and the Rights of Man* (New York: Alfred A. Knopf, 1970); William H. Hale, *Horace Greeley: Voice of the People* (New York: Harper, 1950); Gordon Milne, *George William Curtis and the Genteel Tradition* (Bloomington: University of Indiana Press, 1956); Glyndon G. Van Deusen, *Horace Greeley: Nineteenth Century Crusader* (Philadelphia: University of Pennsylvania Press, 1953).

15. "Review of the Works of John C. Calhoun," *North American Review*, 76 (1853), 473, 496.

16. See U.S., Congress, House, *Executive Documents*, no. 13, 25th Cong., 3d sess., 1838, p. 25; ibid., no. 212, 27th Cong., 2d sess., 1842, pp. 294–298; *House Executive Documents*, no. 91, 36th Cong., 1st sess., 1860, p. 3; *House Reports*, no. 313, 25th Cong., 3d sess., 1839, pp. 142–146; Leonard D. White, *The Jacksonians: A Study in Administrative History, 1829–1861* (New York: Macmillan, 1954), pp. 421–422; Alexander B. Callow, Jr., *The Tweed Ring* (New York: Oxford University Press, 1966); Seymour Mandelbaum, *Boss Tweed's New York* (New York: Wiley, 1965); Allan Nevins, *Hamilton Fish: The Inner History of the Grant Administration* (New York: Dodd, Mead, 1937), pp. 638–666, 717–739, 762–837.

17. U.S., Congress, House, *Congressional Globe*, 39th Cong., 2d sess., 1867, pp. 837–839; Resolution of May 27, 1868, quoted in White, *Republican Era*, p. 297; *Senate Reports*, no. 576, 47th Cong., 1st sess., 1882, p. 212; Carl Schurz to E. L. Godkin, December 7, 1879, in *Speeches, Cor-*

respondence, and Political Papers of Carl Schurz, ed. Frederic Bancroft, 6 vols. (New York: G. P. Putnam, 1913), 3: 490–491. See also *New York Times*, July 27, 1868, p. 4.

18. Wendell P. Garrison [1893], quoted in John G. Sproat, *"The Best Men:" Liberal Reformers in the Gilded Age* (New York: Oxford University Press, 1968), p. 243; J. B. M., "A Civil Service Reform Publication Society," *Nation*, 31 (1880), 153; speech of Carl Schurz before the Senate, January 27, 1871, in Bancroft, *Speeches . . . of Carl Schurz*, 3: 123.

19. George W. Curtis, "The Relation between Morals and Politics," in George W. Curtis, *Orations and Addresses*, ed. Charles E. Norton, vol. 2 (New York, 1894), p. 135; idem, "The Last Assault upon Reform," *Harper's Weekly*, 31 (1887), 358; idem, "Party and Patronage," in *Orations and Addresses*, 2: 505. See also "The Week," *Nation*, 22 (1876), 313; F. W. H., "Civil Service Reform Agitation," *Nation*, 31 (1880), 134; "Civil Service Reform Publication Society," *Nation*, 31 (1880), 170–171; "Civil Service Reform Publication Society," *Nation*, 31 (1880), 184–185. See generally Arthur M. Schlesinger, *Political and Social History of the United States* (New York: Macmillan, 1925), p. 315.

20. Curtis, "Party and Patronage," p. 502.

21. See White, *Jacksonians*, pp. 254–258.

22. See Post Office Reform Act of 1872, 17 Stat. 283. On railroads as the principal carriers of domestic mail, see *A History of the Railway Mail Service* (Washington, D.C.: Columbian Correspondence College, 1903), pp. 7–8, 95–98.

23. See *History of the Railway Mail Service*, pp. 81–104, 107–123; Clark E. Carr, *The Railway Mail Service: Its Origin and Development* (Chicago: A. C. McClurg, 1909), p. 25; George R. Taylor and Irene D. Neu, *The American Railroad Network, 1861–1890* (Cambridge, Mass.: Harvard University Press, 1956), pp. 4–48; James E. White, *A Life Span and Reminiscences of Railway Mail Service* (Philadelphia: Deemer & Jaisohn, 1910), pp. 15, 66, 144. For the order including railway mail clerks in the classified civil service, see Excutive Order of January 4, 1889, in James D. Richardson, ed., *A Compilation of the Messages and Papers of the Presidents*, vol. 8 (New York: Bureau of National Literature, 1911), pp. 845–851.

24. *House Executive Documents*, no. 2, pt. 2, 49th Cong., 1st sess., 1885, p. xxv. For the Customs Administration Act, see 26 Stat. 131, 136–139. Uniformity at the judicial level was obtained through the establishment of the United States Court of Customs Appeals in 1909. See Payne-Aldrich Tariff Act of 1909, §29, 36 Stat. 11. See also White, *Republican Era*, pp. 128–129.

25. See Miles O. Price and Harry Bitner, *Effective Legal Research: A Practical Manual of Law Books and Their Use* (New York: Prentice-Hall, 1953), pp. 417–418. For the earlier unavailability of land office records, see White, *Republican Era*, p. 197. The quotation about systematization is from the preface to volume 1 of *Decisions of the Department of the Interior and General Land Office in Cases Relating to the Public Lands* (Washington, D.C., 1883).

26. Rancho el Solbrante, 1 Land Office Decisions 181, 209 (1882); An-

drew Anderson, 1 Land Office Decisions 1, 2 (1881); Trepp v. Northern Pacific R.R., 1 Land Office Decisions 380, 386 (1881); Perkins v. Central Pacific R.R., 1 Land Office Decisions 336, 342 (1882).

27. Quoted in White, *Republican Era*, pp. 199, 203. On the creation of the Board of Law Review, see Milton Conover, *The General Land Office: Its History, Activities, and Organization* (Baltimore: Johns Hopkins University Press, 1923), p. 29.

28. See Price and Bitner, *Effective Legal Research*, pp. 416–420; White, *Republican Era*, pp. 243–246, 255–256, 390.

29. See Robert W. Mardock, *The Reformers and the American Indian* (Columbia: University of Missouri Press, 1971), pp. 1–2, 8–20, 58–61, 129–141, 150–159; Flora W. Seymour, *Indian Agents of the Old Frontier* (New York: D. Appleton-Century, 1941), pp. 40–42, 63–64, 70–71, 374.

30. *Senate Reports*, no. 1848, 50th Cong., 1st sess., 1888, pp. 6, 21. See generally W. Stull Holt, *The Office of the Chief of Engineers of the Army: Its Non-Military History, Activities, and Organization* (Baltimore: Johns Hopkins University Press, 1923), pp. 20–21, 31–34.

31. Quoted in A. B. Stickney, *The Railway Problem* (St. Paul, Minn., 1891), p. iii.

32. See Thomas M. Cooley, "The Railway Problem Defined," in *Compendium of Transportation Theories*, ed. C. C. McCain (Washington, D.C., 1893), pp. 7, 17; Joseph D. Potts, "The Railroad Problem," in ibid., pp. 31, 34; Augustus Schoonmaker, "Unity of Railways and Railway Interests," in ibid., pp. 57, 60.

33. A. B. Stickney, "The Future of the Railroad Problem," in McCain, *Compendium*, p. 51; Martin A. Knapp, "Discrimination by Railways," in ibid., pp. 185, 187; Colins P. Huntington, "A Plea for Railway Consolidation," in ibid., pp. 251, 254–255; Knapp, "Discrimination by Railways," pp. 187–188; Stickney, *Railway Problem,*, pp. 23–34.

34. Stickney, *Railway Problem*, pp. 29, 34; Charles F. Adams, Jr., *The Government and the Railroad Corporations* (Boston, 1871), p. 11; Knapp, "Discrimination by Railways," p. 189; Stickney, "Future of the Railroad Problem," pp. 54–55. See also idem, *Railway Problem*, pp. 34–35.

35. Huntington, "Plea for Railway Consolidation," p. 255; Stickney, "Future of the Railroad Problem," p. 56; idem, *Railway Problem*, p. 24; Charles F. Adams, Jr., "The Interstate Commerce Law," in McCain, *Compendium*, pp. 178, 180.

36. Quoted in *Congressional Record*, 49th Cong., 1st sess., 1885, p. 332.

37. See Adams, *Government and the Railroad Corporations*, p. 23; Cooley, "Railway Problem Defined," pp. 13–19. See also Augustus Schoonmaker, "The Railroad Malady and Its Treatment," in McCain, *Compendium*, pp. 20, 22–25.

38. Schoonmaker, "Railroad Malady," p. 25; idem, "Unity of Railways," p. 58.

39. See Gabriel Kolko, *Railroads and Regulation, 1877–1916* (Princeton: Princeton University Press, 1965), pp. 7–29, 62–63; E. P. Alexander,

"Railroad Consolidation," in McCain, *Compendium*, p. 260; Thomas M. Cooley, "The Interstate Commerce Act—Pooling and Combinations Which Affect Its Operation," in McCain, *Compendium*, p. 242; Huntington, "Plea for Railway Consolidation," p. 251.

40. Alexander, "Railroad Consolidation," p. 264.

41. Adams, "Interstate Commerce Law," pp. 178, 180; Stickney, "Future of the Railroad Problem," p. 56. For the Interstate Commerce Act, see 24 Stat. 379.

42. Interstate Commerce Act, §§1, 2–4.

43. See Interstate Commerce Comm'n v. Cincinnati, New Orleans & Texas Pacific Ry., 167 U.S. 479, 511 (1897); Cincinnati, New Orleans & Texas Pacific Ry. v. Interstate Commerce Comm'n, 162 U.S. 184, 196–197 (1896); Interstate Commerce Comm'n v. Baltimore & Ohio R.R., 43 Fed. 37 (C.C.S.D. Ohio 1890), aff'd, 145 U.S. 263 (1892).

44. Quoted in Schoonmaker, "Railroad Malady," pp. 28–29; House, *Congressional Record*, 48th Cong., 2d sess., 1883, p. 533 (remarks of Congressman Reagan); Shelby M. Cullom, "The Public and the Railways," in McCain, *Compendium*, pp. 39, 41; idem, "The Federal Control of Railways," in ibid., pp. 80, 82; idem, "The Public and the Railways," pp. 43–44.

45. Cullom, "Federal Control of Railways," p. 81; Schoonmaker, "Railroad Malady," p. 28; Thomas M. Cooley, quoted in ibid., p. 29.

46. People v. Board of Supervisors, 4 Barb. 64, 71 (N.Y. Sup. Ct. 1848); Thorne v. Cramer, 15 Barb. 112, 120 (N.Y. Sup. Ct. 1851); Oakley v. Aspinwall, 3 N.Y. 547, 568 (1850).

47. Wynehamer v. People, 13 N.Y. 378, 428 (1856) (opinion of Selden, J.); People v. Gallagher, 4 Mich. 244, 266 (1856) (dissenting opinion); Hay v. Cohoes Co., 2 N.Y. 159, 160 (1849).

48. Argument by Joseph P. Bradley before the Board of Trustees of Rutgers College [ca. 1836], quoted in Charles Fairman, "The Education of a Justice: Justice Bradley and Some of His Colleagues," *Stanford Law Review*, 1 (1949), 217, 229; address by Joseph P. Bradley at Newark, N.J., July 4, 1848, quoted in Charles Fairman, "Mr. Justice Bradley," in *Mr. Justice*, ed. Allison Dunham and Philip B. Kurland (Chicago: University of Chicago Press, 1956), pp. 69, 78.

49. See Charles Fairman, "What Makes a Great Justice? Mr. Justice Bradley and the Supreme Court, 1870–1892," *Boston University Law Review*, 30 (1950), 49, 58. New Jersey was the only free state in which the Republicans did not win all the electoral votes in the election of 1860. See James G. Randall and David H. Donald, *The Civil War and Reconstruction*, 2nd ed. (Lexington, Mass.: D. C. Heath, 1969), p. 134.

50. Ex parte Newman, 9 Cal. 502, 523–524 (1858) (dissenting opinion).

51. See Phillip S. Paludan, *A Covenant with Death: The Constitution, Law, and Equality in the Civil War Era* (Urbana: University of Illinois Press, 1975), pp. 249–252, 257–258; John P. Reid, *Chief Justice: The Judicial World of Charles Doe* (Cambridge, Mass.: Harvard University Press, 1967), pp. 66–69; Carl B. Swisher, *Stephen J. Field: Craftsman of the Law* (Washington,

D.C.: Brookings Institition, 1930), pp. 110–111, 116; Fairman, "Education of a Justice," pp. 244–245. For brief biographies of several other post–Civil War judges having strong antislavery backgrounds, see *The Justices of the Supreme Court, 1789–1969: Their Lives and Major Opinions*, ed. Leon Friedman and Fred L. Israel, vol. 2 (New York: Chelsea House, 1969), pp. 990, 1046, 1114–1116, 1221, 1381 (Justices Swayne and Davis, Chief Justice Chase, Justices Hunt and Gray).

52. United States v. Hall, F. Cas. No. 15,282, at 80–81 (C.C.S.D. Ala. 1871).

53. Ho Ah Kow v. Nunan, F. Cas. No. 6546, at 255–257, 265 (C.C.D. Cal. 1879).

54. Leeper v. Texas, 139 U.S. 462, 468 (1891); Ex parte Jackson, 96 U.S. 727, 733 (1877); State ex rel. St. Joseph & D.C.R.R. v. Nemaha County, 7 Kan. 542, 555 (1871) (dissenting opinion); State ex rel. Liversey v. Judge of Civil District Court, 34 La. 741, 743 (1882).

55. Railroad Co. v. Lockwood, 84 U.S. 357, 378–379 (1873); Adams v. Yazoo & M.V.R.R., 77 Miss. 194, 277, 25 So. 200, 216 (1898) (language reported in *Southern Reporter* slightly different from language quoted in text).

56. Live-Stock Dealers' & Butchers' Ass'n v. Crescent City Live-Stock Landing & Slaughter-House Co., F. Cas. No. 8408, at 652 (C.C.D. La. 1870).

57. Slaughter-House Cases, 83 U.S. 36, 113, 116 (1873) (Bradley, J., dissenting); ibid., 105 (Field, J., dissenting). See also ibid., 115–116 (Bradley, J., dissenting).

58. Butchers' Union Co. v. Crescent City Co., 111 U.S. 746, 754 (1884) (Field, J., concurring); Pollock v. Farmers' Loan & Trust Co., 157 U.S. 429, 534 (1895) (argument of Joseph H. Choate for appellant); Chicago B. & Q.R.R. v. Chicago, 166 U.S. 226, 236 (1897); *Railway and Corporation Law Journal*, 10 (1891), 281. For similar statements on taxation and appropriation of private property see Monongahela Navigation Co. v. United States, 148 U.S. 312, 324 (1893); Loan Association v. Topeka, 87 U.S. 655, 664 (1874); People ex rel. Detroit & H.R.R. v. Salem, 20 Mich. 452, 473 (1870); Boston C. & M.R.R. v. State, 60 N.H. 87, 94 (1880); Morrison v. Manchester, 58 N.H. 538, 539 (1879) (argument for plantiff).

59. Brief for plaintiff in error, pp. 2–3, Walker v. Sauvinet, 92 U.S. 90 (1876); Braceville Coal Co. v. People, 147 Ill. 66, 71, 35 N.E. 62, 63 (1893); In re Leach, 134 Ind. 665, 668, 34 N.E. 641, 642 (1893); Butchers' Union Co. v. Crescent City Co., 111 U.S. 746, 757 (1884) (Field, J., concurring).

60. "Note," *American Law Review*, 28 (1894), 269; Arthur v. Oakes, 63 Fed. 310, 317 (7th Cir. 1894); Farmers' Loan & Trust Co. v. Northern Pacific R.R., 60 Fed. 803, 822 (C.C.E.D. Wis. 1894); Toledo, A.A. & N.M. Ry. v. Pennsylvania Co., 54 Fed. 730, 737 (C.C.N.D. Ohio 1893) (opinion of Taft, J.); Coeur d'Alene Consol. & Mining Co. v. Miners' Union, 51 Fed. 260, 263 (C.C.D. Idaho 1892); Old Dominion S.S. Co. v. McKenna, 30 Fed. 48, 50 (C.C.S.D.N.Y. 1887); In re Higgins, 27 Fed. 443, 445 (C.C.N.D. Tex. 1886). Accord, Casey v. Typographical Union

No. 3, 45 Fed. 135, 143 (C.C.S.D. Ohio 1891).

61. Joel P. Bishop, *The First Book of the Law* (Boston, 1868), §§87–88; John F. Dillon, *Laws and Jurisprudence of England and America* (Boston, 1895), 13 n. 1, 17, 19.

62. A. Ferris Rihani, "Stare Decisis," *Albany Law Journal*, 57 (1898), 392, 396; William D. Guthrie, *Lectures on the Fourteenth Article of Amendment to the Constitution of the United States* (Boston, 1898), p. 106; Thomas M. Cooley, *Treatise on the Constitutional Limitations*, 4th ed. (Boston, 1878), pp. 378, 432.

63. Wynehamer v. People, 13 N.Y. 378, 391–392 (1856) (Comstock, J., concurring); Passmore Williamson's Case, 26 Pa. 9, 30 (1855) (Lowrie, J., concurring). The other Pennsylvania case was Sharpless v. Mayor of Philadelphia, 21 Pa. 147 (1853). For similar approaches rejecting higher-law arguments see United States v. Hanway, F. Cas. No. 15,299 (C.C.E.D. Pa. 1851); Oliver v. Kauffman, F. Cas. No. 10,497 (C.C.E.D. Pa. 1850); Sim's Case, 61 Mass. 285 (1851).

64. See Morton J. Horwitz, "The Emergence of an Instrumental Conception of American Law, 1780–1820," *Perspectives in American History*, 5 (1971), 285, 311–316.

65. Walter I. Hover, "Stare Decisis,"*Albany Law Journal*, 52 (1895), 73; "Address by Christopher C. Langdell to the Harvard Law School Association, 1886," in Arthur E. Sutherland, *The Law at Harvard: A History of Ideas and Men, 1817–1967* (Cambridge, Mass.. Harvard University Press, 1967), p. 175; Karl Pearson, *The Grammar of Science* (New York, 1895), p. 7; Christopher C. Langdell, *A Selection of Cases on the Law of Contracts*, 2nd ed. (Boston, 1879), p. ix; John C. Gray, "Remoteness of Charitable Gifts," *Harvard Law Review*, 7 (1894), 406, 414; A. Lawrence Lowell, "The Status of Our New Possessions—A Third View," *Harvard Law Review*, 13 (1899), 155; Gray, "Remoteness of Charitable Gifts," p. 414. See also William A. Keener, quoted in "Methods of Legal Education," *Yale Law Journal*, 1 (1892), 139, 144.

66. Christopher C. Langdell, *A Selection of Cases on the Law of Contracts*, 8 vols. (Boston, 1871). For primary cases only, the distribution is 92 percent British, 8 percent American. Other casebooks of the late nineteenth century, though rarely so extreme, also rely heavily on British cases: James B. Ames and Jeremiah Smith, *A Selection of Cases on the Law of Torts*, 2 vols. (Cambridge, Mass., 1893) (50 percent); Melville M. Bigelow, *Leading Cases on the Law of Torts Determined by the Courts of America and England* (Boston, 1875) (50 percent); John C. Gray, *Select Cases and Other Authorities on the Law of Property*, 6 vols. (Cambridge, Mass., 1888–1892) (70 percent); Samuel Williston, *A Selection of Cases on the Law of Contracts*, vol. 2 (Boston, 1894) (41 percent; note, however, that this book was designed as a supplement to Langdell). Typical modern casebooks contain far fewer British cases: Lon L. Fuller and Melvin A. Eisenberg, *Basic Contract Law*, 3d ed. (St. Paul: West Publishing, 1972) (16 percent); Charles O. Gregory and Harry Kalven, Jr., *Cases and Materials on Torts* (Boston: Little, Brown, 1959) (15 percent); Friedrich Kessler and Grant Gilmore, *Contracts: Cases and Materials*,

2nd ed. (Boston: Little, Brown, 1970) (14 percent); William L. Prosser and Young B. Smith, *Cases and Materials on Torts*, 4th ed. (Brooklyn: Foundation Press, 1967) (7 percent). In addition, the *American Law Review*, described as "probably the most important" American legal periodical of its day, was "as much concerned with developments in the law of England as with the current American scene." Mark DeW. Howe, *Justice Oliver Wendell Holmes*: *The Shaping Years, 1841–1870* (Cambridge, Mass.: Harvard University Press, 1957), p. 264.

67. J. I. Clark Hare, "Notes of a Course of Lectures on Contracts Delivered in the Law Department of the University of Pennsylvania, 1882" (Biddle Law Library, University of Pennsylvania, Philadelphia), pp. 131–133.

68. M'Culloch v. Eagle Insurance Co., 18 Mass. (1 Pick.) 278, 281 (1822); Christopher C. Langdell, "Summary," in *Selection of Cases*, pp. 985, 995–996, 1025; Pynchon v. Stearns, 52 Mass. (11 Met.) 304, 312 (1846); Gaines v. Green Pond Iron Mining Co., 33 N.J. Eq. 603 (E. & A. 1881).

69. Davies v. Mann, 10 M. & W. 546, 152 Eng. Rep. 588 (Exch. 1842); "Book Review," *Law Quarterly Review*, 2 (1886), 506, 507. See generally G. Edward White, *Tort Law in America*: *An Intellectual History* (New York: Oxford University Press, 1980), pp. 41–49.

70. On Brown and Peckham see Walter F. Pratt, "Rhetorical Styles on the Fuller Court," *American Journal of Legal History*, 24 (1980), 189. For examples of higher-law language used by Cooley and Dillon, see People ex rel. Detroit & H.R.R. v. Salem, 20 Mich. 452, 473 (1870); Arnold M. Paul, *Conservative Crisis and the Rule of Law: Attitudes of Bench and Bar, 1887–1895* (Ithaca, N.Y.: Cornell University Press, 1960), pp. 79–81. For examples of scientific analysis by Cooley and Dillon, see Thomas M. Cooley, *A Treatise on the Law of Torts* (Chicago, 1879); John F. Dillon, *Treatise on the Law of Municipal Corporations* (Chicago, 1872). For a perceptive analysis of Cooley's career, see Phillip S. Paludan, *A Covenant with Death*: *The Constitution, Law, and Equality in the Civil War Era* (Urbana: University of Illinois Press, 1975), pp. 249–273.

71. Oliver W. Holmes, "Privilege, Malice, and Intent," *Harvard Law Review*, 8 (1894), 1, 3, 7, idem, "The Path of the Law," *Harvard Law Review*, 10 (1897), 457, 465. See also Bishop, *First Book of the Law*, §§85–86.

72. Roberson v. Rochester Folding Box Co., 171 N.Y. 538, 561, 64 N.E. 442, 449 (1902) (dissenting opinion).

73. See Alfred Z. Reed, *Training for the Public Profession of the Law* (New York: Carnegie Foundation for the Advancement of Teaching, 1921), p. 442.

74. Theodore Dwight, quoted in *A History of the School of Law, Columbia University*, ed. Julius Goebel, Jr. (New York: Columbia University Press, 1955), p. 35; statement of James B. Ames, in *Reports of the American Bar Association*, 31 (1907), 1025.

75. See Reed, *Training for the Public Profession*, p. 206.

76. Samuel J. Tilden, quoted in George W. Martin, *Causes and Conflicts: The Centennial History of the Association of the Bar of the City of New York, 1870–*

1970 (Boston: Houghton Mifflin, 1970), p. 37; "The Bar Association of New York," *Albany Law Journal*, 1 (1870), 203.

77. Samuel J. Tilden, quoted in Martin, *Causes and Conflicts*, pp. 15, 38; "The Bar Association of New York," p. 203.

78. Editorial, *New York Times*, June 20, 1869; quoted in Martin, *Causes and Conflicts*, p. 37.

79. Dorman B. Eaton, quoted in Reed, *Training for the Public Profession*, p. 222; quoted in Edson R. Sunderland, *History of the American Bar Association and Its Work* (n.p., 1953), pp. 12–13; Reed, *Training for the Public Profession*, p.228.

80. Holmes, "Path of the Law," pp. 457, 466, 468.

81. Marbury v. Madison, 5 U.S. (1 Cranch) 137 (1803); Scott v. Sandford, 60 U.S. (19 How.) 393 (1857).

82. See Lawrence M. Friedman, *A History of American Law* (New York: Simon and Schuster, 1973), p. 311; Morton Keller, *Affairs of State: Public Life in Late Nineteenth Century America* (Cambridge, Mass.: Harvard University Press, 1977), p. 362; Margaret V. Nelson, *A Study of Judicial Review in Virginia, 1789–1928* (New York: Columbia University Press, 1947), pp. 54, 80; Edward S. Corwin, "The Extension of Judicial Review in New York: 1783–1905," *Michigan Law Review*, 15 (1917), 281, 283–285; Oliver P. Field, "Unconstitutional Legislation in Indiana," *Indiana Law Journal*, 17 (1941), 101; James M. Rosenthal, "Massachusetts Acts and Resolves Declared Unconstitutional by the Supreme Judicial Court of Massachusetts," *Massachusetts Law Quarterly*, 1 (1916), 301.

83. See Corwin, "Extension of Judicial Review," pp. 304–306; Charles G. Haines, "Judicial Review of Legislation in the United States and the Doctrine of Vested Rights and of Implied Limitations of Legislatures," *Texas Law Review*, 2 (1924), 257 and 282, n. 54; ibid., 3 (1924), 1, 39–43. See generally Paul, *Conservative Crisis*.

84. Legal Tender Cases, 79 U.S. 457, 580 (1871); Slaughter-House Cases, 83 U.S. 36, 88–89 (1873); Pollock v. Farmers' Loan & Trust Co., 157 U.S. 429, 596 (1895).

85. 198 U.S. 45 (1905).

86. Barbier v. Connolly, 113 U.S. 27, 31 (1885); Soon Hing v. Crowley, 113 U.S. 703, 710 (1885). See also Legal Tender Cases, 79 U.S. 457, 561–565 (1871) (Bradley, J. concurring).

87. Slaughter-House Cases, 83 U.S. 36, 88–89 (1873) (dissenting opinion); Butchers' Union Co. v. Crescent City Co., 111 U.S. 746, 761, 766 (1884) (concurring opinion). For a similar view of Justice Field's substantive due process jurisprudence, see Charles W. McCurdy, "Justice Field and the Jurisprudence of Government-Business Relations: Some Parameters of Laissez-Faire Constitutionalism, 1863–1897," *Journal of American History*, 61 (1975), 970.

88. Slaughter-House Cases, 83 U.S. 36, 60 (1873); Loan Association v. Topeka, 87 U.S. 655, 665 (1875). See also Gelpcke v. City of Dubuque, 68 U.S. (1 Wall.) 175 (1864), which arose out of facts similar to those in Loan Association v. Topeka. In *Gelpcke*, an Iowa statute authorized a municipal-

ity to buy railroad bonds. Without considering the substantive due process issue, the Court upheld the statute and gave judgement for the creditor, apparently because railroads, unlike factories, were sufficiently public in character to warrant government investment. See Loan Association v. Topeka, 87 U.S. 655, 660–662 (1875). The issue discussed in *Gelpcke* was whether a federal circuit court in Iowa was bound by a ruling of the Iowa Supreme Court, which reversed its earlier rulings, holding the statute unconstitutional. The U.S. Supreme Court held that the circuit court should have followed the earlier Iowa rulings upholding the state legislation, which were in force when the railroad bonds were issued, rather than the later ruling, which was in force when suit was brought. As Justice Miller noted in his dissenting opinion, this choice-of-law question was the only issue resolved in *Gelpcke*. 68 U.S. at 208–210.

89. 165 U.S. 578 (1897).

90. Wynehamer v. People, 13 N.Y. 378 (1856); People v. Gillson, 109 N.Y. 389, 390 (1888).

91. Mayor and City Council of Baltimore v. State ex rel. Board of Police, 15 Md. 376, 468 (1860). The court indicated that the statute would be unconstitutional if it proscribed people "on account of their political and religious opinions." Ibid., p. 468.

92. See State v. Santee, 111 Iowa 1, 4–7 (1900); Connolly v. Union Sewer Pipe Co., 184 U.S. 540, 558–565 (1902); Matter of Application of Jacobs, 98 N.Y. 98 (1885).

93. William E. Russell, "The Proper Province and Office of Constitutional Law," *American Law Register and Review*, 33 (1894), 481, 482; Pollock v. Farmers' Loan & Trust Co., 157 U.S. 429, 596, 607 (1895) (Field, J., concurring); *Farmers' Review*, quoted in Louis Galambos, *The Public Image of Big Business in America, 1880–1940* (Baltimore: Johns Hopkins University Press, 1975), p. 68; Carl Schurz, "Why James G. Blaine Should Not Be President," in Bancroft, *Speeches . . . of Carl Schurz*, 4: 224, 246.

94. Pollock v. Farmers' Loan & Trust Co., 157 U.S. 429, 596 (1895) (concurring opinion); Bradley v. New York & New Haven R.R., 21 Conn. 294, 306 (1851); Legal Tender Cases, 79 U.S. 457, 580 (1871) (dissenting opinion).

Conclusion: The Unresolved Tensions

1. John L. O'Sullivan, "The Democratic Principle," in *Notions of the Americans, 1820–1860*, ed. David Grimstead (New York: G. Braziller, 1970), pp. 86, 88; Jesse H. Choper, *Judicial Review and the National Political Process: A Functional Reconsideration of the Role of the Supreme Court* (Chicago: University of Chicago Press, 1980), p. 64.

2. 10 U.S. (6 Cranch) 87 (1810).

3. This point is made persuasively in Phillip S. Paludan, *A Covenant with Death: The Constitution, Law, and Equality in the Civil War Era* (Urbana: University of Illinois Press, 1975), pp. 42–45.

4. Quoted in Choper, *Judicial Review*, p. 67.

Index